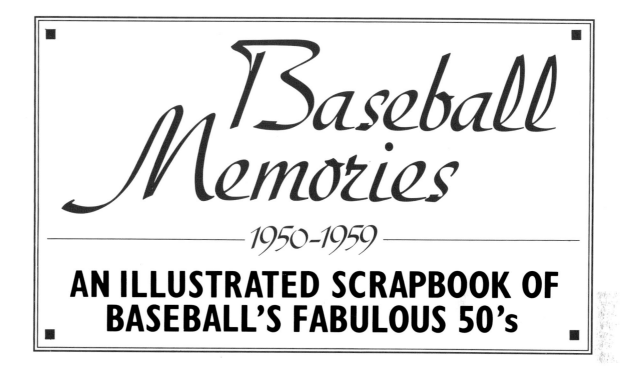

Baseball Memories

1950-1959

AN ILLUSTRATED SCRAPBOOK OF BASEBALL'S FABULOUS 50's

All the Players, Managers, Cities & Ballparks

Marc Okkonen

 Sterling Publishing Co., Inc. New York

ACKNOWLEDGEMENTS

A debt of gratitude to a pair of monumental compilations, the baseball encyclopedias developed by TURKIN & THOMPSON and NEFT & COHEN. With these pioneering research volumes to refer to, the task of gathering player names and the years they played into meaningful rosters for this book was simplified to manageable proportions. And thanks to many individual members of SABR (Society for American Baseball Research) who willingly provided specific pictorial data from their own local sources.

Sources & Contributors:

National Baseball Library, Cooperstown, NY
AAF Library, Los Angeles
Library of Congress, Washington, D.C.
Muskegon County Library, Muskegon, MI
Hackley Library, Muskegon, MI
Art Ahrens
Dennis Anderson
Clarence Blasco

Bob Brown
Peter Capolino
Bob Davids
Joe Dittmer
Jim Eby
Morris Eckhouse
Larry Gerlach
Ed Johnson

Lloyd Johnson
Ed Koller
Jack Lang
Bob Littlejohn
Ron Pesch
Paul Pogharian
Rich Tourengeau

Design & paste-up assembly:
Marc Okkonen

Typesetting:
Sharon Tingley

Photocopy work:
PROFESSIONAL COLOR SERVICE, Muskegon, MI
BRIDGES NETWORK, Muskegon, MI

Photos xerographed from files of the National Baseball Library, microfilm copies of period newspapers, club yearbooks, and various miscellaneous sources.

Original line art (uniform illustrations) copyrighted by the author.

Published by Sterling Publishing Company, Inc.
387 Park Avenue South, New York, N.Y. 10016
© 1993 by Marc Okkonen
Distributed in Canada by Sterling Publishing
℅ Canadian Manda Group, P.O. Box 920, Station U
Toronto, Ontario, Canada M8Z 5P9
Distributed in Great Britain and Europe by Cassell PLC
Villiers House, 41/47 Strand, London WC2N 5JE, England
Distributed in Australia by Capricorn Link Ltd.
P.O. Box 665, Lane Cove, NSW 2066
Printed and Bound in Hong Kong
All rights reserved

Sterling ISBN 0-8069-0427-5

10 9 8 7 6 5 4 3 2 1

Library of Congress Cataloging-in-Publication Data

Okkonen, Marc.
   Baseball memories, 1950–1959 : an illustrated
scrapbook of baseball's fabulous 50's : all the players,
managers, cities & ballparks / Marc Okkonen.
       p.   cm.
   Includes index.
   ISBN 0-8069-0427-5
   1. Baseball—United States—History—20th century.
I. Title.
GV863.A10385   1993
796.357'0973—dc20   93-4749
                                                 CIP

TABLE OF CONTENTS

BASEBALL'S AMERICA
OF 1950-59

A DECADE OF TRANSITION AND DRAMA

Modern historians have labeled the decade of the 1950s as that of the "quiet generation." Perhaps this is justified by comparison with the decades that preceded and followed, but a closer examination of headlines from 1950 to 1959 reveals a "potpourri" of events and developments that had a profound influence on American history in general and baseball in particular. It was, rather, a decade of transition in many respects— the world of 1950 was very much unlike the world of 1959 and the 10-year period was punctuated by mini-events and mini-crises that were not always "quiet," but often dramatic if not traumatic.

Harry Truman ushered in the new decade as U.S. President. He chose not to run for re-election in 1952, and the Democrats picked Illinois' Adlai Stevenson to challenge Eisenhower's bid for the White House.

The fifties had barely begun when the invasion of South Korea once again placed the entire nation on a state of military alert and American troops were quickly sent to battle. The "cold war" suddenly heated up and fearful anxieties about a possible third world war were on everyone's mind. The terrifying prospect of a nuclear confrontation with the Soviet bloc was a distinct by-product of the Korean conflict and only subsided with an eventual stalemate in the fighting and the subsequent armistice in 1953. But the war of nerves continued throughout the balance of the decade and every "brush fire" seemed to offer an invitation to world conflict. The first two years of the decade, with Harry Truman in the White House, marked the end of an unprecedented 20-year run of Democratic administrations, finally over in 1952 with the convincing victory of the Republican candidate, Dwight D. Eisenhower. Ike proved to be a popular president and served out the balance of the decade, restoring the public's acceptance of a GOP Chief Executive. Eisenhower's campaign promise to end the Korean conflict and his reluctance to further commit U.S. combat forces in such cold-war "hot spots" as French Indo-China and the Formosa Straits solidified his hold on the presidency. A precarious policy of "Brinksmanship" versus the communist world, orchestrated by Ike's Secretary of State John Foster Dulles, carried the nation through the nervous decade of the fifties without another "Korean-war" adventure.

Newspaper headlines proclaimed Ike's election in 1952—the first Republican to hold the presidency since Herbert Hoover in 1932.

U.S. combat troops were quickly deployed to South Korea in the summer of 1950. The so-called "police action" had a lasting impact on the decade of the 1950s.

At a Wake Island meeting in 1951, Truman paid tribute to the Korean War's Commander Gen. Douglas MacArthur, but not long afterward MacArthur was relieved of command. He returned to a hero's welcome in the U.S.

Eisenhower was a frequent visitor at Griffith Stadium to watch the hometown Senators in the 1950s. He's shown here filling out his scorecard at a 1957 Nats' contest.

'50 OLDS 88

'52 KAISER

'56 CORVETTE

'56 THUNDERBIRD

'56 PACKARD

Packard Clipper Super Hardtop

'58 EDSEL

'59 CADILLAC

Some successful and not-so-successful automobiles of the decade.

The future patterns of American society were redirected in the 1950s by numerous landmark developments. Organized labor was never more influential nor more powerful and the merger of the AFL and CIO in 1955 further strengthened its voice in shaping the politics and the economy of the nation. Significant gains in the struggle to eliminate racial discrimination in American life were reflected in the Supreme Court's decision in 1954 to strike down the separate-but-equal doctrine in public schools. The simple act of courage by Rosa Parks in refusing to seat herself in the "blacks only" section of a public bus in 1955 sparked an historic series of protests that culminated in long overdue civil rights legislation. Racial discrimination in the public schools reached the boiling point in 1957 when President Eisenhower sent federal troops into Little Rock to enforce the new laws regarding school desegregation. The great civil rights movement of the 1960s, under the leadership of Martin Luther King, had its roots in the fifties. The influx of new black stars in baseball played an important role in the restructuring of American attitudes in these crucial years.

The decade of the fifties also featured the dawn of the space age. A spin-off of the cold war arms race, rocketry came of age with the successful launch of Sputnik by the Soviets in 1957. Americans suddenly looked to the heavens and directed their energies to the new frontiers of space. Population growth soared from 151 million in 1950 to 179 million in 1960 as the new states of Alaska and Hawaii were born at the close of the decade. Rural population as a percentage of the National Census was steadily decreasing in the new age of suburban living. The growth of shopping centers threatened the survival of traditional downtown as the focal point of urban life for the average American.

Some domestic headlines that earmarked the decade of the fifties included THE BRINK'S ROBBERY (1950), THE ATTEMPTED ASSASSINATION OF PRESIDENT TRUMAN (1950), the KEFAUVER COMMITTEE HEARINGS (1951), the FIRING OF GENERAL MacARTHUR (1951), EXECUTION OF THE ROSENBERGS (1953), THE MARRIAGE OF JOE DIMAGGIO AND MARILYN MONROE (1954), THE ARMY/McCARTHY HEARINGS (1954), IKE'S HEART ATTACK (1955), THE SALK VACCINE (1955), THE GRACE KELLY MARRIAGE (1956), HURRICANES HAZEL (1954), DIANE (1955) and AUDREY (1957), THE SINKING OF THE ANDREA DORIA (1956), THE KHRUSHCHEV VISIT (1959) and THE TV QUIZ SHOW SCANDALS (1959). World events that captured the attention of Americans included the KOREAN CONFLICT (1950-53), THE RETURN OF CHURCHILL TO POWER (1951), KURT KARLSEN AND HIS SINKING SHIP FLYING ENTERPRISE (1952), THE CONQUEST OF EVEREST (1953), THE CORONATION OF ELIZABETH (1953), THE DEATH OF STALIN (1953), THE FALL OF DIEN BIEN PHU (1954), PERON DEPOSED (1955), THE SUEZ CRISIS (1956), THE HUNGARIAN REVOLT (1956), THE RETURN OF DE GAULLE IN FRANCE (1958), THE BRUSSELS FAIR (1958), CASTRO'S TAKEOVER IN CUBA (1959).

In 1954, the idols of Hollywood and of the baseball world were united in the celebrated marriage of Marilyn Monroe and recently retired Joe DiMaggio.

In Britain, a radiant new queen ascended to the throne in the spring of 1953.

A 1953 movie advertisement promotes the first wide-screen presentation of CINEMASCOPE—a new Hollywood gimmick to combat the emerging threat of home television.

The movie industry, its patronage threatened by the new popularity of television, introduced new gimmicks to attract audiences—VistaVision, 3-D, and Cinemascope. Broadway gave us some memorable shows and popular songs with THE KING AND I, MY FAIR LADY, DAMN YANKEES, THE MUSIC MAN, and WEST SIDE STORY. Popular music was forever transformed with the introduction of so-called "rock and roll," pioneered by Bill Haley's Comets, Elvis Presley, and others. The recording industry also upgraded the quality of listening with improved 45 RPM and 33-1/3 RPM long playing records, plus the introduction of High Fidelity sound systems. But the entertainment industry in America was truly revolutionized by the new medium of television. TV comedy featured such hit shows as MILTON BERLE'S TEXACO THEATER, I LOVE LUCY, and SID CAESAR'S SHOW OF SHOWS. Ed Sullivan, Jackie Gleason, Perry Como, and Steve Allen were headliners with their popular variety shows. The quality of TV programming during the decade varied from low-budget, juvenile situation comedies to fine documentaries like VICTORY AT SEA and a number of exemplary live dramas on programs such as PLAYHOUSE 90. The televising of sports events also had its highs and lows ranging from coverage of mindless events like wrestling and roller derby to steadily improving images of boxing, professional football, and of course baseball. Mel Allen was synonymous with NBC's annual coverage of the World Series and Dizzy Dean became a media folk hero with his "country bumpkin" style of delivery on ABC and later CBS's Game of the Week. The 1950s were truly television's "Golden Age," a novelty when the decade began and an institution by 1959.

John Cameron Swayze gave us the evening news in his nightly 15-minute NBC telecast in the mid-fifties.

Baseball's Chuck Connors became a TV folk hero in his hit western TV series THE RIFLEMAN, one of many popular "oaters" of the mid-late fifties. Another ex-major leaguer who crossed over to TV was GENERAL HOSPITAL's John Berardino.

In the late fifties, a show business phenomenon named Elvis Presley took the recording industry by storm with a succession of hit records.

America's new entertainment medium became a family preoccupation, as portrayed in this 1950 advertisement scene. The TV sets were all black and white and all American-made.

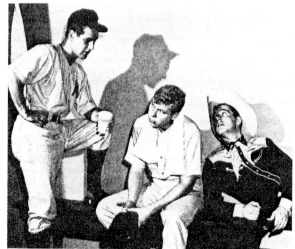

In 1956, TV's U.S. Steel Hour aired a poignant and potent baseball drama, BANG THE DRUM SLOWLY. Starring (L to R) were Paul Newman, Albert Salmi, and George Peppard.

Sports in the U.S.A. were alive and well in the 1950s. In football, Bud Wilkinson's Oklahoma Sooners dominated the collegiate scene with a 47 game win streak in the middle years of the decade. In the NFL, the Cleveland Browns and Detroit Lions each won three championships. CCNY became the only top level college basketball squad to capture both the NCAA title and the then equally prestigious NIT tournament in 1950. George Mikan and the Minneapolis Lakers were the class of the NBA in the first half of the decade, but the Boston Celtics began an incredible domination of professional basketball with the first of eight consecutive championships in 1959. In professional hockey, the Detroit Red Wings with their famed "production line" of Lindsay, Abel and Howe, captured four Stanley Cups in the early fifties, the only U.S.-based NHL team to claim the cup during the decade. Television gave the sport of boxing a tremendous boost during the 1950s. Almost nightly telecasts of boxing cards made instant sports heroes of Rocky Marciano, the reigning heavyweight; Sugar Ray Robinson, the classy middleweight; and many others. Ben Hogan, Cary Middlecoff, Sam Snead, and newcomer Arnold Palmer were the big names in golf. Bill Vukovich won consecutive Indianapolis 500 auto races in 1953-54 before his tragic death in the 1955 race. Pole vaulter Bob Richards and shot-putter Parry O'Brien gave the U.S.A. gold medals in both Olympiads of 1952 (Helsinki) and 1956 (Melbourne).

Coach Bud Wilkinson's Oklahoma Sooners were the "cream" of collegiate football in the mid '50s.

Dr. Cary Middlecoff was one of the decade's top pro golfers.

Pro football's Detroit Lions were a big winner in the fifties. Stars Leon Hart (center) and Doak Walker (right) are shown on the sidelines at Detroit's Briggs Stadium, with the familiar center field bleachers and scoreboard in the background.

Ohio State's 1950 Heisman Trophy back Vic Janowicz went on to a brief baseball career with the Pirates.

Coach Paul Brown (left) of the NFL's Cleveland Browns became a football legend with winning teams and a string of championships carried over from the AAFL of the late forties. On the right are his stellar receivers Dante Lavelli (56) and Mac Speedie (58).

Sugar Ray Robinson gave TV audiences some memorable boxing bouts in the 1950s.

Rocky Marciano was the reigning heavyweight for most of the decade.

Guard Bob Cousy was the first of a galaxy of cage stars that formed a budding dynasty for the Boston Celtics.

Pole vaulter/Decathlon star Bob Richards brought home Olympic gold in 1952 and 1956.

A 1950 Rawlings ad illustrated the latest in contemporary baseball gloves as the decade began.

A similar ad by Wilson in 1958 reflects significant changes—less padding, longer and more contoured fingers.

Detroit catcher Matt Batts models a revolutionary lighter mask design in 1952, holding the older model in his hands.

Slugger Frank Thomas in the all-fiberglass game cap worn by the Pirates in the mid-fifties. This cap style was eventually discarded, but batting helmets became mandatory by the end of the decade.

In 1950, the prop-driven Lockheed constellation was the "Cadillac" of air travel, as this TWA ad illustrates. Some major league clubs were already flying to their scheduled destinations by this time.

By the end of the decade, the Boeing 707 jet airliners were in service—cutting travel time in half and making coast-to-coast baseball a reality.

STATUS OF BASEBALL IN THE FIFTIES

Transportation and urban life in America underwent a significant transformation between 1950 and 1959. Public transport in the larger cities suffered significantly from the increasing popularity of private automobiles. Streetcars, buses, and light rail systems (except in the very large cities) experienced a noticeable loss in patronage. High-speed freeway systems were triggering growth of the suburbs and altering the living patterns of urban America. The Interstate Highway Act of 1955 further stimulated the use of the automobile for long distance travel and contributed to a significant decline in passenger train service. Even the once unaffordable concept of two or more autos per family became a reality in the fifties. The increasing growth of air travel during the decade, climaxed by the later introduction of passenger jets, accelerated the decline of railroad passenger trains and had an historic impact on the geography of major league baseball as well. The national game became truly national at the major league level with franchise relocations to the West Coast late in the decade.

But it was not just the transportation revolution that affected baseball in the fifties. The proliferation of television viewing and even a new upsurge in radio audiences had a monumental impact on baseball. The opportunity to witness baseball games in the comfort of living rooms or neighborhood taverns was a mixed blessing for baseball as a business. The increased exposure created legions of new fans, but the convenience of following the sport without leaving home had disturbing effects on attendance. Even without the televising of baseball, America's preoccupation with the new entertainment medium became a distraction from all public events that depended on gate receipts for survival. Televised major league baseball suddenly expanded the territories of loyal fans to rural America, but this new exposure threatened to destroy the once-healthy structure of the professional minor leagues. By the end of the decade, many of the lower minor leagues had disappeared and even the higher minor leagues were struggling to survive. Total attendance of major league baseball, after a post-war period of phenomenal increase, began to level off and even declined slightly in the early fifties. Only the franchise shifts to new, lucrative markets in the mid-late fifties reversed the steady decline in total attendance in the major leagues. The revenues from TV coverage, though miniscule in comparison with current contracts, helped offset the disappointing gate receipts for many major league clubs.

Much like radio coverage in the 1930s, the policies and attitudes of each team varied considerably in their willingness to provide "free" viewing of games. Most clubs were reluctant to televise home games and limited their coverage to road games, which represented no threat to attendance. For a time, Pittsburgh and later Milwaukee and Kansas City took an ultra-conservative position and refused to televise any games. The most liberal policies were in New York and Chicago where even home games were televised on a regular basis. The major TV networks entered the baseball market in the early fifties. While NBC provided national coverage of the World Series and All Star games, first ABC in 1953 and then CBS presented a selected Saturday game of the week during the regular season. Dizzy Dean and Buddy Blattner handled the announcing chores for ABC/CBS. In 1957, NBC countered with their own game of the week telecasts featuring recently retired Giants Manager Leo Durocher and veteran sportscaster Lindsey Nelson. The introduction of compatible color telecasts by NBC in the late fifties stimulated further interest in TV sports coverage and underscored the commercial value of TV exposure for major league baseball. The era of lucrative, exclusive contracts between major league baseball and NBC were just around the corner as the decade ended.

TV sets became a fixture in taverns across the USA in the 1950s. Big league baseball found a whole new audience and the impact of televised contests was monumental to the game's future.

A TV crew with primitive camera equipment "on location" for a game at New York's Polo Grounds in the early fifties.

Jack Brickhouse was a TV sports institution in Chicagoland with his pleasing commentary on both Cubs and Sox telecasts as well as other major sports in the Windy City.

National radio network broadcasts of selected daily major league contests were already competing with local radio coverage as the decade began. The Liberty Broadcasting System, a maverick network with colorful owner/announcer Gordon McLendon at the mike, sent regular random radio accounts to a nationwide baseball audience in the early 1950s until they were in effect "squeezed out" by the body politic of major league baseball. McLendon, self-dubbed "the Old Scotchman," was a master of recreating games via teletype using realistic sound effects. Local radio announcers for many individual team broadcasts also used this inexpensive method to cover road games in the forties, but as the new decade began, more and more team announcers began to travel with the clubs for live broadcasting all season long. The Mutual Radio Network with Gene Kirby and Al Helfer at the mike, rivaled the Liberty broadcasts with national coverage of a pre-selected "game of the day" by 1950. Increased revenues from radio coverage also resulted in more two-man and even three-man announcing teams. In the early years of TV coverage, some teams used the radio accounts for the audio portion, coining the term "simulcast." Eventually it was determined that the non-stop radio description was ill-suited for video coverage and separate announcers were employed for each form of media. Most clubs widened their listening audience with sizable networks of affiliated stations to complement their local anchor station. By the end of the decade, all games were covered live by radio and all clubs provided at least minimal telecasts—except in Milwaukee, where phenomenal attendance continued unabated.

Al Helfer teamed with Gene Kirby for Mutual Radio's "game of the day," heard by a national audience.

Mel Allen's "sugary" voice was synonymous with nationally televised World Series and All-Star games over NBC-TV in the fifties.

During the regular season, a far-flung national TV audience followed the "game of the week" with baseball legend Dizzy Dean at the mike.

After retiring from managing in 1955, Leo Durocher inaugurated NBC's version of a nationally televised "game of the week" in 1957.

Gordon McLendon had a successful but brief tenure with radio accounts of big league games on his Liberty network in the early '50s.

The breakdown of color barriers in the late forties resulted in a steady influx of talented black stars in the fifties, especially in the National League. The old patterns of discrimination persisted longer in the American League as the Detroit and Boston clubs did not showcase a black player until 1958 and 1959. Only the utter superiority of the powerful New York Yankee teams (with first black Elston Howard added to the roster in 1955) prevented a clear dominance by the National League and its numerous standout black performers who surfaced in the 1950s. The Dodger franchise, which had opened the door to blacks with the signing of Jackie Robinson, claimed a monopoly of talented blacks and was subsequently rewarded with five pennants and two world championships during the ten-year period. Most of baseball's superstars who debuted in the fifties were black National Leaguers— namely Willie Mays, Hank Aaron, Roberto Clemente, Bob Gibson, Frank Robinson, Ernie Banks, and many others. By 1960, professional baseball had permanently erased the stigma of racism and many of baseball's accepted folk heroes were blacks.

In 1958, the Detroit Tigers became the next-to-last club to include blacks on their roster with the signing of Ossie Virgil (left), shown here with Manager Jack Tighe (center) and Herb Moford. The Red Sox showcased their first black player the following year to join the rest of baseball in ending such discrimination.

For most of the major league fans outside the sphere of the New York City-based clubs, the 1950s was a decade of frustration and disappointment. Every team had its heroes and highlights, perhaps enough to sustain fan interest. But championships were destined to be the exclusive property of New York City fans as every World Series during the fifties involved at least one if not both clubs from "the Big Apple." Only in 1959 did the Fall Classic exclude a New York based team, and even then the winning Los Angeles Dodgers were a chronological extension of the old Brooklyn franchise. Casey Stengel's Yankees were invincible from 1950 to 1953 and only a remarkable 111-win season by Cleveland in 1954 denied yet another flag for the Bronx Bombers. And, of course, the fates awarded the world championship to the New York Giants that fall in a stunning four-game sweep over the tribe. The Milwaukee Braves finally wrested the top honors from New York in 1957, but the Yankees returned the favor in 1958. The monopoly of championships made the decade of the fifties a golden era for New York area fans while the "have nots" settled for individual hero worship of home team standouts and memorable moments of baseball drama, despite the failures to capture the seasons' final prizes of first place finishes. The prevailing frustration of non-New York fans perhaps explains the popular appeal of the hit musical "Damn Yankees," a fantasy that suggested an actual winning scenario for the perennial cellar-dwellers, the Washington Senators.

Washington's fictitious new baseball hero Joe Hardy (Stephen Douglas) is tempted by the seductive Lola (Gwen Verdon) in the 1956 Broadway hit musical DAMN YANKEES.

PRINTED MEDIA COVERAGE OF THE GAME

By the 1950s, the number of daily newspapers that covered baseball in the major league cities had dwindled down to half the number of the pre-radio/TV era. New York City, of course, still offered the largest selection of dailies while many of the lesser cities were down to only two or three papers. Many of the once-prosperous big city newspapers were by this time struggling to survive in a period of steady decline in the profitability of the business. Indeed, many traditional dailies became extinct or were absorbed by competing papers during the decade of the fifties. However, the daily reporting of games was still an established staple for baseball fans and a vital ingredient in assuring successful circulation for the newspaper industry. The regular beat writers, all members of the Baseball Writers Association (BBWAA), often worked for neighboring or suburban dailies that considered coverage of the local major league club important enough to justify exclusive writer assignments to baseball. More remote papers relied on shared reports by independent wire services that were also provided by full time baseball reporters who attended all games with eyewitness accounts and stories. Even some of the "out of the mainstream" journals, such as the Daily Worker in New York, had a beat writer assigned to baseball. Many famous writers of the period, such as Fred Lieb, Red Smith, and H. G. Salsinger, were considered institutional names in the baseball world and their written word was eagerly digested by baseball fans everywhere. Although use of four-color photography in regular editions was still a decade away, black and white photo coverage was generously used in the sports pages of papers in the fifties and many news photographers devoted their talents exclusively to baseball during the summer months. The use of cartoonists, both serious and whimsical, was a dying art form in the newspaper sport pages by the 1950s. Once as popular as photographs, fewer and fewer works of line artists appeared to complement the baseball news of the day. Only a handful of established sports artists such as Tom Paprocki ("PAP") and Willard Mullin were able to make a profitable living off their craft via nationwide syndication.

The undisputed source for baseball dope all year round was the old reliable SPORTING NEWS, the weekly tabloid newspaper which had roots going back to the 19th century. The 1950s were the final decade of nearly exclusive year-round attention to baseball alone for the St. Louis-based publication. The familiar front page format with full-size cartoon (very often by the ever-popular Willard Mullin) was a fixture on newsstand racks nationwide. All the news about every level of the national game was published by a first-rate staff of in-house editors plus regional news by established local correspondents from the big daily newspapers of the period. The complete history of baseball in the fifties, or from previous decades for that matter, can be found in the back issues of the Sporting News and researchers need look no further for the important facts about the national pastime. It was truly the "Baseball Bible," or as its subtitle proclaimed, "The Baseball Paper of the World."

When the old Spalding/Reach annual guide books went out of circulation at the beginning of WWII, the Sporting News had already begun to fill the void by publishing an equivalent version of annual record books along with their counterpart, the Dope Book. Just as it was in earlier decades with the Spalding/Reach Guides, the Sporting News annual guide books became a "must" for any complete baseball library. Along with other versions of annual guidebooks, several independently published annual magazines were also popularly circulated every spring—most notably by Street & Smith and Dell. The once-popular monthly BASEBALL magazine suffered a serious decline in readership in the early fifties and after struggling through changes in ownership and desperate attempts to revitalize its format, it finally disappeared forever by 1958. BASEBALL DIGEST, a pocket-size monthly with a more modest format, fared better and continues to be published to this day. Two of the more popular all-sports monthly magazines with slicker formats and some full-color photography were well received by baseball readers during the fifties—the established SPORT magazine plus the brand new SPORTS ILLUSTRATED in 1954. And younger fans eagerly purchased the popular annual sets of baseball cards that provided a visual collection of all the baseball heroes of the day. Of course, the hobby of card collecting in the 1950s was still basically a childhood pastime then and by no means the million-dollar business that it has transformed itself into today.

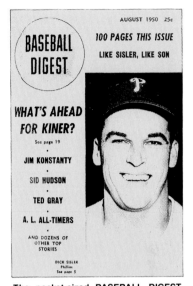

The pocket-sized BASEBALL DIGEST has endured to this day as a fan favorite.

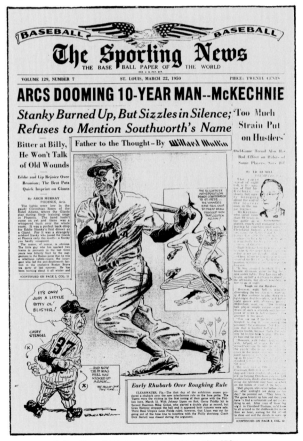

A familiar sight on newsstands in the '50s.

The once-venerable BASEBALL MAGAZINE came to the end of a 50-year run in 1958. In its last years, the cover design bore little resemblance to the familiar look of earlier decades.

SPORT and SPORTS ILLUSTRATED gave baseball fans plenty of color photography of their heroes and quality articles on all aspects of the game.

THE BALLPARKS

The decade of the fifties was the grand climax of the era of classical concrete and steel baseball parks. All of these historic facilities had unique personalities and construction quirks despite their sameness in basic features; i.e., grandstands with full concrete upper decks supported by numerous posts and fully covered by rooftops, also post-supported. Manually operated scoreboards, numerous billboards on the outfield walls, massive banks of incandescent lights (except for Chicago's Wrigley Field), natural grass, and hard outfield walls were all standard. But, except for the newly built parks in the cities with relocated franchises, they were already showing their age. Most of these ballparks dated back to the teen years of the century and despite their seemingly endless durability and veneration by fans, most of them were doomed to obsolescence by the following decades. Despite the many improvements and comforts that are features of these old parks' contemporary replacements, long-time fans in places like Cincinnati and Pittsburgh speak reverently of and recall fondly the pleasures of attending games at old Crosley Field and Forbes Field. Maybe this is simply the usual "good old days" sentiment of

older fans, but then maybe not. After an endless series of circular, look-alike, all-purpose big league stadiums surfaced in the late sixties and seventies, the newest parks in Chicago's South Side and, more dramatically, the new Orioles Park at Camden Yards have attempted to resurrect the ambience of the ballparks of the fifties. Although the numerous support posts and poor sight lines have been basically eliminated along with manually operated scoreboards in these new parks, the architectural eccentricities and sense of neighborhood have been deliberately preserved and joyously received by fans and critics alike.

Four of the older classic era parks have not been significantly remodeled and are still in business— Cleveland Municipal Stadium, Tiger (Briggs) Stadium, Fenway Park, and Wrigley Field. The least tampered with are Wrigley and Fenway and even today the experience of visiting these ballparks is very much like revisiting the 1950s. Today's Yankee Stadium is only partially recognizable as the old Bronx park of the fifties after the massive rebuilding project in the seventies. Tiger Stadium is still the same structure, but the gleaming white exterior and the predominantly bright blue interior have somehow destroyed its more

comfortable memory of soft gray on the outside, standard green on the inside as it was in the 1950s. Also, the surrounding neighborhood has suffered from urban decay and a nearby freeway has carved out a huge strip of the familiar Corktown area. The rapid deterioration of the surrounding neighborhood of some of the now-extinct parks had as much to do with their demise as the shortcomings of the structures themselves. Some good examples of this seemingly hopeless blight appeared in St. Louis and Cincinnati and a good case could have been made for abandoning Yankee Stadium for the same reasons. Cleveland's venerable oval, the so-called "mistake on the lake," has survived intact but its days are numbered as a baseball facility as plans are underway for a new ballpark. A partially recreated version of Crosley Field currently exists in suburban Cincinnati as a nostalgic reminder of the Reds' home in the fifties. In Boston, a small section of the old Braves Field facility is still standing as another reminder of the early 1950s, when there were two major league teams in the Hub. Gone forever are the Polo Grounds, Ebbets Field, Griffith Stadium, old Comiskey Park, Shibe Park (Connie Mack Stadium), Forbes Field, and Sportsman's Park (Busch Stadium, the first version).

Manually operated scoreboards, like this one at Detroit's Briggs Stadium, were the norm in 1950. By 1959, most were converted to electronic operation.

A couple of major league ballpark scenes from the 1950s that could be passed off as current photos, since both parks have changed very little. On the left, Chicago's Wrigley Field, and below, Detroit's Briggs (Tiger) Stadium.

Relocation of franchises in the fifties gave baseball two brand new ballparks, two hastily upgraded minor league parks, and the abominable adaptation of the Los Angeles Coliseum. Milwaukee's County Stadium was not particularly unique in its appearance, just the newest version of the standard concrete and steel double-decked grandstand that was a continuation of the old classic parks then in existence. However, unlike its predecessors, it was totally insulated from its surroundings by a vast parking area—a symptom of the rapidly expanding automobile population of that decade. Baltimore's Memorial Stadium reflected another consideration that influenced future ballpark construction. The coming of the new Orioles in 1954 was the catalyst in approving the new facility but from the beginning it was intended to also be the new home of the NFL Colts—thus deliberately designed as a multi-sport facility. This rationale deprived the new structure from inheriting the inviting configurations and "personality" that could have identified it as a pure baseball park. The new Oriole Park at Camden Yards has more than made amends for this shortcoming.

Kansas City's Blues Stadium as it was for the last years of AAA ball, before the new upper deck and other modifications were made to ready it for the arrival of the Athletics in 1955. It was then renamed Municipal Stadium.

Kansas City's Municipal Stadium, the new home of the Athletics for the 1955 season, was merely a face-lift and expansion of the home field of the AAA Blues that was originally built in the twenties. Kansas City fans not only inherited an historic franchise, but shared a similar experience with existing major league cities by attending games in an already historic facility. Although not blessed with a sparkling new stadium, KC fans were no worse off than most of the existing ML cities and no one complained. A similar scenario greeted the arrival of the transplanted Giants in San Francisco in 1958. Plans were already underway to construct a brand new major league ballpark, but in the meantime the SF fans flocked to tiny Seals Stadium, former home of the now-extinct PCL club, to root for their new major leaguers. The frenzy of excitement over the long-awaited appearance of major league baseball in the Bay area completely drowned out any complaints about having to temporarily play in an inadequate, small park. In Los Angeles, the excitement was even more tumultuous and the likewise temporary inconvenience of watching the Dodgers play their games in an inadequate, oversized bowl that was in no way "baseball friendly" failed to keep fans from pouring into the Coliseum in record numbers. Despite the phenomenal fan support that greeted the Dodgers in their early years in Los Angeles, it is very unlikely that the LA fans who continued to flock to the new Dodger Stadium in the sixties would ever lust for the return of the Coliseum experience.

THE TEAMS AND THE PLAYERS

Many baseball sentimentalists look back fondly at the era of the 1950s as a "golden age" of big league baseball. Who can argue that the decade showcased as many star players and dramatic moments as any other era in the history of the game? But this definition of the decade leans heavily on geography and particularly the legions of fans in the New York area. Ask any longtime Boston Red Sox fan or Chicago Cub fan if the fifties was a golden age and you may get an argument. Sure, there were memorable moments and unforgettable players like Ted Williams and Ernie Banks, but for many fans the fifties also symbolized frustration—the hopeless scenario of somehow stealing a pennant from the perennial champions, the Yankees, the Dodgers, or the Giants. The complete dominance of the New York Yankees had its appeal even to somewhat neutral fans outside the New York sphere who worshipped them as the personification of excellence. But their continual successes also eroded any sense of parity in the American League and many fans in other cities lost interest. The Yanks' success was a mixed blessing for overall attendance. Of course, Yankee Stadium enjoyed healthy gate receipts and the powerful Bronx Bombers drew good crowds whenever they "barnstormed" around the circuit. Despite the resentment and envy they generated in other American League towns, fans were captivated by their roster of headline players and looked forward to the prospect of a home team upset. But at the same time, the competition between the other seven teams in the American League degenerated into a battle for second place, not much to hope for for die-hard fans. Despite the monopoly of Dodgers/Giants pennants during the decade, neither of these clubs seemed invincible to NL fans as were the Yankees in the junior circuit.

An all-too-familiar sight for non-New York fans . . . another Dodger/Yankee World Series with the opposing managers congratulating each other.

Tiny Seals Stadium in San Francisco offered no fan protection from the elements nor from the afternoon sun.

Casey Stengel's Yankee teams in the fifties set a standard for winning consistently that may never be matched. They seemed incapable of a mortal losing streak or an off-season that even the great Yankee teams of the past occasionally experienced. And they possessed that rare blend of team chemistry and experience that never failed them in clutch situations. Even when they yielded an AL pennant to the surprising Indians in 1954, they still won 103 games. Finally in 1959, they showed signs of mortality and possibly age by finishing third, barely over .500. Stengel had the luxury of generously platooning a squad of versatile talent and he used this strategy like a magician. The Yankees were blessed with wealthy owners Dan Topping and Del Webb plus the crafty general manager George Weiss. This front office team very often procured experienced veterans like Johnny Mize, Johnny Sain, and Enos Slaughter at just the right moment to strengthen the team for the pennant run. Veteran hurlers Ed Lopat, Vic Raschi and Allie Reynolds provided a solid pitching rotation in the early years of the decade. When this trio began to fade, the younger Whitey Ford, Bob Grim, Bob Turley, and Tom Sturdivant continued the tradition of dependable starting pitchers. Mickey Mantle and Yogi Berra provided most of the offensive firepower during the decade, but the lineup had few weak spots and every hitter in the Yankee lineup was a threat to break up a ball game. For die-hard Yankee fans and "closet" Yankee fans throughout the league, the 1950s were truly the "golden age" of the franchise, a record of excellence that will probably never be seen again.

As for the American League "also rans" of the decade, only Cleveland and Chicago managed to break the monopoly of Yankee pennants. The Indians had the strongest pitching in baseball, arguably superior to the New York staff for most of the decade. Bob Feller, Bob Lemon, Early Wynn, Mike Garcia and ever-so-briefly Herb Score, supported by ace relievers Don Mossi and Ray Narleski, gave the tribe six second-place finishes and one pennant during the 1950-59 period. They also featured some heavy artillery with Ray Boone, Al Rosen, Dale Mitchell, and Larry Doby. But their lineup could not match the balance and depth of the New Yorkers and could not sustain them through the late stages of the pennant chase. However, in 1954 everything meshed perfectly for manager Al Lopez and the Indians piled up a league record of 111 victories, giving the impression that a new dynasty was at hand. The bubble was promptly burst by Leo Durocher's Giants in the post-season classic, as the Indians were swept in four games. They finished another strong second the following year with 93 wins, but never recaptured the amazing chemistry of 1954 and even slipped into the second division by 1957.

The Chicago White Sox emerged from second-division obscurity in the late forties to become the most exciting team to watch in the 1950s. Flamboyant Frank Lane, the master trader, became GM in 1949 and revamped the roster with a series of brilliant player acquisitions. Pitcher Billy Pierce was virtually "stolen" from Detroit and the new keystone combination of shortstop Chico Carrasquel and second baseman Nelson Fox were key arrivals via the frenzied trading of Lane. Slugging first baseman Eddie Robinson, outfielder/infielder Minnie Minoso, and catcher Sherman Lollar were other important ingredients in the transformation into the new "Go-Go" Sox of the early fifties. New field manager Paul Richards arrived in 1951 to complete the picture. The blend of speed, power, defense and solid pitching made the White Sox a serious contender for second place throughout the decade and they finally captured the big prize in 1959 under Al Lopez. Chicago's South Side followers were treated to an exhilarating brand of baseball in the "Go-Go" years—even the bland, monotone broadcasts of radio voice Bob Elson could not conceal the ongoing drama that was offered to long-suffering Sox fans.

The 1954 Cleveland Indians established an AL season record with 111 victories. TOP (L to R): Doby, Wynn, Garcia, Grasso, Newhouser, Westlake, Hooper, Houtteman, Strickland, Lemon, Regalado. 3RD ROW (L to R): Mossi, Feller, Philley, Majeski, Rosen, Wertz, Mitchell, Hegan, Trainer Bock. 2ND ROW (L to R): Narleski, Naragon, Coach Cuccinello, Mgr. Lopez, Coach Kress, Coach Lobe, Coach Harder. SEATED (L to R): Smith, Hoskins, Glynn, Avila, Pope, Dente, Batboy Klug.

Yankees' pilot Stengel (center) with two key ingredients in the team's recipe for winning: Mickey Mantle on the left, Yogi Berra on the right.

General Manager Frank Lane chats with one of his key acquisitions for the "go-go" White Sox team of the early fifties, Minnie Minoso.

The Boston Red Sox and Detroit Tigers, both solid pennant contenders as the forties drew to a close, "burned out" in the early fifties and finished out the decade in the middle of the pack. Even the genius of veteran manager Joe McCarthy could not rally the talented but aging Red Sox to wrest the pennant from the Yankees and surprising Detroit in 1950. The pitching staff, led by Mel Parnell, proved no match for the solid Yankee rotation and even a team .302 batting average could not overcome a 4.88 staff ERA. The incomparable Ted Williams continued to hit with a vengeance throughout the decade, but all-stars Dom DiMaggio, Bobby Doerr, Johnny Pesky, and Vern Stephens all succumbed to age and were gone by 1953. By the late fifties, the rebuilt Red Sox presented a fairly solid roster of talented players like Jackie Jensen, Jimmy Piersall, Frank Malzone, and Sammy White, but as before were unable to assemble a strong rotation of starting pitchers to seriously challenge the front-runners. Meanwhile, the Detroit club began the decade with a rush. Manager Red Rolfe had his Bengals in first place for most of the 1950 season, but they finally faded badly at the end to finish three games behind the New Yorkers. The acquisition of second baseman Jerry Priddy and outstanding seasons for Tiger mainstays Kell, Wertz, Evers, Groth, Lipon, and Houtteman gave Detroit fans plenty to cheer about that year as they drew a record 1.9 million into Briggs Stadium. But it was all downhill following the 1950 season as the Tigers plummeted to their very first residency of the American League cellar in 1952. The club seemed suddenly cursed as popular radio announcer Harry Heilmann died in 1951 and owner Walter O. Briggs passed on in early 1952. Even a desperate series of multi-player trades involving front-line stars in 1952 did not have much effect as they simply exchanged over-the-hill veterans for more over-the-hill veterans and youngsters that failed to live up to their potential. Tiger fans stayed home in droves and were slow to generate interest in following the games of the hapless Tigers as described by Heilmann's replacement, Van Patrick. Things picked up slowly as the decade rolled on and, as in Boston, a new crop of solid players like Ray Boone, Steve Gromek, Harvey Kuenn, Frank Bolling, Frank Lary, Jim Bunning, and 18-year-old outfielding phenom Al Kaline improved the team to respectable .500 status. Even Van Patrick, in truth a fine announcer, won back a full audience of listeners by the end of the decade. New ownership by John Fetzer and Fred Knorr in 1957 restored some stability to the organization after a hectic period under the heirs of the Briggs estate.

In the nation's capital, major league baseball remained a necessary patriotic formality throughout the 1950s. Under veteran manager Bucky Harris, they actually played .500 ball and finished as high as fifth place in 1952 and 1953. They looked around in awe and then promptly nosedived back to their customary cellar occupancy for four of the last five years of the decade. Their lineup was occasionally blessed with a sprinkling of established position players like Mickey Vernon, Eddie Yost, Gil Coan, Pete Runnels, Roy Sievers, and young Harmon Killebrew. They also on rare occasions got major league pitching from Bob Porterfield and the two Latinos Pedro Ramos and Camilio Pascual. The death of veteran owner Clark Griffith in 1955 changed the destiny of the franchise as his more realistic heir Calvin Griffith soon became tempted by the thought of greener pastures for the team.

The Red Sox power men of 1950—Williams, Doerr, and Dropo after a 29-4 drubbing of the hapless Browns.

Manager Jack Tighe (left) with new Tiger heroes of the late fifties—Al Kaline (center), Harvey Kuenn (right).

Connie Mack celebrated his incredible 50th year at the helm of the Philadelphia Athletics as the decade began. Mack then stepped down as field manager, relinquishing the job to one time A's player and coach Jimmy Dykes. The A's were by this time a troubled franchise as the more exciting Phillies, the pennant-winning "Whiz Kids" of 1950, were badly outdrawing the American Leaguers at their shared facility, Shibe Park. Dykes managed to lead the team briefly into the first division in 1952, led by some great pitching from little Bobby Shantz and some decent hitting by Ferris Fain, Elmer Valo and young slugger Gus Zernial. But the spread of talent just wasn't there and in tandem with a general lack of excitement, the franchise hit rock bottom in 1954. It became clear that Philadelphia could no longer support two major league teams, so Mack put the club up for sale. Arnold Johnson was the winning bidder and he immediately announced that the club would transfer to Kansas City for the 1955 season. It was the end of the road for the Connie Mack odyssey, which began with the formation of the American League back in 1901 and gave Philadelphia fans many unforgettable baseball heroes and some legendary teams. Mack himself passed away in early 1956, as if to add the final nail in the coffin.

THE WHITE HOUSE
WASHINGTON

April 11, 1950

Dear Connie Mack:

The Massachusetts country boy has gone places in baseball since he started his career as catcher on the home town team in those faraway days of the early eighties of the last century.

Gladly do I join the friends and legion of fans who are to gather in your honor at Philadelphia on Thursday evening, April twentieth, to celebrate the fiftieth anniversary of your association with big league baseball. In you American sport has had an exemplar whose record has been an inspiration to our youth for a full half century. Best of all, you are going strong at fourscore and seven with eyes always to a hopeful future. May your shadow never grow less.

Cordially and sincerely,

Harry Truman

Connie Mack's 50th year as boss of the Athletics was not overlooked by the White House.

Kansas City fans eagerly received the Athletics, despite their lowly standing in the league. New manager Lou Boudreau was able to get some extra mileage from a melting pot of veteran players in their first year, but after that they settled into the bottom of the heap for the balance of the decade. Without a productive farm system to build a contending team from within, a revolving door of journeyman players came and went through annual trades that seldom created any winning chemistry for the Athletics. Many of these player trades were consummated with the New York Yankees, usually to the Yanks' advantage, and the club was cynically accused by many to be a pseudo-farm team of the New Yorkers. Kansas City fans lamented the frequent transfer of potential "marquis" players like Bob Cerv, Hector Lopez, Enos Slaughter, and Bobby Shantz to New York in exchange for Yankee players with marginal contributions to Casey Stengel's magic formula for winning pennants. Even the arrival of Billy Martin, a proven sparkplug for winning teams in the Bronx who managed to get in Stengel's "doghouse," was a disappointment and he was traded to Detroit the following season. The fruits of finally acquiring the major league variety of baseball for Kansas City fans gradually developed a sour taste as the front office seemed incapable of assembling a winning or even a respectable team.

Another AL franchise that shared the same futility as the Athletics when the fifties began was the St. Louis Browns. The co-tenants of Sportsman's Park were unable to attract the healthy following of the perennially respectable NL Cardinals, who enjoyed a long tradition of pennant winning teams and showcased popular superstars like Stan Musial, Enos Slaughter, and Red Schoendienst. Hopelessly trapped at the bottom of the standings, even flamboyant owner-promotor Bill Veeck was unable to recreate anything close to the success he enjoyed in Cleveland in the late forties. Only pitcher Ned Garver stood out as a proven major leaguer, winning 20 games for the last place Brownies of 1951. The balance of the roster consisted of a handful of washed-up veterans, some capable journeymen, and youngsters of high minor league qualifications. Veeck's occasional gimmicks, like the insertion of midget Eddie Gaedel into the lineup in a '51 game, got headlines but did little to attract new fans. Nor did the acquisition of the ageless wonder Satchel Paige to the roster. Veeck's antics became a nuisance and an embarrassment to other more conservative AL owners, and after the Braves' transfer to Milwaukee proved to be a financially successful venture, Veeck was forced out and the franchise was sold to a group of investors in Baltimore.

A sparkling new stadium was ready and waiting and Baltimore returned to the American League after an absence of 52 seasons. The 1954 player roster bore only limited resemblance to the St. Louis Browns of 1953. The front office busied itself in the preseason and assembled a new team of mostly veteran players that managed to lose 100 games but escaped the dreaded cellar. Baltimore management proved more productive than Kansas City in recruiting a winning club as they enticed Paul Richards from the White Sox to double as general manager and field manager for 1955. Their scouting efforts, along with Richards' shrewd judging of needed talent, began to pay off with the signing of future stars like Gus Triandos, Billy Gardner, Milt Pappas and a "franchise" third baseman named Brooks Robinson. The likes of Pappas, Billy O'Dell and later Hoyt Wilhelm began to provide some decent pitching and the Orioles gradually elevated themselves into the first division by 1960.

Some of the ex-Browns who continued their careers with the transplanted Orioles of 1954—(L to R): Vic Wertz, Marlin Stuart, Neil Berry, Lou Kretlow, and Don Lenhardt.

The ageless immortal, Satchel Paige, proved to Brownie fans and the rest of the American League that he still had some juice in his pitching arm by winning 18 games from 1951 to 1953.

In the senior circuit, the Dodgers were clearly the "cream at the top" for most of the decade. Except for a lapse in 1958, their maiden season in Los Angeles, they produced five pennants and two world championships and were always a factor, if not an outright contender, in the pennant chase. In fact, only final game heroics by the Phils' Dick Sisler in 1950 and the Giants' Bobby Thomson in 1951 prevented Brooklyn from matching the Yanks' five consecutive pennants from 1949 to 1953. The genius of Branch Rickey had assembled an all-star lineup in the late forties that served them well through the decade of the fifties. An important ingredient in producing this winning aggregation was the early recruitment of negro stars like Jackie Robinson, Roy Campanella, Don Newcombe, and Joe Black. On paper, no team in baseball (including the Yankees) could claim a superior array of balance and depth, both offensively and defensively, as the "boys of summer"—Hodges, Robinson, Reese, Cox, Furillo, Snider, Campanella, et al. The pitching staff was extraordinarily deep in quality starters and managers Shotton, Dressen, and Walter Alston enjoyed the luxury of five and even six man rotations to keep the team in peak condition over the long season. Their combined ERA was seldom impressive and they did not showcase consistent 20-game winners as did Cleveland, for example, but they got enough offensive support to get the job done. Preacher Roe, Carl Erskine, and Don Newcombe were the workhorses during the early/mid decade, backed up by some fine relief work by Jim Hughes and Clem Labine. Toward the end of the decade Johnny Podres and Don Drysdale carried the pitching load. Newcomer Sandy Koufax was unimpressive in the late fifties—his control betrayed him and temporarily delayed the spectacular pitching he displayed in the sixties. The franchise was also blessed with one of the soundest business operations in baseball under the guidance of owner Walter O'Malley.

The Dodgers' traditional rivals, the Giants, also enjoyed a successful tenure in the fifties, especially in the first half of the decade. Leo Durocher won pennants in 1951 and 1954 and retired after the 1955 season with a career winning record of well over .500. Bill Rigney's first two years as manager were disappointing but when the franchise relocated to San Francisco, the team returned to contention. Following the Dodgers' lead, the Giants did not hesitate to sign black stars once the color barrier was ended and it paid immediate dividends. Hank Thompson and Monte Irvin made solid contributions from the start but the big prize was signing Willie Mays in 1951. The "Say Hey" kid was an instant idol of the fans and his amazing feats at the bat, on the base paths, and in the outfield became the talk of baseball. No other player in the National League, with the possible exception of Stan Musial, became more identified as the symbol of his team. As Willie went, so went the Giants as they stumbled into fifth place during Mays' absence due to military service in 1953; then reclaimed the NL flag upon his return in 1954. Of course, the New Yorkers had a lineup of first-rate players to complement Willie—Lockman, Dark, Mueller, Westrum, to mention a few. Sal Maglie, Jim Hearn, Larry Jansen, and Hoyt Wilhelm were the backbone of a fine pitching corps that kept them contending in the early years of the decade. Johnny Antonelli, Ruben Gomez, Sam Jones, and Jack Sanford made up the nucleus of the staff in the early San Francisco years. New sluggers Orlando Cepeda and Willie McCovey joined the team in SF and helped revitalize the West Coast version of the Giants as a legitimate pennant threat.

The opening season of the decade (1950) gave National League fans a rare treat. The sudden emergence of Philadelphia's "whiz kids" as pennant contenders captured the attention of fans throughout the league. They finally won out, but only after holding off an unbelievable late season surge by the Brooklyn club that produced a classic finale. In the last day of the season (pitting the two contenders as the fates of the schedule graciously permitted) the Phils' Dick Sisler homered in the tenth to give Philadelphia fans their first flag in 35 years. The outfield of Sisler, Richie Ashburn, and Del Ennis provided the hitting to back up a fine pitching trio of Robin Roberts, Curt Simmons, and Bob Miller. But the key that opened the door to the flag was bespectacled relief pitcher Jim Konstanty, who came out of nowhere to win 16 games and save 22 others. Konstanty was voted league MVP and started the first game of the World Series due to Curt Simmons' unfortunate recall to military service. Manager Eddie Sawyer was unable to sustain the magic the following season and was replaced by Steve O'Neill in early 1952. But win or not, the legend of the "Whiz Kids" gave Phillie fans plenty of thrills well into the decade and provided some long-lost optimism in the City of Brotherly Love. The perennially strong pitching tandem of Roberts and Simmons kept the Phillies respectable for most of the decade, but they finally faded into the cellar in 1958-59, and, as if to provide "bookends" for the 10-year span, Eddie Sawyer was rehired to finish out the 1950s.

Duke Snider, Carl Erskine, and Manager Chuck Dressen celebrating a World Series game victory in 1952.

The one and only Willie Mays, the catalyst for New York Giants pennants in 1951 and 1954.

The hard-hitting outfield that sparked the 1950 Phillies "Whiz Kids" to an NL flag—Dick Sisler, Richie Ashburn, and Del Ennis.

In Boston, Braves' owner Lou Perini had watched the gradual deterioration of his 1948 pennant winners to a second division club by 1952 and so did many Boston fans, but not from the seats at Braves Field as attendance dwindled dramatically to crisis levels. It became clear that Boston had become exclusively a Red Sox town and something had to give. Despite a handful of solid veterans, including Warren Spahn, Earl Torgeson, Sid Gordon, and Walker Cooper and the arrival of coming stars Eddie Mathews, Johnny Logan, and Lew Burdette, the team was unable to sustain fan interest. The ruling body politic of the National League grudgingly consented to alter the 50-year alignment of major league teams and granted Perini permission to transfer the team to Milwaukee for the 1953 season. Little Milwaukee responded with a phenomenal first year attendance total of almost 2 million, nearly sevenfold over the 1952 Braves Field figures and erasing any doubts about the financial wisdom of rearranging baseball's status quo. Charlie Grimm's newborn Braves also responded to the warm reception by finishing in second place and continued to challenge for the pennant for the balance of the decade. The pitching trio of Warren Spahn, Lew Burdette, and Bob Buhl developed into a formidable starting corps. The acquisition of veterans Joe Adcock, Red Schoendienst, and Andy Pafko along with Mathews and young outfielder Hank Aaron rewarded manager Fred Haney with a pennant and world's championship in 1957. The Braves repeated as NL champs the following year and were denied a third in a playoff with the Dodgers to close out the decade. Milwaukee fans continued to fill County Stadium in record numbers, completing the scenario of baseball's biggest financial success story of the 1950s.

The Milwaukee Braves combined great pitching and run production for winning seasons. Shown are (L to R): Jack Dittmer, Johnny Logan, Ed Mathews, Jim Pendleton, and Del Crandall after hammering out a record eight homers in a game vs. Pittsburgh in 1953.

The St. Louis Cardinals during the fifties never seriously threatened to occupy first place, but stayed respectable for most of the decade. Beer Baron August Busch purchased the club in 1953 and the operation subsequently floundered under master trader Frank Lane, whose not-so-brilliant player shuffling was unable to improve the club's fortunes. The enduring skills of Stan Musial continued to carry the burden of the offense after many of the old Cardinal favorites retired or were traded off. The Redbird pitching corps was held together during the decade by Gerry Staley, "Vinegar Bend" Mizell, Harvey Haddix, and Brooks Lawrence. Ken Boyer, Don Blasingame, and Wally Moon arrived in the latter half of the fifties to add some punch. But the resurgence of the Cardinals would have to wait until the next decade when new heroes like Curt Flood and Bob Gibson, late arrivals in the '50s, would help soften the blow of Musial's retirement from the game. The real story of the Cardinals of the fifties was the people's choice, Stan the Man, who added four batting championships to his career total of seven and his mere presence in the lineup made the Cardinals a top gate attraction. The signing of new general manager Bing Devine in 1958 finally gave the club an architect to orchestrate the steady improvement of Cardinal fortunes.

In Cincinnati, General Manager Gabe Paul assembled a lineup of power hitters in the mid-fifties that provided some excitement for Reds fans but was unable to lift the team much over .500, except for a strong run in 1956 under Birdie Tebbetts. Ted Kluszewski, Wally Post, Gus Bell, rookie Frank Robinson, and Ed Bailey were the big guns in producing a record tying total of 221 homers in '56. Johnny Temple and Roy McMillan were arguably the premier keystone combination of the decade. Cincinnati fans, in their frenzy to showcase their hometown heroes, created a national controversy when they "stuffed" the ballot boxes for the 1957 All-Star game selections. Fans outside the Cincinnati area were outraged by the practically all-Reds starting lineup and forced a change in the method of future balloting. Reds' pitching was pretty much "ho-hum" during the '50s. Ken Raffensberger and Ewell Blackwell were the mainstays in the early years, followed by Brooks Lawrence, Joe Nuxhall, and Bob Purkey. The signing of Freddie Hutchinson in mid-1959 to manage the Reds was an omen of better things to come for Cincinnati in the 1960s.

The decade of the fifties was truly a forgettable stretch for the Chicago Cubs and Pittsburgh Pirates. They spent most of the 10-year period jockeying for last place in the standings. Their fortunes and even the makeup of their teams followed a remarkably similar path. Both clubs suffered from a dreadful lack of quality pitching for most of the decade, especially the Cubs. The Pirates finally assembled a decent staff in the late '50s with the likes of Bob Friend, Vern Law, Harvey Haddix and Roy Face—and they began to creep up into the alien world of the first division as the decade ended. Both teams understandably experienced a revolving door of managerial changes, the usual "quick fix" that seldom transforms legitimate losers. They both featured individual home run sluggers in their lineups: for the Cubs it was first Hank Sauer, then Ernie Banks; for the Pirates first Ralph Kiner, then Frank Thomas. For Cub fans, the only consistent highlights were provided by shortstop Banks, who came up in late 1953 and averaged 40 homers a season for the balance of the decade. For the Pirates, the future was much brighter as they gradually assembled a stable of stars like Bill Mazeroski, Roberto Clemente, and Bill Virdon to complement their improved pitching. Danny Murtaugh arrived in 1957 to lead the team fortunes upward to a pennant in 1960.

Muscular Reds first baseman Ted Kluszewski, in his patented bare-shouldered look, was the backbone of the long-ball wrecking crew from Cincinnati in the mid-fifties.

SPRING TRAINING SITES 1950-1959	
BALTIMORE ORIOLES	Yuma AZ 1954, Daytona Beach FL 1955, Scottsdale AZ 1956-58, Miami FL 1959
BOSTON/ MILWAUKEE BRAVES	Bradenton FL 1950-59
BOSTON RED SOX	Sarasota FL 1950-58, Scottsdale AZ 1959
BROOKLYN/ LOS ANGELES DODGERS	Vero Beach FL 1950-59
CHICAGO CUBS	Catalina Island CA 1950-51, Mesa AZ 1952-59
CHICAGO WHITE SOX	Pasadena CA 1950-52 (also Palm Springs CA 1951 and El Centro CA 1952), El Centro CA 1953, Tampa FL 1954-59
CINCINNATI REDS	Tampa FL 1950-59
CLEVELAND INDIANS	Tucson AZ 1950-59
DETROIT TIGERS	Lakeland FL 1950-59
NEW YORK/ SAN FRANCISCO GIANTS	Phoenix AZ 1950, St. Petersburg FL 1951, Phoenix AZ 1952-59
NEW YORK YANKEES	St. Petersburg FL 1950, Phoenix AZ 1951, St. Petersburg FL 1952-59
PHILADELPHIA/ KANSAS CITY ATHLETICS	West Palm Beach FL 1950-59
PHILADELPHIA PHILLIES	Clearwater FL 1950-59
PITTSBURGH PIRATES	San Bernardino CA 1950-52, Havana CUBA 1953, Ft. Pierce FL 1954, Ft. Myers FL 1955-59
ST. LOUIS BROWNS	Burbank CA 1950-52, San Bernardino CA 1953
ST. LOUIS CARDINALS	St. Petersburg FL 1950-59
WASHINGTON SENATORS	Orlando FL 1950-59

THE MANAGERS

Casey Stengel's remarkable run of championships places him at the head of the class of big league pilots during the 1950-59 period. The old "professor," with his delightfully cryptic manner of speech, responded to the unending media attention as if he were placed in the spotlight by central casting. Even if the monotonous winning habits of the Yankees as a team sometimes wore thin in the press, an interview or a quote from Casey was always good copy. His rhetoric was seldom fully understood and his strategy was often unpredictable, but the results spoke for themselves. His earlier tenure as a manager in the National League in the thirties was a dismal failure, a fact which made his appointment with New York in 1949 a huge question mark. An argument can be made that the vast reservoir of talented Yankee players would have made any manager look like a genius, but the fact remains that Stengel got the maximum results on the field and could never be accused of managing the New Yorkers out of a pennant that they should have won.

Leo Durocher also possessed a personality that produced good copy for the baseball reporters, but Leo was cut from the old John McGraw mold. His abrasive, flamboyant behavior irritated as many people as it attracted. Durocher made many enemies, but he knew how to win and further, he knew how to assemble and maneuver a cast of players into a winning combination. His managerial record speaks for itself, but perhaps his most notable achievement in the early fifties was his paternal development of young superstar Willie Mays into a leadership role with the Giants. Across the way in Brooklyn, Chuck Dressen guided the talented Dodgers to consecutive pennants in the early fifties. Dressen was as combative and sometimes as ill-tempered and impatient as Durocher, but without the swashbuckling personality of Leo the Lip. His successor, Walter Alston, continued the Dodgers' winning tradition in a contrastingly quiet manner. Alston's introverted demeanor belied his abilities to execute sound baseball strategy and communicate effectively with his team. He went on to serve for 23 seasons as one of the most productive managers in the history of the Dodger franchise.

Grizzled baseball veteran Casey Stengel made up for a dismal managerial record in the National League by piloting the Yankees to five straight world championships and eight pennants in the decade of the '50s.

Walter Alston came out of the Dodger farm system in 1954 to embark on a long tenure as a successful manager.

Leo Durocher sharpened his credentials as a winning field boss with two NL pennants for the Giants in the early fifties.

Among the other big-league field managers who produced pennant winners in the fifties, Senor Al Lopez deserves top ranking. He kept the Cleveland Indians in contention from 1951 to 1956 and managed them to a record 111 victories in the 1954 pennant-winning season. From there he moved on to Chicago and brought the White Sox their first AL flag since 1919. Fred Haney, who succeeded the popular Charlie Grimm at Milwaukee in 1956, brought some heavy baggage as the pilot of the pathetic Pirates of 1953-55. But a year later the Braves were the world champions and like Stengel, Haney was able to erase his image as a manager of losers and strengthened his reputation as a sound field general with a follow-up pennant in '58 and a near miss in '59. Eddie Sawyer was the other pennant-winning manager of the decade, piloting the Philadelphia Phillies in the 1950 season. Sawyer departed in 1952 but returned to his old post as Phils' manager in 1958, replacing Mayo Smith, who went on to manage the Cincinnati Reds in 1959.

"Senor" Al Lopez, the only AL manager besides Stengel to win pennants in the 1950s.

Fred Haney led Milwaukee to two flags in '57 and '58, including a W/S victory over the "invincible" Yanks.

A discussion of major league field managers in the 1950s would be disrespectful to the history of the game without mentioning a pair of legendary figures that survived to guide losing clubs in the 1950s. The illustrious career of Connie Mack, baseball's "grand old man," finally came to an end in the fifties. Mr. Mack, as he was dutifully addressed by almost everyone, was 88 years young when he surrendered the managerial reins of the Philadelphia Athletics to Jimmy Dykes in 1951. Connie's incredible tenure as A's manager spanned five full decades, all the way back to the birth of the American League in 1901. Even though Mr. Mack was well past his prime years as a field boss, he simply didn't "have the horses" in 1950 to field a competitive team. His advanced age notwithstanding, no one dared challenge his storied credentials as a big league manager, having piloted some of the great dynasties in

Ancient Connie Mack began the 1950s with his last fling at managing at age 87.

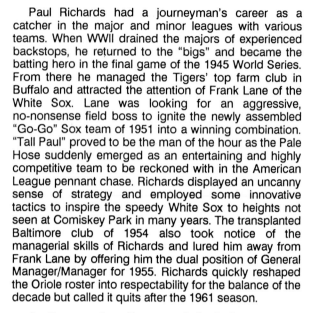

Bucky Harris managed the Nats (for the third time) and the Tigers (for the second) in the fifties.

the twentieth century. His uniqueness was accentuated by his never having donned a uniform in his 50 years with the Athletics. Oddly enough, his last season as manager (1950) was shared with the only other remaining ML manager who preferred street clothes—Burt Shotton of Brooklyn. The other old surviving "war horse," whose managerial career dated back to his "boy manager" years with Washington in the 1920s, was Bucky Harris. Bucky surfaced occasionally as a big league manager in every decade and with mixed results. Very often he was saddled with hopeless clubs, but he did guide the Yankees to a world championship in 1947. He reappeared as Washington manager in 1950 (for the third time) without much success and made his final managerial debut with Detroit in 1955. His fine playing career as a second baseman combined with his long managerial association with major league baseball put him into the baseball Hall of Fame in 1975.

"Tall Paul" Richards led the "GO-GO" SOX, then moved on to Baltimore in 1955.

Lou Boudreau piloted three AL clubs in the decade—Cleveland, Boston, and Kansas City.

Paul Richards had a journeyman's career as a catcher in the major and minor leagues with various teams. When WWII drained the majors of experienced backstops, he returned to the "bigs" and became the batting hero in the final game of the 1945 World Series. From there he managed the Tigers' top farm club in Buffalo and attracted the attention of Frank Lane of the White Sox. Lane was looking for an aggressive, no-nonsense field boss to ignite the newly assembled "Go-Go" Sox team of 1951 into a winning combination. "Tall Paul" proved to be the man of the hour as the Pale Hose suddenly emerged as an entertaining and highly competitive team to be reckoned with in the American League pennant chase. Richards displayed an uncanny sense of strategy and employed some innovative tactics to inspire the speedy White Sox to heights not seen at Comiskey Park in many years. The transplanted Baltimore club of 1954 also took notice of the managerial skills of Richards and lured him away from Frank Lane by offering him the dual position of General Manager/Manager for 1955. Richards quickly reshaped the Oriole roster into respectability for the balance of the decade but called it quits after the 1961 season.

Another one-time "boy wonder" playing manager, Lou Boudreau, piloted three major league clubs during the fifties. He ended a nine-year run as skipper of the Cleveland Indians in 1950 with a strong fourth place finish and moved on to the Red Sox the following season as a player only. When Lou's playing days were at an end, the Boston club enticed him to stay on as field manager. But he was unable to elevate the mixture of over-the-hill veterans and unproven youngsters any higher than fourth place so he signed up to try his hand with the transplanted Athletics in Kansas City for their first year there in 1955. The results were disappointing as the A's plummeted to last place in '56 after an encouraging 6th place finish in '55. Lou departed KC the following year and then signed on with the Cubs as a play-by-play radio announcer. In 1960, he left the radio booth for one last fling at managing (with the hometown Cubs).

Eddie Sawyer gave Phillie fans a rare pennant in 1950. Fired in 1952, he was rehired in 1958.

CLUB OWNERS & EXECUTIVES

The decade of the 1950s witnessed a monumental "changing of the guard" in the ruling elite of several major league clubs. A handful of prominent owners, some of whom dated back to the early years of the century, passed from the baseball scene. Cornelius McGillicuddy, better known as Connie Mack, or the "grand old man of baseball," was instrumental in the formation of the American League in 1901. Mack's association with big league baseball actually reached back as far as the 1880s when he was a catcher with the Washington club in the old National League. He was a part owner with Ben Shibe and other investors in the Philadelphia Athletics in the formative years of the league and was also field manager from the very beginning. He eventually became the principal owner and continued to manage until stepping down after the 1950 season, his 50th year at the helm. He stayed on as club owner through 1954, when he sold the franchise to Arnold Johnson of Kansas City. Mack's dignified, angular presence in street clothes in the Athletics' dugout became an American institution and his impact on the long history of the American League was indelibly imprinted. Even with old Athletics favorite Jimmy Dykes leading the team on the field, it was not the same after Mack stepped down, and when he died in 1956, a glorious era had sadly ended.

Connie Mack, with sons Earle (left) and Roy (right), controlled the destiny of the A's up to their "last hurrah" in Philadelphia (1954).

Clark Griffith's tenure as Washington owner spanned four decades.

Like Mack, Washington owner Clark Griffith's career in the American League paralleled the life of the league itself. An ace pitcher for the Chicago NL team in the 1890s, Griffith was lured by White Sox owner Charles Comiskey to sign on with the fledgling American Leaguers as pitcher/manager in 1901 and he subsequently guided them to a league pennant that first year, winning 24 games on the mound for the Pale Hose. When New York entered the AL arena in 1903,

Griffith transferred over to manage and pitch for the new Highlanders franchise. He briefly jumped back to the National League to pilot the Cincinnati club in 1909 and 1910, but returned to the new league in 1912 as manager and part owner of the Washington Nationals. Soon thereafter he purchased controlling interest in the club and remained in charge until his death in October 1955. His adopted nephew, Calvin Griffith, then took over and finished out the decade as club owner.

Branch Rickey's career as executive and owner with several clubs set high standards for others to emulate. He began the decade with Brooklyn but finished it in Pittsburgh.

In the National League, another legendary baseball executive with a storied past, Wesley Branch Rickey, made his "last hurrah" in the 1950s. Possibly no other executive in the game made more historically significant contributions to baseball than Rickey. After a brief career as a catcher with the St. Louis Browns and New York Highlanders from 1905 to 1907 he attended the University of Michigan Law School and also managed the baseball team there. His star player at Ann Arbor was pitcher George Sisler and when he returned to manage the St. Louis Browns in 1913, he signed the talented Sisler directly off the U of M campus. In 1919 he joined the neighboring St. Louis Cardinals in the same capacity and his gift of oratory and managerial skills soon elevated him to the front office. Rickey became the game's greatest manipulator and collector of baseball talent and built a farm club empire for St. Louis that was eventually emulated by all major league clubs. The idea of outright ownership of a vast chain of minor league operations with most of its players under Cardinal contracts converted the St. Louis franchise from a perennial loser to a solid contender and often a pennant winner in the thirties and forties. He then moved on to Brooklyn, where he used the same methods to mold the Dodger organization into the winning teams of the late forties and early fifties. But unquestionably his best known initiative occurred in 1946 when he finally broke baseball's color line by

signing Jackie Robinson to a Brooklyn contract. He sold his Brooklyn interests to Walter O'Malley in 1951 and joined the Pittsburgh Pirates as vice president and later chairman of the board. At the end of the decade, Rickey announced plans for a third major league, the Continental League, which forced the hand of baseball owners and led to league expansion in the early sixties. The path of major league baseball for decades has been influenced by the legacy of Branch Rickey.

Although legendary pioneer executive Charles Comiskey died in 1931, the Comiskey dynasty lingered into the fifties with the Chicago White Sox under the ownership of daughter-in-law Grace Comiskey and grandson Chuck. After decades of mostly second division futility, the Comiskeys had the good fortune of hiring General Manager Frank Lane in 1949. Lane hastily woke up the sleeping franchise with a non-stop frenzy of player trades and the hiring of Paul Richards as field manager. The Comiskey dynasty came to an end in 1958, one year short of their first pennant in 40 years under new owner Bill Veeck. Another long-term ownership came to an end in the early 1950s with the passing of Detroit's Walter O. Briggs. The inheritance of leadership by W. O. "Spike" Briggs was unstable and short-lived. By the decade's end, the Briggs family no longer had any connection with the club's operation. Cincinnati owner Powell Crosley, like Briggs, had invested heavily from his primary non-baseball enterprises to field competitive teams with limited success. The Crosley name had been synonymous with various successful products like affordable radios and the patented "Shelvador" refrigerators. But for Crosley and the Reds it was "no cigar" in the fifties—only a power-laden lineup that made one serious threat in 1956.

Detroit owner W. O. Briggs, shown here in 1951 with a perplexed GM Charley Gehringer, watching his 1950 contenders collapse into mediocrity.

Powell Crosley held the reins in Cincinnati for over two decades.

Several major league clubs retained their traditional ownerships throughout the decade of the fifties and beyond. The best known names in this group were Horace Stoneham of the Giants, Phillip K. Wrigley of the Cubs, and Tom Yawkey of the Red Sox. Stoneham inherited the New York club upon the death of his father, Charles Stoneham, in the mid-thirties. He is best remembered for his collaboration with Dodgers owner Walter O'Malley in the historic relocation of both franchises to the West Coast in 1958. Wrigley, like Stoneham, inherited the Cubs ownership from his father, William Wrigley, the chewing gum tycoon. The junior Wrigley's stewardship was unable to produce any more pennants after WWII and the Cubs settled to the bottom of the standings for the decade of the fifties. Among other things, Wrigley is remembered for his refusal to install lights at the Cubs home park, the only club to resist the lure of night baseball by the 1950s. Red Sox owner Tom Yawkey also had an ancestral link to big league ownership—his uncle (by adoption) Bill Yawkey once owned the Detroit club. Yawkey was the last of the big spenders with unfortunately only one AL pennant (1946) to show for it. He spent the early years of his presidency procuring established top players for cash and fielded some star-studded lineups in the post-war years but by the 1950s, the Red Sox rosters became more reliant on developing home grown talent and were basically a .500 ball club for most of the decade.

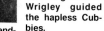

Gum magnate Phil Wrigley guided the hapless Cubbies.

Tom Yawkey, free-spending Red Sox owner.

Walter O'Malley, who left Brooklyn for West Coast gold.

Among the newer magnates of the fifties, Walter O'Malley of the Dodgers set a new standard for business-like operation of a ball club. Along with capable general manager Buzzy Bavasi, he kept the team in contention and kept the operation profitable without relying on funds from other personal business ventures. Even though his Brooklyn club had solid fan support, he saw the opportunity to seize the enormous revenue awaiting on the West Coast and uprooted his team in 1957. The abrupt departure did not endear him to Flatbush followers, but no one could question the financial wisdom of the relocation. The St. Louis

Cardinals entered a new era in 1953 when millionaire brewer August Busch purchased the team from Fred Saigh. His first move was to purchase Sportsman's Park from the failing Browns and rename it Busch Stadium. The Browns were history after 1953 and two great St. Louis traditions, the Busch brewery and the popular Cardinals, were united and became synonymous for decades to come. But the most successful front office in baseball was unquestionably in the Bronx, where construction moguls Dan Topping and Del Webb reaped the profits of a consistent winning club with the largest market base in baseball. They were also blessed with arguably baseball's shrewdest general manager, George Weiss.

Owner Bill Veeck (left), shown with White Sox pilot Al Lopez (center) and GM Hank Greenberg in 1959, won the hearts of Southside fans by delivering a long-savored pennant to Comiskey Park.

Without question, the most newsworthy and colorful club owner of the fifties was Bill Veeck. An unconventional maverick, Veeck stood out conspicuously among the many staid, businesslike front office execs of his era. After a short but spectacular run as owner of the Cleveland Indians in the late forties, Veeck resurfaced as owner of the struggling St. Louis Browns franchise in 1951. Veeck had already established a reputation as a master huckster, but his innovative promotions failed to fully resurrect pitiful attendance at Sportsman's Park and he grudgingly relinquished ownership to Baltimore interests in 1953. Many of his bizarre stunts like the celebrated insertion of midget Eddie Gaedel into a game in 1951 had been frowned upon by other more conservative owners and he was in a sense temporarily "blacklisted" by major league baseball. When the Detroit club went on the market in the late fifties, Veeck made the highest bid but was turned down because of his "P.T. Barnum" reputation. Undaunted, he tried again when the Comiskey heirs put the White Sox club on the block in 1959. He not only won approval, but had the good fortune of giving Chicago's south side their first pennant since 1919.

Despite the disfavor he invited from other owners, Veeck was a "fan's owner" and was easily the most popular executive in major league baseball. Many of the special promotional "days" he introduced have since become an accepted and profitable practice by other clubs.

Many very skilled and capable general managers were visible in the decade of the fifties. Gabe Paul in Cincinnati, Chub Feeney in New York, and John Quinn in Milwaukee (besides the aforementioned Weiss and Bavasi) each had as much to do with the successful and/or profitable club operations as did the team owners. Several ex-players exhibited front office talent—most notably Hank Greenberg, Joe Cronin, and Paul Richards. Even a former umpire, Billy Evans, ran the affairs of the Detroit club in the first years of the fifties. But the one general manager that made the most headlines was trader Frank Lane. Lane was hired in 1949 to revitalize the comatose Chicago White Sox franchise and he soon startled the baseball scene with a seemingly continuous frenzy of player trades that within two years transformed the Pale Hose into an exciting and contending team. The revolving door of roster changes was sometimes so frantic that the White Sox even had the services of the same player twice in one season via the trade route. Lane proved to be either extremely shrewd or extremely lucky as most of the transactions seemed to favor the White Sox. They wound up with an exceptional blend of front-line stars like Billy Pierce, Nelson Fox, and Minnie Minoso without surrendering players of equal potential. The flamboyant Lane's reckless style worked against him though as he wore out his welcome in the Windy City by 1955. From there he went on to the St. Louis Cardinals and Cleveland Indians, but despite his ongoing penchant for player shuffling he was unable to work the same magic for these clubs and he soon drifted back to the minor leagues from whence he came.

"Trader" Frank Lane did his frantic player shuffling with three different teams as a GM in the '50s.

The Yankees' winning formula was orchestrated by GM George Weiss.

ALL-STAR GAMES

By 1950, the All-Star game had become a midsummer fixture—a popular showcase for the top talent in both leagues. The American League had dominated the first 16-year tour through the major league parks since 1933 and the game returned to its original site, Chicago's Comiskey Park, in 1950 to begin its second cycle. The National Leaguers served notice that the AL domination was over as they pulled out a thrilling 14-inning victory on Red Schoendienst's clutch home run. By 1959, the senior circuit stars had won 7 of the 11 classics during the new decade. One factor that may have tipped the scales in favor of the resurging NL's fortunes was the presence of numerous black stars that were more eagerly recruited by National League clubs. Many American League rosters remained exclusively white until late in the decade when, coincidentally, the AL won three of the last four games. Aging superstars Stan Musial and Ted Williams plus Yogi Berra made the most appearances during the decade. Robin Roberts of the Phillies topped decade hurlers with five appearances. Bob Friend and Gene Conley had the unique distinction of having been both the winning and losing pitcher of an All-Star game during the 10-year span. Stan Musial hit the most All-Star home runs (3), including a 12th inning game winner at Milwaukee in 1955.

Relocation of franchises gave the midsummer classic three new host ballparks during the 1950s—Milwaukee in 1955, Baltimore in 1958, and Los Angeles in 1959. After Cincinnati fans inundated the ballot boxes to present a nearly all-Reds starting lineup in 1957, the All-Star voting method was taken from the fans and turned over to the managers, coaches, and players the following year. In a further attempt to eliminate favoritism, nominations could not include players from their own clubs. The financial success of the games prompted owners and players to add a second All-Star game to the schedule in 1959, a controversial decision that survived for another three seasons until it was scrapped in favor of the traditional single game. The Gillette Safety Razor Company played a vital role in promoting and broadcasting the All-Star games in the fifties. They produced and publicized fan balloting as well as sponsoring the radio accounts and telecasts of the games. The Mutual Radio Network carried the games up to 1957 with Al Helfer and Bob Neal as the principal announcers. NBC, which took over radio coverage from Mutual in 1957, televised the All-Star games exclusively throughout the decade. Mel Allen did the TV play-by-play for 10 of the 11 All-Star games, backed up by Jack Brickhouse, Al Helfer, and others.

Burt Shotton, winning pilot of the NL in the 1950 All-Star game, points to the hitting heroes of the contest at Chicago's Comiskey Park. Ralph Kiner (left) tied the game with a homer in the 9th and Red Schoendienst (right) sealed the victory with a circuit blast in the 14th.

A capacity crowd filled every corner of Cincinnati's Crosley Field for the 1953 midsummer classic. The National Leaguers prevailed once again, 5-1.

1950-59 DECADE ALL-STAR TEAMS

American League

Outfielders:	Ted Williams, Mickey Mantle, Al Kaline, Larry Doby, Minnie Minoso, Hank Bauer

Third Basemen:	**Shortstops:**	**Second Basemen:**
George Kell	Phil Rizzuto	Nelson Fox
Al Rosen	Chico Carrasquel	Bobby Avila

First Basemen:	**Catchers:**	**Pitchers:**
Ferris Fain	Yogi Berra	Early Wynn
Bill Skowron	Sherm Lollar	Billy Pierce
		Whitey Ford
		Bob Lemon
		Jim Bunning
		Billy O'Dell

National League

Outfielders:	Stan Musial, Willie Mays, Duke Snider, Hank Aaron, Ralph Kiner, Enos Slaughter

Third Basemen:	**Shortstops:**	**Second Basemen:**
Eddie Mathews	Peewee Reese	Red Schoendienst
Ken Boyer	Ernie Banks	Jackie Robinson

First Basemen:	**Catchers:**	**Pitchers:**
Gil Hodges	Roy Campanella	Robin Roberts
Ted Kluszewski	Del Crandall	Warren Spahn
		Don Newcombe
		Ewell Blackwell
		Johnny Antonelli
		Bob Friend

THE FARM SYSTEMS AND THE MINOR LEAGUES

One of the more historically significant developments of the decade of the fifties was the dramatic contraction of the minor leagues. In 1950 there were 58 professional leagues—by the end of the decade there were only 24 left, less than half the 1950 total. The attendance boom of the post-war years peaked in 1949, then sharply plummeted throughout the decades of the fifties and sixties. Without question television, both as a recreational preoccupation by itself and its rapidly expanding coverage of major league baseball, was the chief culprit. Even without the emerging popularity of TV, baseball as a spectator sport in the smaller markets probably could not have sustained the following it enjoyed in the post-war period. A severe recession in 1949 certainly contributed to the drop-off in minor league patronage and the outbreak of the Korean War in 1950 created a national distraction in the early fifties. At first, the troubled executives were quick to blame the war effort and its deportment of players (and even a sizable number of fans) as the reasons for the temporary losses, but as the war ended and the decade rolled on the decline continued. It became clear that the salad days of minor league baseball were gone forever and an era of constant realignment and down-scaling was at hand. Major league franchise relocations and expansion to the West Coast further deepened the crisis for the higher minor leagues. The Pacific Coast League yielded its two major markets, Los Angeles and San Francisco, to the majors and its unique identity as a near third major league was undermined. The stable alignment of all of the high minors was badly shaken and entered a period of constant changes. The once healthy AAA cities of Kansas City, Milwaukee, Baltimore, and shortly Minneapolis/St. Paul were transformed into major league markets overnight. The top level AAA circuit followed the lead of the big leagues by seeking out new territories in far-flung cities like Ottawa, Canada and even Havana, Cuba. Some of the more successful mid-level towns like Omaha were suddenly elevated to AAA status to replace departed or troubled member cities. These shake-ups also trickled down into the lower echelons of minor league ball, which were already experiencing a serious decline of gate receipts at all levels.

1950-59 MINOR LEAGUE AFFILIATIONS (AAA, AA, A)

BALTIMORE ORIOLES (1954-59)
AAA – Vancouver 1956-59, Louisville 1958, Miami 1959
AA – San Antonio 1954-58, Amarillo 1959
A – Lewiston 1954, Wichita 1954-55, Columbus (GA) 1956, Knoxville 1957-58

BOSTON RED SOX
AAA – Louisville 1950-55, San Francisco 1956-57, Minneapolis 1958-59
AA – Birmingham 1950-52, Oklahoma City 1957, Memphis 1958
A – Scranton 1950-51, Albany 1952-54, 1956-57, Montgomery 1955, Allentown 1958-59

BOSTON/ MILWAUKEE BRAVES
AAA – Milwaukee 1950-52, Toledo 1953-55, Wichita 1956-58, Louisville 1959, Sacramento 1959
AA – Atlanta 1950-59, Austin 1956-59
A – Hartford 1950-52, Denver 1950-51, Jacksonville 1953-59, Lincoln 1954, Topeka 1957-58

BROOKLYN/ LOS ANGELES DODGERS
AAA – Montreal 1950-59, St. Paul 1950-59, Hollywood 1950, Portland 1956, Los Angeles 1957, Spokane 1958-59
AA – Mobile 1950-55, Ft. Worth 1950-56, Monterrey (Mex.) 1955, Victoria (BC) 1958-59
A – Elmira 1950-55, Pueblo 1950-57, Macon 1956-59, Des Moines 1958

CHICAGO CUBS
AAA – Los Angeles 1950-56, Springfield 1950-53, Portland 1957-58, Ft. Worth 1959
AA – Nashville 1950-51, Beaumont 1954, Tulsa 1956, Memphis 1957, Fort Worth 1957-58, San Antonio 1959
A – Grand Rapids 1950-51, Des Moines 1950-57, Macon 1952-55, Pueblo 1958, Lancaster 1959

CHICAGO WHITE SOX
AAA – Sacramento 1950-51, Charleston (WV) 1953-54, Indianapolis 1957-59
AA – Memphis 1950-56
A – Colorado Springs 1950-58, Charleston (SC) 1959

CINCINNATI REDS
AAA – Syracuse 1950, Havana (Cuba) 1955-59, Seattle 1956-59
AA – Tulsa 1950-54, Nashville 1955-59, Monterrey (Mex.) 1957-58
A – Charleston (WV) 1950-51, Columbia (SC) 1950-55, Savannah 1956-59, Albuquerque 1958

CLEVELAND INDIANS
AAA – San Diego 1950-51, Indianapolis 1952-56, San Diego 1956-59
AA – Oklahoma City 1950, Dallas 1951-52, Tulsa 1955, Mobile 1956-59
A – Dayton 1950, Wilkes-Barre 1950-51, Wichita 1951-52, Reading 1952-59, Montgomery 1956

DETROIT TIGERS
AAA – Toledo 1950-51, Buffalo 1952-55, Charleston (WV) 1956-59
AA – Little Rock 1950-55, Birmingham 1957-59

DETROIT TIGERS (continued)
A – Flint 1950, Williamsport 1950-52, Montgomery 1952-53, Wilkes-Barre 1954, Augusta 1955-58, Syracuse 1956, Lancaster 1958, Knoxville 1959

NEW YORK/ SAN FRANCISCO GIANTS
AAA – Minneapolis 1950-57, Jersey City 1950, Ottawa (Can.) 1951, Phoenix 1958-59
AA – Nashville 1952-54, Dallas 1955-57, Corpus Christi 1958-59
A – Jacksonville 1950-52, Sioux City 1950-55, 1958, Wilkes-Barre 1955, Johnstown 1956, Springfield (Mass.) 1957-59

NEW YORK YANKEES
AAA – Kansas City 1950-54, San Francisco 1951, Denver 1955-58, Richmond 1956-59
AA – Beaumont 1950-52, Birmingham 1953-56, New Orleans 1957-58
A – Muskegon 1950-51, Binghamton 1950-59

PHILADELPHIA/ KANSAS CITY ATHLETICS
AAA – Buffalo 1950, Ottawa (Can.) 1952-54, Columbus (OH) 1955-56, Buffalo 1957-58, Portland 1959
AA – Little Rock 1957-58, Shreveport 1959
A – Lincoln 1950-52, Savannah 1950-55, Williamsport 1953, Columbia (SC) 1956-57, Albany 1958-59

PHILADELPHIA PHILLIES
AAA – Toronto 1950, Baltimore 1951-53, Syracuse 1954-55, Miami 1956-58, Buffalo 1959
AA – Tulsa 1957-58
A – Utica 1950, Schenectady 1951-57, Spokane 1953-54, Williamsport 1958-59

PITTSBURGH PIRATES
AAA – Indianapolis 1950-51, Hollywood 1951-52, Columbus (OH) 1957-59, Salt Lake City 1958-59
AA – New Orleans 1950-56, Mexico City 1956-58
A – Albany 1950, Charleston (SC) 1950-53, Denver 1952-54, Williamsport 1954-56, Lincoln 1955-58, Columbus (GA) 1959

ST. LOUIS BROWNS (1950-53)
AAA – Baltimore 1950, Toronto 1951-52
AA – San Antonio 1950-53
A – Wichita 1950, Dayton 1951, Scranton 1952, Wichita 1953

ST. LOUIS CARDINALS
AAA – Rochester 1950-59, Columbus (OH) 1950-54, Omaha 1955-59
AA – Houston 1950-58, Tulsa 1959
A – Omaha 1950-54, Columbus (GA) 1950-55, 1957, Allentown 1954-56, Sioux City 1956, York 1958-59

WASHINGTON SENATORS
AAA – Louisville 1956
AA – Chattanooga 1950-59
A – Augusta 1950, Scranton 1953, Charlotte 1954-59

But major league baseball was and always will be dependent upon the minor leagues as a proving ground for developing and nurturing talent. This symbiotic necessity proved to be the salvation of what was left of the minor league structure in the late fifties. Major League affiliation or outright ownership became no longer a bonus but indeed a necessity for most minor league franchises. And big league clubs were reluctant to reduce or abandon their minor league pastures that were so critical in providing an outlet for their young prospects to develop into major leaguers, so they were more than willing to subsidize even marginal franchises to keep them in operation. However, even the larger networks of farm teams of, for example, Brooklyn and the St. Louis Cardinals, were victims of minor league deterioration and were somewhat reduced in number by 1959. The size of the farm system very often determined the consistent quality of teams like Brooklyn and the Cardinals, each with the luxury of two AAA affiliates for most of the decade. In the forties, these clubs had farm teams at every level down to class D, often sponsoring two teams at several levels. All major league teams had a top AAA level club at one time or another during the decade. The teams with weaker working agreements with ever-changing locales seemed to reflect their poorer performance during the decade. A good example of an inferior farm system would be the Washington Senators, who relied on their AA Chattanooga club to develop top prospects for most of the decade and their perennial second division status reflected their almost non-existent farm system. Even a top notch staff of scouts could not guarantee a rich supply of talented players if the farm system was inadequate for their development. The Dodgers' and Cardinals' ability to retain their deep rosters of farmed out players by the end of the decade paid dividends for them in the following decade as they continued to field contending teams. The minor leagues continued to diminish in number in the sixties, but the preservation of at least skeleton farm systems by the healthier major league operations helped check their headlong rush to extinction.

THE BASEBALL COMMISSIONER

During the 1950s, the high post of baseball commissioner was held first by A. B. "Happy" Chandler, then by Ford C. Frick. Chandler had succeeded the late Judge Landis in 1945. He presided during the historic post-war period that witnessed the breakdown of baseball's color barrier with the signing of Jackie Robinson in 1946. After the long era of near-despotic rule by Landis, the owners were inclined to choose a more resilient and amicable leader to better serve the more stable and more prosperous climate of baseball in the forties. Chandler, a former governor and U.S. Senator from Kentucky, seemed an ideal choice. He blended a media-friendly disposition with a resolve to make difficult and often unpopular decisions "in the best interests of baseball." But by 1950, the honeymoon was all but over as owners soured on Happy and refused to renew his contract. Among other misgivings, some paranoid owners feared that some of Chandler's edicts would invite legislative scrutiny and thereby threaten the legal sanctuary of the reserve clause. Their fears seem to be well-founded as baseball was bombarded by an almost annual series of hearings and inquiries during the 1950s, but it can be argued that other developments more profound than Chandler's conduct had more to do with the legal challenges that faced the national pastime.

Chandler stubbornly refused to resign immediately and remained in office well into the summer of 1951. The owners chose to select a replacement from within the ranks, naming long-time NL President Ford Frick to succeed Chandler. More cerebral and scholarly, Frick also was more subservient to the whims of the more influential owners like Brooklyn's Walter O'Malley. Frick was a baseball insider who had paid his dues as sportswriter, broadcaster, journalist, and top executive. His appointment redefined the role of commissioner as a professional administrator answering primarily to the needs and wishes of club owners as a body. But Frick proved to be a very capable and effective commissioner for the times, responding firmly yet with restraint to the decisions that faced him. Although not regarded as the "fan's commissioner" as Chandler before him, he was generally respected by all parties. Frick seldom took the initiative on the larger issues but reacted responsibly when the game's best interests were at stake. He stayed in the background during the monumental franchise relocations of the decade and was often criticized for not interceding on behalf of New York area fans during the Dodger/Giants move.

A. B. "HAPPY" CHANDLER
commissioner 1950-51

FORD FRICK
NL president 1950-51
commissioner 1951-59-

WARREN GILES
NL president 1951-59

WILL HARRIDGE
AL president 1950-58

JOE CRONIN
AL president 1959-

Major League Umpires 1950-59

AMERICAN LEAGUE

CHARLIE BERRY 1950-59
JAMES BOYER 1950
NESTOR CHYLAK 1954-59
JAMES DUFFY 1951-55
JOHN FLAHERTY 1953-59
GROVER FROESE 1952-53
BILL GRIEVE 1950-55
JIM HONOCHIK 1950-59
CAL HUBBARD 1950-51
ED HURLEY 1950-59
BILL McGOWAN 1950-54
BILL McKINLEY 1950-59
LARRY NAPP 1951-59
JOE PAPARELLA 1950-59
ART PASSARELLA 1950-53
JOHN RICE 1955-59
SCOTTIE ROBB 1952-53
ED ROMMEL 1950-59
ED RUNGE 1954-59
HANK SOAR 1950-59
JOHN STEVENS 1950-59
ROBT. STEWART 1959
BILL SUMMERS 1950-59
FRANK TABACCHI 1956-59
FRANK UMONT 1954-59

**Umpire-in-Chief
TOM CONNOLLY
1950-53**

**CAL HUBBARD
Supervisor 1952-53
Umpire-in-Chief
1954-59**

NATIONAL LEAGUE

WM. P. BAKER 1957
LEE BALLANFANT 1950-57
AL BARLICK 1950-55, 1958-59
DUSTY BOGGESS 1950-59
KEN BURKHART 1957-59
JOCKO CONLAN 1950-59
SHAG CRAWFORD 1956-59
FRANK DASCOLI 1950-59
VIC DELMORE 1956-59
HAL DIXON 1953-59
AUGIE DONATELLI 1950-59
WM. ENGELN 1952-56
LARRY GOETZ 1950-57
ART GORE 1950-56
TOM GORMAN 1951-59
ANGELO GUGLIELMO 1952
BILL JACKOWSKI 1952-59
LOUIS JORDA 1950-52
STAN LANDES 1955-59
BABE PINELLI 1950-56
SCOTTIE ROBB 1950-52
LEN ROBERTS 1953-55
FRANK SECORY 1952-59
VINCE SMITH 1957-59
BILL STEWART 1950-54
ED SUDOL 1957-59
ANTHONY VENZON 1957-59
LON WARNEKE 1950-55

**Chief-of-Staff
BILL KLEM
1950-54**

In a 1950 game at Brooklyn, Art Gore calls out sliding Gus Bell of the Pirates.

CHARLIE BERRY

JIM HONOCHIK

ED HURLEY

LEE BALLANFANT

AL BARLICK

DUSTY BOGGESS

BILL McGOWAN

BILL McKINLEY

JOE PAPARELLA

JOCKO CONLAN

FRANK DASCOLI

AUGIE DONATELLI

John Stevens explains his decision to Washington Manager Lavagetto in a 1958 game.

ED ROMMEL

HANK SOAR

BILL SUMMERS

TOM GORMAN

FRANK SECORY

BILL STEWART

LON WARNEKE

THE CITIES &
THE BALLPARKS

BALTIMORE 1954-59

Baltimore skyline from Federal Hill

Fort McHenry and Baltimore Harbor

Mount Vernon Place and Washington Monument

THE NEWSPAPERS:

BALTIMORE 1954-59 (continued)

THE BASEBALL REPORTERS:

GEORGE BOWEN Jr.
AP

RALPH BRACKBILL
Evening Sun

A. DOUGLAS BROWN
Evening Sun

CARL BUCHELE
Sun

AL COSTELLO
News-Post

JAMES ELLIS
Evening Sun

NEAL ESKRIDGE
News Post

CLAUDE GIBBS
Sun

LOUIS HATTER
Sun

ART JANNEY
News-Post

JESSE LINTHICUM
Sun

BOB MAISEL
Sun

PAUL MENTON
Evening Sun

STEVE O'NEILL
News Post

RODGER PIPPEN
News Post

JOHN STEADMAN
News Post

HUGH TRADER Jr.
News Post

MURRAY WEIMAN
Evening Sun

GORDON BEARD *AP*
ED BURL *Sun*
HENRY KNOCH *Sun*
SAM LACY

THE BROADCASTERS:
radio & television:

ERNIE HARWELL
1954-59

HOWIE WILLIAMS
1954

BAILEY GOSS
1954-56

CHUCK THOMPSON
1955-56

LARRY RAY
1957

HERB CARNEAL
1957-59

BALTIMORE—Memorial Stadium 1954-59

Like Cleveland's Municipal Stadium, the elliptical contour of the stands was designed to accommodate football, namely the Baltimore Colts of the NFL. Unlike Cleveland, the upper deck was not roofed.

A full house of almost 50,000 witnessed the grand opener in 1954.

Vice President Richard Nixon threw out the first ball to welcome the Orioles back to the American League after an absence of five decades.

The new grandstand under construction in 1953.

A magnificent aerial view of a night game in August 1954. A new lighting system had only recently been completed. In 1956, a new fence was erected to shorten the center field dimensions.

The grand facade at the south end of the new giant horseshoe.

BOSTON

Boston Harbor waterfront

Symphony Hall, Horticultural Hall
and Huntington Avenue

Washington Street, theatre district at night

THE NEWSPAPERS:

BOSTON (continued)

THE BASEBALL REPORTERS:

JOE CASHMAN	WILL CLONEY	ED COSTELLO	JOHN GARRO	MICHAEL GILLOOLY	HY HURWITZ	JOSEPH McHENRY	MIKE McNAMEE	ROY MUMPTON	ED RUMILL
Record	Herald, Post	Herald		American	Globe		Advertiser		C.S. Monitor

ROBERT AJEMIAN *American*
JIM BAGLEY *INS*
ART BALLOU *Globe*
JOHN BARRY *Globe*
GENE BASSET *Post*
ROGER BIRTWELL *Globe*
PHIL BISSELL *Globe*
AL BLACKMAN *INS*
JOHN BROOKS *Record*
GORDON CAMPBELL *Traveler*
GEORGE CARENS *Traveler*
LARRY CLAFLIN *American*
SAM COHEN *Record*
BOB COYNE *Post, Record*
BILL CUNNINGHAM *Herald*
ED CUNNINGHAM *Herald*
NICK DEL NINNO *Traveler*
JOHN DROHAN *Traveler*
DAVE EGAN *Record*
HERB FINNEGAN *American*
JACK FROST *UP*
ROBERT GATES *C.S. Monitor*
JOHN GILLOOLY *Record*
BOB GREEN *AP*
BILL GRIMES *American*
JOHN HANLON
JOHN HARTNETT *AP*
GERRY HERN *Post*
AL HERSHBERG *Post*
PAUL HINES *Post*
PRESCOTT HOBSON
ROBERT HOLBROOK *Globe*
BOB HOOBING *AP*
TIM HORGAN *Traveler*

VICTOR JOHNSON *Herald*
HAROLD KAESE *Globe*
CLIFF KEANE *Globe*
MATT KEANY *Record*
JOE KELLEY *AP*
ROBERT KIERSTEAD *Traveler*
W. R. KING *AP*
MURRAY KRAMER *Record*
AUSTEN LAKE *American*
WM. LISTON *Traveler*
JOE LOONEY *Herald*
GENE MACK *Globe*
ALEX MacLEAN *Record*
JOHN MALANEY *Post*
FRANKLIN MATZEK
HENRY McKENNA *Herald*
JOE McKENNEY *Post*
HENRY MINOTT *UP*
HARRY MOLTER *C.S. Monitor*
LEO MONAHAN *Record*
TOM MONAHAN *Traveler*
GERALD MOORE *Post*
W. J. MORSE *C.S. Monitor*
JERRY NASON *Globe*
DAVID O'HARA *AP*
STEVE O'LEARY *American, Record*
JOE PHELAN *UP*
LINWOOD RAYMOND
BOB REMER *Herald*
BOB SALMON *UP*
ART SAMPSON *Herald*
FRANK SARGENT
ART SIEGEL *Traveler*
HOWELL STEVENS *Post*

MELVILLE WEBB *Globe*
WALLACE WEEKS *AP*
RALPH WHEELER *Herald*
LEO WHITE *American*

THE BROADCASTERS:

BOSTON BRAVES

radio:

JIM BRITT
1950-52

LES SMITH
1951-52

TOM HUSSEY
1950

LEO EGAN
1950

BUMP HADLEY
1951

television:

JIM BRITT
1950-52

TOM HUSSEY
1950

BUMP HADLEY
1950-52

LES SMITH
1951

BOSTON RED SOX

radio:

TOM HUSSEY
1950-54

JIM BRITT
1950

LEO EGAN
1950

CURT GOWDY
1951-59

BOB DELANEY
1951-53

BOB MURPHY
1954-59

BILL CROWLEY
1958-59

television:

JIM BRITT
1950

BUMP HADLEY
1950

BOB DELANEY
1951-53

BILL CROWLEY
1958

TOM HUSSEY
1950-54

CURT GOWDY
1951-59

BOB MURPHY
1954-59

BOSTON—Braves Field 1950-52

A postcard view of a night game, probably taken in the 1940s.

The main entrance building on Gaffney Street.

A view from behind the right field foul pole on opening day 1950.

Looking out toward the first base bleachers.

The left field fence and scoreboard. Braves Field probably led the league in billboards during the fifties.

The right field fence and bleacher section.

BOSTON—Fenway Park

A postcard view from above as the park looked in the 1940s.

The main entrance on Jersey Avenue still looks very much like it did in 1912, when Fenway was built.

A view from the right field corner.

A more contemporary aerial view showing rebuilt light standards and additional rooftop structures. The freeway paralleling Landsdown St. is a new addition.

Another aerial view from above the right field bleachers illustrates the eccentric configuration of the Red Sox home park.

BROOKLYN 1950-57

Brooklyn Bridge Plaza, Washington St. Post Office

THE NEWSPAPERS:

BROOKLYN EAGLE

(LONG ISLAND DAILY PRESS, DAILY ADVOCATE, STAR-JOURNAL)

THE BROADCASTERS:
radio & television:

RED BARBER
1950-53

CONNIE DESMOND
1950-56

VIN SCULLY
1950-57

ANDRE BARUCH
1954-55

AL HELFER
1956-57

JERRY DOGGETT
1957

THE BASEBALL REPORTERS:

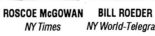

HAROLD BURR
Eagle

SID FRIEDLANDER
NY Post

MIKE GAVEN
NY Journal-American

ROGER KAHN
NY Herald Tribune

JACK LANG
L.I. Daily Press

ROSCOE McGOWAN
NY Times

BILL ROEDER
NY World-Telegram

DICK YOUNG
NY Daily News

DAVID ANDERSON *Eagle*
GEORGE BURTON
JACK BUTLER
RICHARD CARMODY
CHARLES FEENEY Jr.
BEN GOLD *Eagle*
TOMMY HOLMES *Eagle*
MURRAY JANOFF
JOE LEE *Eagle*
MICHAEL LEE
AL LIEBERMAN

JAMES MURPHY *Eagle*
LOU NISS *Eagle*
LOUIS O'NEILL
AL PALMA *NY Journal-American*
JOHN POWERS
MARSHALL REED
STEPHEN ROGERS
JACK SCHWARTZ
DONALD SMITH
JERRY TWOHIG
STAN WYMAN *Daily*

BROOKLYN—Ebbets Field 1950-57

An aerial view revealing much of the surrounding neighborhood.

The main entrance with its "gingerbread" arched windows was a cherished feature of Brooklyn's revered ballpark.

The Ebbets Field press box.

The left field wall, looking towards center.

Dodger fans lining up along the sidewalk for a chance at World Series tickets.

CHICAGO

Michigan Avenue, looking north from the Art Institute

The Tribune Tower at night

The Chicago River

THE NEWSPAPERS:

Yanks Shut Out by A's

CHICAGO (continued)

THE BASEBALL REPORTERS:

WARREN BROWN
American

ED BURNS
Tribune

JOHN CARMICHAEL
Daily News

DAVID CONDON
Tribune

ROBERT CROMIE
Tribune

DAN DESMOND
American

RICHARD DOZER
Tribune

CHARLES DUNKLEY
AP

JAMES ENRIGHT
American

LEO FISCHER
American

NEIL GAZEL
Daily News

DICK HACKENBERG
Sun-Times

JOHN HOFFMAN
Sun-Times

JERRY HOLTZMAN
Sun-Times

PAT JOYCE
INS

GENE KESSLER
Sun-Times

JOHN KUENSTER
Daily News

JERRY LISKA
AP

EDGAR MUNZEL
Sun-Times

KEN OPSTEIN
INS

ED PRELL
Tribune

HOWARD ROBERTS
Daily News

ED SAINSBURY
UP

WILFRED SMITH
Tribune

IRVING VAUGHAN
Tribune

ARCH WARD
Tribune

DAVE WALSH
Herald-American

WILLIAM BECKER *American*
GENE BLUDEAU *UP*
TOM BRANAGAN *AP*
TIM CANTY *UP*
CHARLES CHAMBERLAIN *AP*
JOHN CLARKE *Sun-Times*
RUSS COWAN
DALE COYLE *Howe N.B.*
TED DAMATA *Sun-Times*
CHARLES EINSTEIN *INS*
WILLIAM FURLONG *Daily News*
ROBERT GLASS *INS*
ED GREENE *American*
GERALD HEALEY *INS*
EARL HILLIGAN

FRED HOWE *Howe N.B.*
JACK MABLEY *Daily News*
HOWARD MARTIN *Tribune*
HARRY McNAMARA *American*
JOE MOOSHIL *AP*
JOHN PHILLIPS *Howe N.B.*
FRANCIS J. POWERS *Daily News*
LORNE RAY *Howe N.B.*
JOE REIN *Daily News*
JOHN F. RYAN *Daily News*
SEYMOUR SHUB *Sun-Times*
HERB SIMONS
WENDELL SMITH *American*
GEORGE STRICKLER *Tribune*
TED TRYBA

THE BROADCASTERS:

CHICAGO CUBS *radio:*

BERT WILSON
1950-55

BUD CAMPBELL
1950-51, 53

GENE ELSTON
1954-57

JACK QUINLAN
1955-59

MILO HAMILTON
1956-57

LOU BOUDREAU
1958-59

television (both clubs):

JOE WILSON
1950-51

JACK BRICKHOUSE
1950-59

HARRY CREIGHTON
1950-56

VINCE LLOYD
1950, 54-59

MARTY HOGAN
1951

CHICAGO WHITE SOX *radio:*

BOB ELSON
1950-59

DICK BINGHAM
1952

DON WELLS
1953-59

CHICAGO—Comiskey Park

The ornate brick work and open archways from the original construction in 1910 were a familiar feature to Southside fans. Here is the main entrance on the SW corner at 35th & Shields.

A bird's eye view reveals the charming symmetry of Comiskey Park.

A night game in progress sometime in the 1950s.

Another view of a game from behind home plate with a good look at the center field scoreboard and bleachers, where only Hank Greenberg had reached with a homer up to that time.

CHICAGO—Wrigley Field

An aerial view of the "friendly confines"—not much different from today, except for no lights. It was originally built in 1914 to serve the "outlaw" Federal League club.

Time has truly stood still at Wrigley Field . . . same vine-covered outfield wall, same manually-operated scoreboard, same bleachers (except for today's block-out section that helps batters see a pitched ball).

The main entrance at Clark & Addison, decked out for the 1947 All-Star game. It still looks the same, even the sign.

The novel "people mover" ramps to the upper deck—installed in 1956.

Upper deck boxes along the third base line.

CINCINNATI

The Ohio River and Cincinnati skyline viewed from Kentucky

Fountain Square in downtown Cincinnati

The Greyhound Bus Terminal

THE NEWSPAPERS:

CINCINNATI (continued)

THE BASEBALL REPORTERS:

SI BURRICK
Dayton News

RITTER COLLETT
Dayton J/H

ROBERT FIRESTONE
Times-Star

PAT HARMON
Post

EARL LAWSON
Times-Star

BOB PILLE
Post

LOU SMITH
Enquirer

TOM SWOPE
Post

WALTER BRINKMAN *Times-Star*
GEORGE BRISTOL *Times-Star*
NIXON DENTON *Times-Star*
JAMES FERGUSON
DICK FORBES *Enquirer*
WILLIAM FORD *Enquirer*
FRANK GRAYSON *Times-Star*
DAVE GROTE *NLSB*
HAROLD HARRISON *AP*
FRITZ HOWELL
BOB HUSTED *Enquirer*
LOU LAWHEAD *Enquirer*

RICHARD MACKE *Enquirer*
JACK MOLLOY *Enquirer*
ED O'NEILL
HARRY RECKNER *Post*
HAROLD RUSSELL *Enquirer*
LESLIE SKINNER *Times-Star*
SAUL STRAUS *Enquirer*
JAMES TAYLOR
CLARENCE WIESE *Post*
CLAUDE WOLFF *AP*

THE BROADCASTERS:

radio:

WAITE HOYT
1950-59

BOB GILMORE
1952-54

JACK MORAN
1955-59

television:

WAITE HOYT
1950-55

BOB GILMORE
1952-54

JACK MORAN
1955

MARK SCOTT
1956

GEORGE BRYSON
1956-59

FRANK McCORMICK
1958-59

CINCINNATI—Crosley Field

First known as Redland Field when it was built in 1912, it occupied the same property at Western & Findlay as its predecessors dating back to the 1880s. First ML night game played here in 1935.

The Reds' office building adjoined the main grandstand structure along Findlay Street.

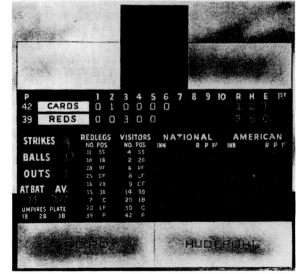

A view from the right field corner—c. 1958.

A brand new scoreboard was erected for 1957.

The famous "sun deck" bleacher section in right field, bordering Western Avenue.

CLEVELAND

The city skyline from Lake Erie

East Sixth Street, looking north

High Level Bridge across the Cuyahoga

An aerial view of the Stadium and downtown area

THE NEWSPAPERS:

CLEVELAND (continued)

THE BASEBALL REPORTERS:

ROBERT AUGUST
Press

ED BANG
News

GORDON COBBLEDICK
Plain Dealer

BEN FLEIGER
Press

FRANK GIBBONS
Press

HARRY JONES
Plain Dealer

HAL LEIBOWITZ
News

ED McAULEY
News

JIM SCHLEMMER
Akron Beacon/Journal

HENRY ANDREWS *Press*
HOWARD BABCOCK *INS*
MARTIN BERCK *AP*
JACK CLOWSER *Press*
BOB CUBBEDGE *INS*
LOU DARVAS *Press*
MILT DOLINGER *UP*
JIM DOYLE *Plain Dealer*
RICHARD DUGAN *UP*
JOE DURBIN *UP*

MILT ELLIS *Plain Dealer*
RICHARD FALES *UP*
MATT FENN *News*
HERM GOLDSTEIN *News*
ZOLTON GOMBOS
PHIL HARTMAN *Press*
CHARLES HEATON *Plain Dealer*
CHARLES HORNIK *AP*
STEVE HOWICK *UP*
PAUL JACOBS *News*
WALTER JOHNS
CLETUS JONES *AP*
ED KATZ *Plain Dealer*
MILT LAPINE *Press*
JACK LEDDEN *News*
WILLIAM LEVY *INS*
FRANKLIN LEWIS *Press*
WILLIAM LOFTUS *UP*
REGIS McAULEY *News*
JOHN MORGENTHALER *AP*

ROBERT MORRISON *UP*
ISI NEWBORN *Press*
ADOLPH PONIKVAR *INS*
HOWARD PRESTON *News*
FRED REINERT *Plain Dealer*
WILLIAM RITT
JAMES SIBBISON *AP*
LARRY SMITH *AP*
RICHARD SMITH *AP*
JOHN SORDS
ELLIS SPRUNGER *AP*
DAN TAYLOR *Press*
TED VIROSTKO *INS*
EUGENE WHITNEY *Plain Dealer*
ROBERT YONKERS *Press*
ALEX ZIRIN *Plain Dealer*

THE BROADCASTERS:

radio:

JACK GRANEY
1950-53

JIMMY DUDLEY
1950-59

AL HOEGLER
1950-52

ED EDWARDS
1954-55

TOM MANNING
1956

BOB NEAL
1957-59

television:

JIMMY DUDLEY
1950

JACK GRANEY
1950
AL HOEGLER
1950
HAL NEWELL
1951
LARRY ALLEN
1951
RED JONES
1952-53

BOB NEAL
1952-53

JIM BRITT
1954-57

KEN COLEMAN
1954-59

BILL McCOLGAN
1958-59

CLEVELAND—Municipal Stadium

Crowds entering the SW corner gate A for a big game in 1953.

The often-maligned giant oval opened for business in 1932 and has served Indians fans well through the decades. When the Tribe had winning seasons, they also set attendance records and with few complaints from the spectators.

Over 65,000 faithful at the 1950 opening game vs. Detroit—not an unusual turnout when the Indians fielded exciting teams and their crowds were the envy of other AL club owners.

A view of a game in progress from directly behind the backstop.

DETROIT

An aerial view from the forties, Briggs Stadium in the foreground—without lights and neighboring freeways

Grand Circus Park, in the heart of downtown Detroit

Downtown's Washington Boulevard at night

THE NEWSPAPERS:

DETROIT (continued)

THE BASEBALL REPORTERS:

E. A. BATCHELOR Sr.

TOMMY DEVINE
Free Press

DAVE DILES
AP

JOE FALLS
Times, AP

SAM GREENE
News

EDGAR HAYES
Times

HAL
MIDDLESWORTH
Free Press

H. G. SALSINGER
News

LYALL SMITH
Free Press

WATSON
SPOELSTRA
News

GEORGE VAN
Times

W. E. ANDERMAN *Times*
JACK BERRY *UP*
CHARLES CAIN *AP*
PAUL CHANDLER *News*
MARSHALL DANN *Free Press*
HARRY DAYTON
ART DORANZIO *Free Press*
JAMES EASTHORNE *Free Press*
DOC GREENE *News*
ED JONES
HAROLD KAHL *Times*
LEE KAVETSKI *News*
VINCE KLOCK *Free Press*
JOE KNACK
BOB LATSHAW *Free Press*
HARRY LEDUC *News*
LEO MacDONNELL *Times*
JOHN MANNING *Times*
GEORGE MASKIN *Times*
ROBERT McCLELLAN *Times*
TOM MERCY

BOB MURPHY *Times*
LLOYD NORTHARD *UP*
GEORGE PUSCAS *Free Press*
ADAM SARNACKI
BOB SIEGER *AP, News*
BOB SMITH *Free Press*
FRANK SNYDER *INS*
HENRY STAPLER *News*
RICHARD THOMPSON *Free Press*
DOUG VAUGHAN
HARRY WADE *News*
CHARLES WARD *Times*
DAVID WILKIE *AP*
DON WOLFE
BOB WOOD *News*
JAMES ZERILLI *Free Press*

THE BROADCASTERS:

radio & television:

TY TYSON
1951

VAN PATRICK
1952-59

PAUL WILLIAMS
1951

HARRY HEILMANN
1950

DIZZY TROUT
1953-55

MEL OTT
1956-58

GEORGE KELL
1959

DETROIT—Briggs Stadium

When the 1950s began, the center field scoreboard was manually operated and topped with a circular clock.

The historic corner of Michigan & Trumbull—where Tiger baseball was first played in 1896. The 1950s version had a soft gray exterior and all-green seating on the inside.

40 seats were sacrificed in the RF corner boxes in 1955 to give star right fielder Al Kaline more room to roam and to minimize collisions that could result in injury.

By 1959, the big scoreboard had been "electrified" and later widened to offer more fan information. A new square clock replaced the circular version.

A panoramic view from behind home plate of a 1956 contest that drew a near-capacity crowd. The rooftop third deck that nearly encircled the grandstand was one of Briggs Stadium's novel features.

An aerial view from 1959 of the major leagues' only completely double-decked baseball facility.

KANSAS CITY 1955-59

Union Depot in the foreground, downtown KC in the distance

Kansas City's Municipal Airport, near the heart of the city

Petticoat Lane

THE NEWSPAPERS:

KANSAS CITY 1955-59 (continued)

Municipal Stadium

THE BASEBALL REPORTERS:

JOHN JOHNSON
Call

BERNARD McDONALD

JOE McGUFF
Star

ERNEST MEHL
Star

JAMES BROWN *Call*
ROBERT BUSBY *Star*
WILLIAM CLARK *UPI*
FRANK CORRIE *AP*
JERE COX *UPI*
FRANK CRAWFORD *AP*
L. L. EDGE *UPI*
PAUL O'BOYNICK *Star*
LYLE SCHWILLING *UPI*
GARRETT SMALLEY
News-Press

CHARLES NETHAWAY

SKIPPER PATRICK
AP

JOHN THOMSON
Kansan

For the impending arrival of big league baseball in 1955, Kansas City rebuilt and added an upper deck to their existing AAA facility (Blues Field) to raise its capacity to 31,000.

THE BROADCASTERS:

radio:

MERLE HARMON
1955-59

LARRY RAY
1955-56

ED EDWARDS
1957-58

BILL GRIGSBY
1959

television:
MERLE HARMON
1959
BILL GRIGSBY
1959

Enthusiastic crowds often filled the newly refurbished park to support the somewhat inept Athletics in their earlier years in Kansas City. This view is from the left field corner.

LOS ANGELES 1958-59

LA International Airport in the 1950s

The Harbor Freeway, a symbol of Southern California

Downtown LA at dusk, with the famous City Hall in view

THE NEWSPAPERS:

LOS ANGELES 1958-59 (continued)

THE BASEBALL REPORTERS:

PHIL COLLIER
S.D. Union

FRANK FINCH
Times

BOB HUNTER
Examiner

AL KAHN
UPI

GEORGE LEDERER
L.B. Press-Telegram

BOB MYERS
AP

JOHN OLD
Herald Examiner

CHARLEY PARK
Mirror News

BONNIE COHEN
PAUL CORCORAN *UPI*
CHARLES CURTIS *Times*
GEORGE DAVIS *Herald Express*
CHARLES DENTON
MELVIN DURSLAG *Examiner*
BRAVEN DYER *Times*
VINCENT FLAHERTY *Examiner*
BUD FURILLO *Herald Express*
DAN HAFNER *Examiner*
KARL HUBENTHAL *Examiner*
DICK HYLAND *Times*
CHARLES MAHER *AP*
PATRICK McNULTY *AP*
MORTON MOSS *Examiner*

CLAUDE NEWMAN
BOB OATES *Examiner*
BOB PANELLA
HANK RIEGER *UPI*
RUBE SAMUELSON
SAM SCHNITZER *Examiner*
JOE ST. AMANT *INS*
MAXWELL STILES *Mirror News*
COY WILLIAMS *Mirror News*
AL WOLF *Times*
BEN WOOLBERT *Examiner*
SID ZIFF *Mirror News*
PAUL ZIMMERMAN *Times*

THE BROADCASTERS:

radio:

VIN SCULLY
1958-59

JERRY DOGGETT
1958-59

television:

VIN SCULLY
1959

JERRY DOGGETT
1959

LOS ANGELES—Memorial Coliseum 1958-59

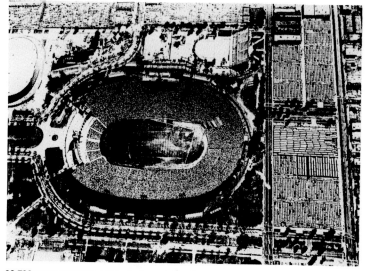

Los Angeles Dodger fans, hungry for big league baseball under any conditions, had to settle for far-distant seats (mostly benched) totally unprotected from the summer sun and a horribly aborted field configuration. A high screen had to be erected in left field to compensate for the 251-ft. distance from home plate.

92,700 persons filled up the giant amphitheatre to witness the fifth game of the 1959 World Series.

The famous peristyle end of the Coliseum reminded everyone that this facility was an "imposter" and an affront to the sport of baseball.

This view from behind home plate documents the first pitch of major league baseball in Los Angeles—the Giants' Jim Davenport at bat, Carl Erskine pitching.

MILWAUKEE 1953-59

Downtown Milwaukee, from the air

Wisconsin Ave. looking west, library on the right

THE NEWSPAPERS:

MILWAUKEE SENTINEL
State Weather
Partly cloudy, slightly warmer.
★ ★ ★ ★ ★ FINAL Dedicated to Truth, Justice and Public Service 5 Cents
One of the Oldest Business Institutions in Milwaukee — Founded June 27, 1837
VOLUME CXVI, NO. 250 TUESDAY, APRIL 14, 1953 64 PAGES IN FOUR SECTIONS

THE MILWAUKEE JOURNAL
Seventy-fifth Year 94 Pages Thursday, October 3, 1957 Pay No More Latest Edition
Burdette Stops Yanks, Evens Series

THE BASEBALL REPORTERS:

AUSTEN BEALMAR	CHARLES CAPALDO	LOUIS CHAPMAN	RAY DOHERTY	RAY GRODY	CHARLES JOHNSON
AP	*AP*	*Sentinel*	*UPI*	*Sentinel*	*Journal*

OLIVER KUECHLE	LLOYD LARSEN	FRED LINDECKE	FRANK MARASCO	AL RAINOVIC	A. T. "RED" THISTED
Journal	*Sentinel*	*UPI*	*Sentinel*	*Journal*	*Journal*

DONALD TRENARY	CLEON WALFOORT	STEVE WELLER	BOB WOLF	LOUIS ZIMMERMAN
Journal	*Journal*	*Journal*	*Journal*	

GEORGE ARMOUR *UPI*
CHRIS EDMONDS *AP*
DION HENDERSON *AP*
MIKE KUPPER
SAM LEVY *Journal*
RUSSELL LYNCH *Journal*
RICHARD McFARLANE *UPI*
FRED PARKER *UPI*
PETE SCHMITT
BOB SPATT

THE BROADCASTERS:

radio: (no television)

BOB KELLY
1953

BLAINE WALSH
1954-59

EARL GILLESPIE
1953-59

MILWAUKEE—County Stadium 1953-59

Milwaukee's brand new stadium was standard "state of the art" concrete and steel classic, but it broke precedent by being located far from downtown and surrounded by vast acreage for automobile parking—unique for a pure baseball park.

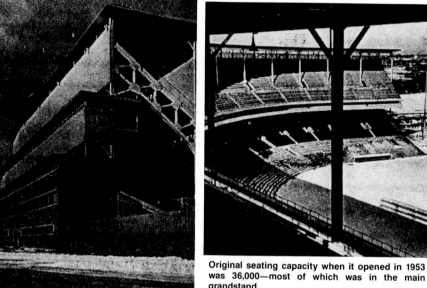

Original seating capacity when it opened in 1953 was 36,000—most of which was in the main grandstand.

A close-up look at the grandstand construction.

The main grandstand as seen from the outfield.

A fine aerial view of the nearly finished product in early 1953. An astonishing total of 1.8 million fans would flock to the new park in its first year.

NEW YORK CITY

THE NEWSPAPERS:

The Empire State Building, the world's tallest in the fifties, overlooks the towers of Manhattan

World-famous Times Square

The same view of Times Square after dark

NEW YORK CITY (continued)

THE BASEBALL REPORTERS:

GEORGE BURTON
L.I. Daily Press

DAN DANIEL
World Telegram

WM. DAUGHERTY
Newark News

JOHN DREBINGER
Times

LOUIS EFFRAT
Times

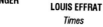
BEN EPSTEIN
Mirror

CHAS. "CHUB" FEENEY
L.I. Star-Journal

TIL FERDENZI
Journal-American

HY GOLDBERG
Newark News

HARRY GRAYSON

MILTON GROSS
Post

ROGER KAHN
NY Herald Tribune

JOE KING
World Telegram

BARNEY KREMENKO
Journal-American

JAMES McCULLEY
Daily News

JERRY MITCHELL
Post

ARCH MURRAY
Post

JAMES OGLE
Newark Star-Ledger

HAROLD ROSENTHAL
Herald Tribune

ED SINCLAIR
Herald Tribune

KEN SMITH
Mirror

JOSEPH TRIMBLE
Daily News

JOE WILLIAMS
World Telegram

J. P. ABRAMSON *Herald Tribune*
DAVID ANDERSON *Journal-American*
JOSEPH ARATA
JOHN BARRINGTON *INS*
JAMES BECKER *AP*
FRED BENDEL *Newark News*
RICHARD BENNETT *Elias*
JOHN BILLI
CLIFFORD BLOODGOOD *BB Mag*
WILLIAM BLOOME *World Telegram*
FRANK BLUNK *Times*
HUGH BRADLEY *Journal-American*
JIMMY BRESLIN
WILLIAM BRIORDY *Times*
LESTER BROMBERG *World Telegram*
AL BUCK *Post*
LEWIS BURTON *Journal-American*
JIMMY CANNON *Post*
LAWTON CARVER *INS*
CLARENCE CASSIN *Mirror*
HAROLD CLASSEN *AP*
LEONARD COHEN *Post*
BOB CONSIDINE *INS*
ROBERT COOKE *Herald Tribune*
BILL CORUM *Journal-American*
JACK CUDDY *UP*
ARTHUR DALEY *Times*
JAMES DAWSON *Times*
FRED DeLUCCA *INS*
CHARLES DEXTER *Daily Worker*
FRED DOWN *UP*
PAUL DURKIN
JOHN EBINGER *Daily News*
FRANK ECK *AP*
CARLOS FERRO
OSCAR FRALEY *UP*
SID FRIEDLANDER *Post*
ED FRIEL
HUGH FULLERTON Jr. *AP*
TONY GALLI *INS*
MICHAEL GAVEN *Journal-American*
IKE GELLIS *Post*
GEORGE GIRSCH *Mirror*
HARRY GLASER *Journal-American*
LESTER GOODMAN *Elias*
HERB GOREN
FRANK GRAHAM *Journal-American*
SID GRAY *Herald Tribune*

JAY GRAYSON
JOHN GRAYSON
JOHN GRIFFIN *UP*
WILL GRIMSLEY *AP*
BERT GUMPERT *Post*
SAM GUNST
JACK HAND *AP*
W. C. HEINZ *Sun*
JOHN HENIGAN *Mirror*
HARRY HENNESSY *Reuters*
JOE HIRSCH *Morning Telegram*
CHARLES HOERTER *Daily News*
TOMMY HOLMES *Herald Tribune*
PAUL HOROWITZ *Newark News*
JAMES HURLEY *Mirror*
JERRY IZENBERG
HERB JAFFE
JAMES KAHN *Sun*
MAX KASE *Journal-American*
RAYMOND KELLY *Times*
CHRIS KIERAN *Daily News*
WILLIE KLEIN
LEONARD KOPPETT *Post*
SID KRONISCH *AP*
AL LANEY *Herald Tribune*
JOHN LARDNER
WM. LAUDER *Herald Tribune*
FRANK LEONARD
LEONARD LEWIN *Mirror*
CARL LUNDQUIST *UP*
JACK LYNN *Post*
WM. MARDO
IRVING MARSH *Herald Tribune*
WHITNEY MARTIN *AP*
WILLIAM MATHIAS *Daily News*
ALAN MAVER
PAT McDONOUGH *World Telegram*
ROSCOE McGOWAN *Times*
LEO MEALIA *Daily News*
TOM MEANY *Morning Telegraph*
TED MEIER *AP*
LOU MILLER *World Telegram*
NORMAN MILLER *UP*
ED MILLS
DANA MOZLEY *Daily News*
WILLARD MULLIN *World Telegram*
ED MURPHY *Sun, World Telegram*
JAMES MURPHY *World Telegram*

NEW YORK CITY (continued)

BARNEY NAGLER *Morning Telegraph*
JOSEPH NICHOLS *Times*
JOE O'DAY *Daily News*
BEN OLAN *AP*
MURRAY OLDERMAN
STAN OPTOWSKI *UP*
TOM O'REILLY *Morning Telegraph*
JACK ORR
WARREN PACK *Journal-American*
AL PALMA *Journal-American*
TOM PAPROCKI *AP*
DAN PARKER *Mirror*
LAWRENCE PERRY
LEO PETERSON *UP*
JOHN PIEROTTI *Post*
FRANCIS PORTELA
JAMES POWERS *Daily News*
JOHN POWERS
WM. QUINN
MARSHALL REED
JOE REICHLER *AP*
BUD RENNIE *Herald Tribune*
GRANTLAND RICE
LESTER RICE *Journal-American*
ARTHUR RICHMAN *Mirror*
MILT RICHMAN *UP*
JAMES ROACH *Times*
ORLO ROBERTSON *AP*
PAT ROBINSON *INS*
LESTER RODNEY *Daily Worker*
WM. ROEDER *World Telegram*
SAUL ROOGOW *Herald Tribune*
MURRAY ROSE *AP*
LEONARD SCHECHTER *Post*
IRA SEEBACHER *Morning Telegraph*
CHAS. SEGAR
EMERSON SEIBOLD *Post*
JOE SHEEHAN *Times*
HOWARD SIGMOND *INS*
HENRY SINGER *Post*
SEYMOUR SIWOFF
WALTER SMITH *Herald Tribune*
TED SMITS *AP*
STEVE SNIDER *UP*
LAWRENCE SPIKER *Times*
GUS STEIGER *Mirror*
BOB STEWART *World-Telegram*
GAYLE TALBOT *AP*

FRANK TRUE *Sun*
JAMES TUITE *Times*
HY TURKIN *Daily News*
JOE VAL *World Telegram*
AL VERMEER
ED WADE *Post*
CHRISTY WALSH
DAVID WALSH *INS*
FRED WEATHERLY *Mirror*
WILL WEDGE *Sun*
HAROLD WEISMAN *Mirror*
JOHN WHEELER
GORDON WHITE *Times*
ED WILKS *AP*
WILBUR WOOD *Sun*
STAN WOODWARD
MEL WOODY
DICK YOUNG *Daily News*

THE BROADCASTERS:

NEW YORK GIANTS
radio & television:

RUSS HODGES
1950-57

ERNIE HARWELL
1950-53

BOB DELANEY
1954-57

JIM WOODS
1957

NEW YORK YANKEES

radio:

MEL ALLEN
1950-59

CURT GOWDY
1950

DIZZY DEAN
1951

ART GLEESON
1951-52

BILL CROWLEY
1951-52

JIM WOODS
1953-56

JOE E. BROWN
1953

RED BARBER
1954-59

PHIL RIZZUTO
1957-59

television:

MEL ALLEN
1950-59

CURT GOWDY
1950

DIZZY DEAN
1950-51

ART GLEESON
1951-52

BILL CROWLEY
1951-52

JOE E. BROWN
1953

JIM WOODS
1953-56

RED BARBER
1954-59

PHIL RIZZUTO
1957-59

NEW YORK CITY—Polo Grounds 1950-57

The elongated "horseshoe" configuration was the most unusual stadium layout in the majors, an evolutionary growth from the original ball diamond of 1890. By the 1950s, high-rise apartments had replaced the old train repair yards on the north. Old Manhattan Field on the south was now a huge parking lot.

A view toward the far-distant (475 ft.) center field bleachers and the familiar Chesterfield sign.

The Polo Grounds was a popular scheduled stop for commuter trains northward bound to the Bronx, just across the Harlem River.

The Eighth Avenue street-level entrance was the main inlet for Giant fans, even though it was the bleacher end of the park.

NEW YORK CITY—Yankee Stadium

The "House That Ruth Built" was a magnificent cathedral of baseball tradition. The spirits of great Yankee players and teams of past generations figuratively "haunted" the place.

The latticework trimmings on the grandstand roof were a familiar feature to Yankee Stadium visitors in the fifties.

An aerial view looking west across the Harlem River reveals the proximity of the neighboring Giants' home park (Polo Grounds) in upper Manhattan.

PHILADELPHIA

Looking southeast, down Benjamin Franklin Parkway toward the heart of the city

Independence Square

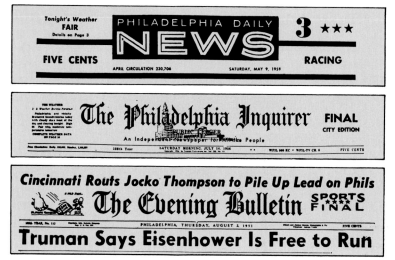

Municipal Auditorium and Convention Hall

THE NEWSPAPERS:

PHILADELPHIA (continued)

THE BASEBALL REPORTERS:

STAN BAUMGARTNER
Inquirer

HUGH BROWN
Bulletin

FRED BYROD
Inquirer

DON DANIELS
Inquirer

ED DELANEY
Daily News

SANDY GRADY
Daily News

JOHN HAYES
Daily News

RAYMOND KELLY
Bulletin

ALLAN LEWIS
Inquirer

LANSING McCURLEY
Daily News

LARRY MERCHANT
Daily News

ARTHUR MORROW
Inquirer

JACK ORR
Daily News

ED POLLOCK
Bulletin

LEO RIORDAN
Inquirer

JOHN WEBSTER
Inquirer

FRANK YEUTTER
Bulletin

HERB ALTSCHULL *AP*
RALPH BERNSTEIN *AP*
TOM BRADSHAW *AP*
JEROME CARSON *Bulletin*
AL CARTWRIGHT
JOHN CLANCY *UP*
GRANT DOHERTY *Daily News*
DONALD DONAGHEY *Bulletin*
JACK FRIED *Bulletin*
JOHN GAUDIOSI *UP*
S. O. GRAULEY *Inquirer*
RUSS GREEN *UP*
JOE GREENDAY *Daily News*

STAN HOCHMAN *Daily News*
HENRY LITTLEHALES *Inquirer*
JACK McKINNEY *Daily News*
JOHN O'BRIEN *UP*
ORLO ROBERTSON *AP*
EARL ROTH *Bulletin*
ROBERT VETRONE *Bulletin*
WM. G. WEART
CHAS. WELSH Jr. *AP*
DAVID WILSON *Inquirer*
JACK WILSON *Bulletin*

THE BROADCASTERS:

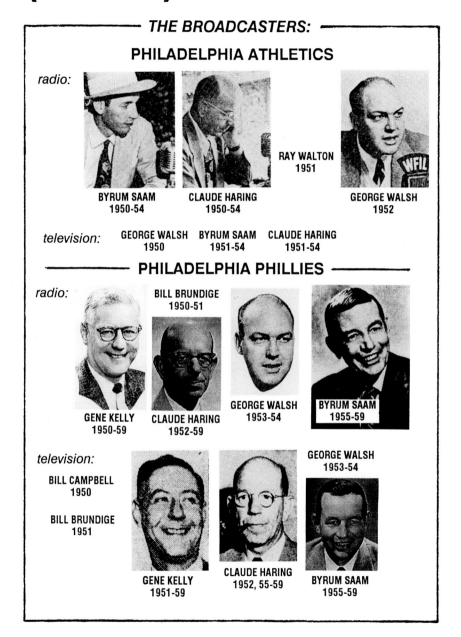

PHILADELPHIA ATHLETICS

radio:

BYRUM SAAM
1950-54

CLAUDE HARING
1950-54

RAY WALTON
1951

GEORGE WALSH
1952

television: GEORGE WALSH   BYRUM SAAM   CLAUDE HARING
1950   1951-54   1951-54

PHILADELPHIA PHILLIES

radio:

BILL BRUNDIGE
1950-51

GENE KELLY
1950-59

CLAUDE HARING
1952-59

GEORGE WALSH
1953-54

BYRUM SAAM
1955-59

television:

BILL CAMPBELL
1950

BILL BRUNDIGE
1951

GENE KELLY
1951-59

CLAUDE HARING
1952, 55-59

GEORGE WALSH
1953-54

BYRUM SAAM
1955-59

PHILADELPHIA—Shibe Park (Connie Mack Stadium)

The venerable old park in North Philly served as home to both AL Athletics and NL Phillies up to 1954, when the A's left town. Originally named Shibe Park when it was built in 1909, it was renamed Connie Mack Stadium in 1953.

A bird's eye view reveals its identity as a true "neighborhood" park, bounded on all four sides by city streets.

The SW corner entrance at Lehigh & 21st Sts. retained the original classic "gingerbread" architecture of 1909, blended in with more austere rooftop offices which were added in later years.

A street-level view looking north along the 21st Street side of the main grandstand.

PITTSBURGH

A downtown view from Mt. Washington

Pittsburgh at night from Duquesne Heights

Liberty Avenue, looking east
from 7th Street

THE NEWSPAPERS:

The Pittsburgh Press — FINAL

PITTSBURGH Sun-Telegraph — FINAL EDITION

Pittsburgh Post-Gazette
One of America's Great Newspapers

PITTSBURGH (continued)

THE BASEBALL REPORTERS:

AL ABRAMS
Post-Gazette

LESTER BIEDERMAN
Press

CHARLES "CHILLY" DOYLE
Sun-Telegraph

JACK HERNON
Post-Gazette

CHESTER SMITH
Press

ED BALINGER *Post-Gazette*
JACK BERGER *Press*
TOM BIRKS *Sun-Telegraph*
JOE BRADIS *AP*
NORMAN BRAUN *UPI*
JACK BURNLEY *Sun-Telegraph*
JOHN CARROLL *UPI*
RUDY CERNKOVIC *UPI*
MYRON COPE *Post-Gazette*
ROBERT DRUM *Press*
HARRY FAIRFIELD *Press*
JOHN GOLIGHTLY *INS*
TROY GORDON *INS*
PHIL GRABOWSKI *Sun-Telegraph*
MERRILL GRANGER
JACK HENRY
JOHN HENRY *Sun-Telegraph*

VINCE JOHNSON *Post-Gazette*
JIM JORDAN *Post-Gazette*
HARRY KECK *Sun-Telegraph*
RAY KIENZL *Sun-Telegraph*
GEO. KISEDA *Sun-Telegraph*
PAUL KURTZ *Press*
FRED LANDUCCI *Press*
DAN McGIBBENY Jr. *Post-Gazette*
JAMES MILLER *Sun-Telegraph*
DUKE MORAN *AP*
DONALD QUAY
GILBERT REMLEY *Post-Gazette*
JACK SELL *Post-Gazette*
GIL STALEY *AP*
AL TEDERSTROM *Press*
DAVIS WALSH *Sun-Telegraph*
CHAS. WELSH Jr. *AP*
ROLLO WILSON

THE BROADCASTERS:

radio:

ROSEY ROWSWELL
1950-54

BOB PRINCE
1950-59

DICK BINGHAM
1955-57

PAUL LONG
1957-59

JIM WOODS
1958-59

television:

BOB PRINCE
1957-59

JIM WOODS
1959

PITTSBURGH—Forbes Field

Forbes Field, named after a Revolutionary War general, was one of the first of a "new wave" of all concrete and steel classic parks when it opened in 1909.

A badly "colorized" postcard view of a night game scene at Forbes Field.

Fans converging on the main entrance for a big game.

The famous "Greenberg Gardens," where the left field fence was shortened in 1947 for sluggers Kiner and Greenberg. It was removed in 1954.

Another view of the main entrance at Bouquet & Sennott Sts.

SAN FRANCISCO 1958-59

The Bay Bridge, from Yerba Buena Island

The Hyde St. cable car, Alcatraz in the distance

Chinatown after dark

THE NEWSPAPERS:

SAN FRANCISCO 1958-59 (continued)

THE BASEBALL REPORTERS:

EMMONS BYRNE
Oakland Tribune

CURLEY GRIEVE
Examiner

JACK HANLEY
INS

WALTER JUDGE
Examiner

ABE KEMP
Examiner

DICK O'CONNOR
Palo Alto Times

BOB STEVENS
Chronicle

PRESCOTT SULLIVAN
Examiner

BUCKY WALTER
News

SCOTT BAILLE *UP*
ALLAN CLINE *AP*
WILL CONNOLLY *Chronicle*
WALTER DALEY *Call-Bulletin*
RAY HAYWOOD *Oakland Tribune*
DAN HRUBY
HARRY JOHANSEN *INS*
BILL LEISER *Chronicle*
JACK McDONALD *Call-Bulletin*
JIM McGEE *Call-Bulletin*
FRANCIS POWERS
ART ROSENBAUM *Chronicle*
DON SELBY *Examiner*
BUD SPENCER *News*
JACK STEVENSON *AP*
ALAN WARD *Oakland Tribune*
ROGER WILLIAMS *News*
HAL WOOD *UP*

THE BROADCASTERS:

radio:

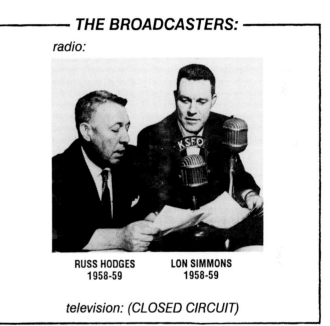

RUSS HODGES
1958-59

LON SIMMONS
1958-59

television: (CLOSED CIRCUIT)

SAN FRANCISCO—Seals Stadium 1958-59

The transplanted Giants of 1958 had to settle for a tiny, hastily refurbished Seals Stadium until their new Candlestick Park was available.

Discounting LA's makeshift use of the non-baseball Coliseum, Seals Stadium was the major leagues' only completely uncovered ballpark. It had served as home for PCL teams since 1931.

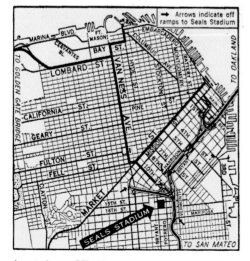

Located near SF's Mission District, trying to find a parking place was an "adventure" for the new Giant fans.

Seals Stadium's seating capacity was upped from 18,500 to almost 24,000 to try to accommodate an eager public. Extra lighting was also added, as well as a new dark green paint job.

ST. LOUIS

Aerial view of downtown St. Louis

The Eads Bridge and the Mississippi River

Park Plaza and Chase Hotel, next to Forest Park

THE NEWSPAPERS:

ST. LOUIS (continued)

THE BASEBALL REPORTERS:

BOB BURNES
Globe Democrat

SID KEENER
Star-Times

J. ROY STOCKTON
Post-Dispatch

ELLIS VEECH
E. St. L. Journal

JOHN ARCHIBALD *Post Dispatch*
HUGO AUTZ *Sporting News*
ALVIN T. BARNES Jr. *Star-Times*
EDGAR BRANDS *Sporting News*
BOB BROEG *Post Dispatch*
ROLAND BURKE *Sporting News*
JOE COPPAGE *Sporting News*
JERE COX *UP*
PAUL DIX *UP*
AL DOPKING *AP*
WM. FAIRBAIRN *Globe Democrat*
DICK FARRINGTON *Post Dispatch*
C. T. FELKER *Sporting News*
HAROLD FLACHSBART *Post-Dispatch*
WM. FLEISCHMAN *Star-Times, Globe Democrat*
LEONARD GETTELSON *Sporting News*
RAY GILLESPIE *Star-Times, Sporting News*
CHARLES GOULD *Globe Democrat*
ED HAGAN *E. St. L. Journal*
RENO HAHN *Globe Democrat*
MARTIN HALEY *Globe Democrat*
JACK HERMAN *Globe Democrat*
ART HUGHES *Sporting News*
ARNOLD IRISH *E. St. L. Journal*
WILLIS JOHNSON *Globe Democrat*
CLIFF KACHLINE *Sporting News*
OSCAR KAHAN *Sporting News*
HOWARD KEE *Globe Democrat*
WM. KERCH *Globe Democrat*
ERNEST LANIGAN *Sporting News*
DENNIS McCARTHY *UP*
PAUL McFARLANE *Sporting News*
WM. McGOOGAN *Post-Dispatch*
LLOYD McMASTER *Post-Dispatch*

DENT McSKIMMING *Post-Dispatch*
ALLAN MERRITT *AP*
MARION MILTON *Star-Times*
HARRY MITAUER *Globe Democrat*
STANTON MOCKLER *UP*
ROBERT MORRISON *Post-Dispatch*
RAY NELSON *Star-Times*
JOE OPPENHEIMER *INS*
BOB PARKIN *UP*
HAROLD PIETY *E. St. L. Journal*
ARTHUR PLAMBECK *Sporting News*
JOE POLLOCK *Globe-Democrat*
RALPH RAY *Sporting News*
LOWELL REIDENBAUGH *Sporting News*
JOHN RICE *Globe Democrat, Post Dispatch*
PAUL RICKART *Sporting News*
CHRIS ROEWE Jr. *Sporting News*
GENE ROGUSKI *INS*
OSCAR RUHL *Sporting News*
NEAL RUSSO *Post-Dispatch*
JIM SCOTT *INS*
RAY SMITH *Globe Democrat*
CHARLES SPINK *Sporting News*
ROBERT SUITS *AP*
BUD THEIS *Globe Democrat*
W. VERNON TIELJEN *Star-Times*
HAROLD TUTHILL *Post-Dispatch*
JAMES VAN VALKENBURG *AP*
GLEN WALLAR *Globe Democrat*
HERMAN WECKE *Post-Dispatch*
FRANZ WIPPOLD *Sporting News*
AMADEE WOHLSCHLAGER *Post-Dispatch*
J. ED WRAY *Post-Dispatch*
THOMAS YARBROUGH *AP*

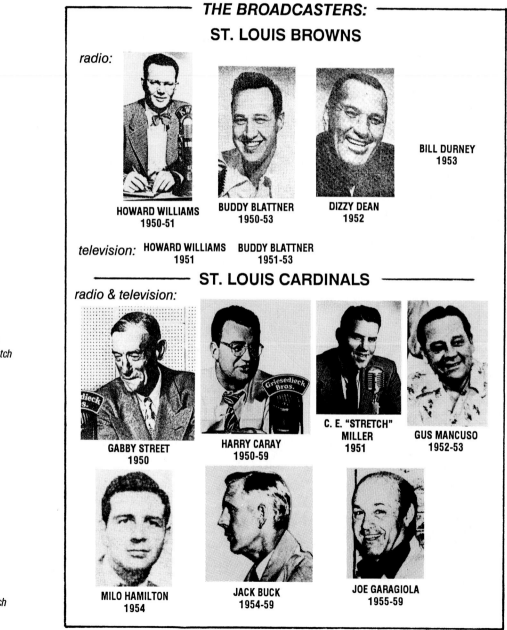

THE BROADCASTERS:
ST. LOUIS BROWNS

radio:

HOWARD WILLIAMS
1950-51

BUDDY BLATTNER
1950-53

DIZZY DEAN
1952

BILL DURNEY
1953

television: **HOWARD WILLIAMS** **BUDDY BLATTNER**
1951 1951-53

ST. LOUIS CARDINALS

radio & television:

GABBY STREET
1950

HARRY CARAY
1950-59

C. E. "STRETCH" MILLER
1951

GUS MANCUSO
1952-53

MILO HAMILTON
1954

JACK BUCK
1954-59

JOE GARAGIOLA
1955-59

ST. LOUIS—Sportsman's Park (Busch Stadium)

A postcard view of Sportsman's Park in the 1940s. Although the site was used for baseball before 1900, the double-decked grandstand and diamond location dated back to 1909. The Browns and Cardinals were co-users of the park from 1920 up to 1954, when the Browns left.

Another aerial shot depicting the park in the late fifties, when it was called Busch Stadium. A rooftop press box and new scoreboard were added features for that decade.

New owner Busch added new lights, new scoreboard, and other improvements for 1954.

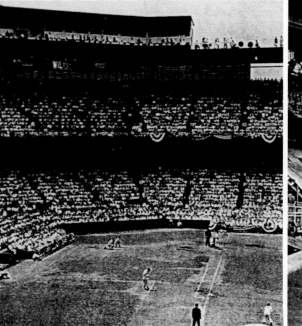

Until 1953, the AL Browns actually owned Sportsman's Park and the Cardinals were paying guests. Cards' owner Busch purchased the park in 1953 and gave it its new name.

A scene from opening day 1950.

Construction on overall park improvements in early 1954.

WASHINGTON DC

The Capitol Building and neighboring landmarks

Pennsylvania Avenue

Washington DC National Airport

THE NEWSPAPERS:

WASHINGTON DC (continued)

THE BASEBALL REPORTERS:

BOB ADDIE
Times-Herald, Post

EDDIE CRANE
Alex. Gazette

CHARLES EGAN
Star

EVERETT GARDNER
Daily News

BUS HAM
Post

BURTON HAWKINS
Star

RICE O'DELL
Daily News

SHIRLEY POVICH
Post

DAVID REQUE
Daily News

MORRIS SIEGEL
Daily News, Post

FRANCIS STANN
Star

JIM TUCKER
N. Va. Sun

WM. AHLBERG *Post*
HERB ALTSCHULL *AP*
LEWIS ATCHISON *Star*
CHARLES BARBOUR *Times-Herald, Star*
ERNEST BARCELLA *UP*
RUSS BENNETT *Daily News*
HERMAN BLACKMAN *Post*
GEORGE CLARK *Star*
GEORGE CLIFFORD *Daily News*
ART EDSON *AP*
SAM FOGG *INS*
HERBERT HEFT *Post*
RAY HILL *Army Times*

JOE IVES *AP*
WHEELER JOHNSON *Star*
JOHN KELLER *Star*
WM. KERWIN *INS*
WM. PEELER *Star*
WHITNEY SHOEMAKER *AP*
DAVID SLATTERY *Daily News*
JACK TULLOCH *Alex. Gazette*
JACK WALSH *Post*
ROBERT WENTWORTH *Times-Herald*
MERRILL WHITTLESEY *Star*
MARTIN ZACHRAVEE *Post*

THE BROADCASTERS:

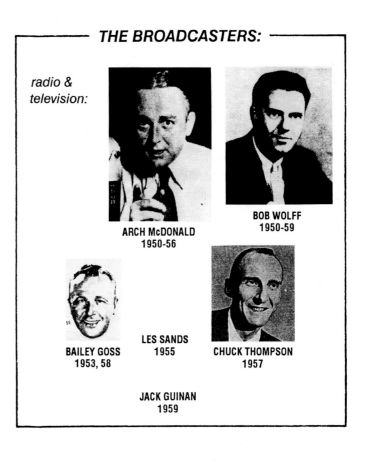

radio & television:

ARCH McDONALD
1950-56

BOB WOLFF
1950-59

BAILEY GOSS
1953, 58

LES SANDS
1955

CHUCK THOMPSON
1957

JACK GUINAN
1959

WASHINGTON DC—Griffith Stadium

A view of the third base stands and double-decked pavilion.

Griffith Stadium was hastily constructed in early 1911 to replace a wooden stand destroyed by fire on the same site. It was bordered on the north by Howard University and Freedman's Hospital (lower right in photo).

Another view looking down the first base line. An identical pavilion mirrored the third base side. The upper deck seating was unusually steep and the roof was noticeably higher than the main grandstand.

A scene from a game in progress from behind home plate.

Another aerial view clearly shows the unusual "notch" in dead center field, where owners of these apartment buildings had refused to sell out to the Washington club.

THE TEAMS

Baltimore Orioles 1954-59

FRONT OFFICE:

CLARENCE W. MILES
president 1954-55

JAMES KEELTY Jr.
president 1956-59-

ARTHUR EHLERS
gen. mgr. 1954

PAUL RICHARDS
gen. mgr./manager
1955-59-

LEE MacPHAIL
gen. mgr. 1959

FIELD MANAGERS:

JIMMY DYKES
1954

PAUL RICHARDS
1955-59-

COACHES:

HARRY BRECHEEN 1954-59
TOM OLIVER 1954
FRANK SKAFF 1954
LUMAN HARRIS 1955-59
AL VINCENT 1955-59
JIMMY ADAIR 1957-59
EDDIE ROBINSON 1957-59

TRAINER:

ED WEIDNER

THE PLAYERS:

CHICO GARCIA
second baseman
1954

BILLY HUNTER
shortstop
1954

VIC WERTZ
outfielder
1954

CLINT COURTNEY
catcher 1954

DICK KRYHOSKI
first baseman
1954

SAM MELE
first base, outfield
1954

JIM FRIDLEY
outfielder
1954

NEIL BERRY
infielder
1954

Baltimore Orioles (continued)

BOB TURLEY
pitcher 1954

BOB CHAKALES
pitcher 1954

HOWIE FOX
pitcher 1954

JOE DURHAM
outfielder
1954, 1957

MARLIN STUART
pitcher 1954

MIKE BLYZKA
pitcher 1954

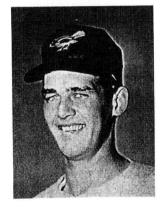

DON LARSEN
pitcher 1954

BOB KENNEDY
third base, outfield
1954-55

FRANK KELLERT
first baseman 1954

VERN STEPHENS
shortstop
1954-55

EDDIE WAITKUS
first baseman
1954-55

DICK KOKOS
outfielder
1954

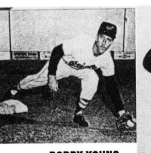

BOBBY YOUNG
second baseman
1954-55

CAL ABRAMS
outfielder
1954-55

GIL COAN
outfielder
1954-55

LES MOSS
catcher
1954-55

JOE COLEMAN
pitcher 1954-55

Baltimore Orioles (continued)

BOB KUZAVA
pitcher
1954-55

DUANE PILLETTE
pitcher 1954-55

LOU KRETLOW
pitcher 1954-55

CHUCK DIERING
outfielder
1954-56

BILLY O'DELL
pitcher
1954, 1956-59

JIM BRIDEWEISER
infielder
1954, 1957

DON JOHNSON
pitcher 1955

BILLY COX
infielder 1955

ED LOPAT
pitcher 1955

SAUL ROGOVIN
pitcher 1955

HARRY BYRD
pitcher 1955

GENE WOODLING
outfielder
1955, 1958-59-

DAVE PHILLEY
outfielder
1955-56

HANK MAJESKI
infielder 1955

DON LEPPERT
second baseman
1955

JIM McDONALD
pitcher 1955

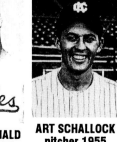

ART SCHALLOCK
pitcher 1955

**ANGELO
DAGRES**
outfielder
1955

FREDDIE MARSH
utility 1955-56

**HAROLD W.
"HAL" SMITH**
catcher
1955-56

Baltimore Orioles (continued)

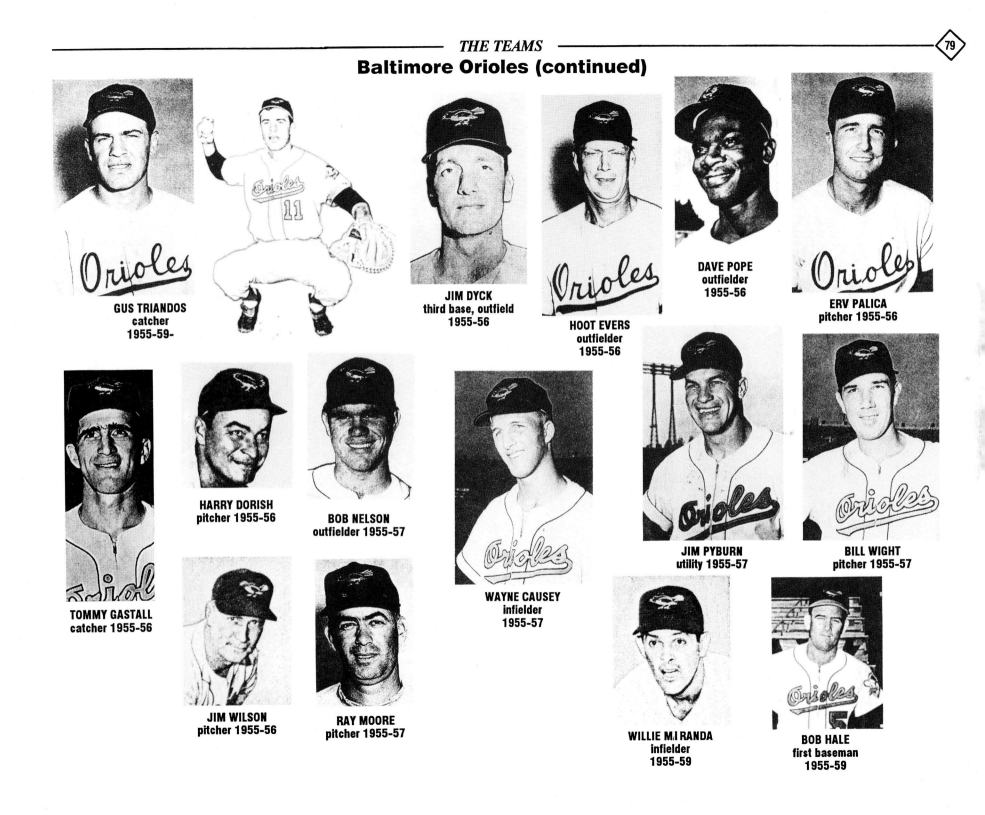

GUS TRIANDOS
catcher
1955-59-

JIM DYCK
third base, outfield
1955-56

HOOT EVERS
outfielder
1955-56

DAVE POPE
outfielder
1955-56

ERV PALICA
pitcher 1955-56

TOMMY GASTALL
catcher 1955-56

HARRY DORISH
pitcher 1955-56

BOB NELSON
outfielder 1955-57

WAYNE CAUSEY
infielder
1955-57

JIM PYBURN
utility 1955-57

BILL WIGHT
pitcher 1955-57

JIM WILSON
pitcher 1955-56

RAY MOORE
pitcher 1955-57

WILLIE MIRANDA
infielder
1955-59

BOB HALE
first baseman
1955-59

BROOKS ROBINSON
third baseman
1955-59-

GEORGE ZUVERINK
pitcher 1955-59

HAL "SKINNY" BROWN
pitcher 1955-59-

MORRIE MARTIN
pitcher 1956

BOBBY ADAMS
infielder 1956

JOE FRAZIER
outfielder 1956

JOHNNY SCHMITZ
pitcher 1956

MIKE FORNIELES
pitcher 1956-57

GEORGE KELL
third baseman
1956-57

CONNIE JOHNSON
pitcher 1956-58

DON FERRARESE
pitcher 1956-57

TITO FRANCONA
first base, outfield
1956-57

CHARLIE BEAMON
pitcher 1956-58

Baltimore Orioles (continued)

DICK WILLIAMS
utility
1956-57, 1958

JOE GINSBERG
catcher 1956-59-

BILLY GARDNER
infielder 1956-59

BOB BOYD
first baseman
1956-59

BILLY LOES
pitcher 1956-59

BOB NIEMAN
outfielder
1956-59

ART CECCARELLI
pitcher 1957

JIM BUSBY
outfielder
1957-58

KEN LEHMAN
pitcher 1957-58

BILLY GOODMAN
infielder 1957

CARL POWIS
outfielder
1957

FRANK ZUPO
catcher 1957-58

JERRY WALKER
pitcher 1957-59-

AL PILARCIK
outfielder
1957-59-

Baltimore Orioles (continued)

MILT PAPPAS
pitcher 1957-59-

LENNY GREEN
outfielder
1957-59

FOSTER CASTLEMAN
utility 1958

JIM MARSHALL
first base, outfield
1958

JACK HARSHMAN
pitcher 1958-59

JOE TAYLOR
outfielder 1958-59

**ARNOLD
PORTOCARRERO**
pitcher 1958-59

HOYT WILHELM
pitcher 1958-59-

RON HANSEN
shortstop 1958-59-

CHICO CARRASQUEL
infielder 1959

BILLY KLAUS
infielder 1959-

ALBIE PEARSON
outfielder 1959-

WALT DROPO
first baseman
1959-

JIM FINIGAN
infielder 1959

LEO BURKE
utility
1958-59

WILLIE TASBY
outfielder
1958-59-

ERNIE JOHNSON
pitcher 1959

BILLY HOEFT
pitcher 1959-

JACK FISHER
pitcher 1959-

BARRY SHETRONE
outfielder 1959-

WHITEY LOCKMAN
utility 1959

Boston Red Sox 1950-59

FRONT OFFICE:

TOM YAWKEY
owner/president
1950-59

EDDIE COLLINS
VP 1950

JOE CRONIN
gen. mgr. 1950-58

BUCKY HARRIS
gen. mgr. 1959

FIELD MANAGERS:

JOE McCARTHY
1950

STEVE O'NEILL
1950-51

LOU BOUDREAU
1952-54

MIKE HIGGINS
1955-59

BILLY JURGES
1959

COACHES:

EARLE COMBS 1950-52
STEVE O'NEILL 1950
PAUL SCHREIBER 1950-58
JOHNNY SCHULTE 1950
GEORGE SUSCE 1950-54
EDDIE MAYO 1951
BILL McKECHNIE 1952-53
OSCAR MELILLO 1952-53
DEL BAKER 1953-59

BUSTER MILLS 1954
JACK BURNS 1955-59
DAVE "BOO" FERRISS 1955-59
MICKEY OWEN 1955-56
RUDY YORK 1959

TRAINER: JACK FADDEN

THE PLAYERS:

DICK LITTLEFIELD
pitcher 1950

KEN KELTNER
third, first base
1950

LOU STRINGER
infielder 1950

AL PAPAI
pitcher 1950

BIRDIE TEBBETTS
catcher 1950

CHARLEY SCHANZ
pitcher 1950

Boston Red Sox (continued)

BOBBY DOERR
second baseman
1950-51

MATT BATTS
catcher 1950-51

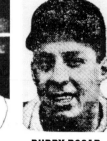

TOM WRIGHT
outfielder
1950-51

BUDDY ROSAR
catcher 1950-51

CHUCK STOBBS
pitcher 1950-51

FRED HATFIELD
infielder 1950-52

JOHNNY PESKY
infielder 1950-52

HARRY TAYLOR
pitcher 1950-52

VERN STEPHENS
shortstop 1950-52

MEL PARNELL
pitcher 1950-56

TED WILLIAMS
outfielder
1950-59-

WALT DROPO
first baseman
1950-52

DOM DIMAGGIO
outfielder
1950-53

Boston Red Sox (continued)

AL ZARILLA
outfielder
1950, 1952-53

JOE DOBSON
pitcher 1950, 1954

CLYDE VOLLMER
outfielder 1950-53

ELLIS KINDER
pitcher 1950-55

BILLY GOODMAN
utility 1950-57

JIM PIERSALL
outfielder
1950, 1952-58

WALT MASTERSON
pitcher 1950-52

CHARLEY MAXWELL
outfielder 1950-54

WILLARD NIXON
pitcher 1950-58

LES MOSS
catcher 1951

LOU BOUDREAU
infielder 1951-52
(manager '52-'54)

MICKEY McDERMOTT
pitcher 1950-53

MEL HODERLEIN
infielder 1951

AL EVANS
catcher
1951

RAY SCARBOROUGH
pitcher 1951-52

Boston Red Sox (continued)

LEO KIELY
pitcher
1951, 1954-59

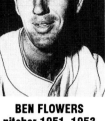

BEN FLOWERS
pitcher 1951, 1953

KARL OLSON
outfielder
1951, 1953-55

GEORGE SCHMEES
utility 1952

DIZZY TROUT
pitcher 1952

BILL WIGHT
pitcher 1951-52

JOHNNY LIPON
shortstop 1952-53

ARCHIE WILSON
outfielder 1952

AL BENTON
pitcher 1952

RALPH BRICKNER
pitcher 1952

HERSH FREEMAN
pitcher 1952-53, 1955

NORM ZAUCHIN
first baseman
1951, 1955-57

GEORGE KELL
third baseman
1952-54

GUS NIARHOS
catcher
1952-53

HOOT EVERS
outfielder
1952-54

DEL WILBER
catcher
1952-54

Boston Red Sox (continued)

GENE STEPHENS
outfielder 1952-53, 1955-59-

DON LENHARDT
outfield, third base
1952, 1954

SID HUDSON
pitcher 1952-54

DICK BRODOWSKI
pitcher 1952, 1955

BILL HENRY
pitcher 1952-55

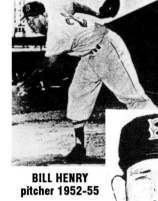

FAYE THRONEBERRY
outfielder 1952, 1955-57

MILT BOLLING
shortstop
1952-57

DICK GERNERT
first base, outfield
1952-59

SAMMY WHITE
catcher 1952-59

TED LEPCIO
infielder
1952-59

Boston Red Sox (continued)

IKE DELOCK
pitcher 1952-59

BILL KENNEDY
pitcher 1953

TOMMY UMPHLETT
outfielder 1953

MARV GRISSOM
pitcher 1953

BILLY WERLE
pitcher 1953-54

FLOYD BAKER
infielder 1953-54

HAL "SKINNY" BROWN
pitcher 1953-55

FRANK SULLIVAN
pitcher 1953-59-

BILLY CONSOLO
infielder 1953-59

HARRY AGGANIS
first baseman
1954-55

TEX CLEVENGER
pitcher 1954

MICKEY OWEN
catcher 1954

TOM HURD
pitcher
1954-56

GRADY HATTON
infielder 1954-56

SAM MELE
first base, outfield
1954-55

Boston Red Sox (continued)

RUSS KEMMERER
pitcher 1954-57

JACKIE JENSEN
outfielder 1954-59-

OWEN FRIEND
infielder 1955

HAYWOOD SULLIVAN
catcher 1955, 1957, 1959

GEORGE SUSCE
pitcher 1955-58

TOM BREWER
pitcher 1954-59

EDDIE JOOST
infielder 1955

PETE DALEY
catcher
1955-59

FRANK BAUMANN
pitcher 1955-59

FRANK MALZONE
third baseman
1955-59-

BILLY KLAUS
shortstop, third base
1955-58

MICKEY VERNON
first baseman
1956-57

GENE MAUCH
infielder
1956-57

Boston Red Sox (continued)

RUDY MINARCIN
pitcher 1956-57

DON BUDDIN
shortstop
1956, 1958-59-

BOB PORTERFIELD
pitcher 1956-58

DAVE SISLER
pitcher 1956-59

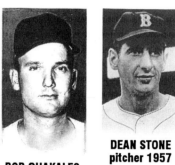

MARTY KEOUGH
outfield, first base
1956-59-

BOB CHAKALES
pitcher 1957

DEAN STONE
pitcher 1957

KEN ASPROMONTE
second baseman
1957-58

MURRAY WALL
pitcher
1950, 1957-59

MIKE FORNIELES
pitcher
1957-59-

LOU BERBERET
catcher
1958

BUD BYERLY
pitcher 1958

BILL RENNA
outfielder
1958-59

**ROBERT W.
"RIVERBOAT"
SMITH**
pitcher 1958

AL SCHROLL
pitcher
1958, 1959

PETE RUNNELS
infielder
1958-59-

Boston Red Sox (continued)

TED BOWSFIELD
pitcher 1958-59-

BILL MONBOQUETTE
pitcher 1958-59-

VIC WERTZ
first baseman
1959-

JIM BUSBY
outfielder
1959-

BOBBY AVILA
second baseman
1959

JACK HARSHMAN
pitcher 1959

NELS CHITTUM
pitcher 1959-

EARL WILSON
pitcher 1959-

JERRY CASALE
pitcher 1958-59-

TED WILLS
pitcher 1959-

BILLY HOEFT
pitcher
1959

GARY GEIGER
outfielder 1959-

PUMPSIE GREEN
shortstop, second base
1959-

JERRY MALLETT
outfielder 1959

Boston/Milwaukee Braves 1950-59

FRONT OFFICE:

LOUIS PERINI
owner, president
1950-59-

JOSEPH CAIRNES
president 1957-59

JOHN QUINN
gen. mgr. 1950-58

JOHN McHALE
gen. mgr. 1959-

FIELD MANAGERS:

BILLY SOUTHWORTH
1950-51

TOMMY HOLMES
1951-52

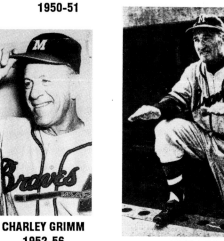

CHARLEY GRIMM
1952-56

FRED HANEY
1956-59

COACHES:

JOHNNY COONEY 1950-55	CHARLEY ROOT 1956-57
JIMMY BROWN 1950-51	CONNIE RYAN 1957
BOB KEELEY 1950-57	BILLY HERMAN 1958-59
BUCKY WALTERS 1950-55	JOHN FITZPATRICK 1958-59
FRED HANEY 1956	GEORGE SUSCE 1958-59
JOHNNY RIDDLE 1956-57	WHITLOW WYATT 1958-59

TRAINER: C. K. LACKS

THE PLAYERS:

MICKEY HAEFNER
pitcher 1950

NORM ROY
pitcher
1950

BOB HALL
pitcher
1950

PETE REISER
third base, outfield
1950

**JOHNNY
ANTONELLI**
pitcher
1950, 1953

CONNIE RYAN
second baseman
1950

PAUL BURRIS
catcher
1950, 1952-53

Boston/Milwaukee Braves (continued)

BOB ELLIOTT
third baseman
1950-51

BUDDY KERR
shortstop, second base
1950-51

TOMMY HOLMES
outfielder
1950-51
(manager 1951-52)

JOHNNY SAIN
pitcher 1950-51

BOB CHIPMAN
pitcher 1950-52

BOB ADDIS
outfielder
1950-51

GENE MAUCH
infielder
1950-51

BOBBY HOGUE
pitcher 1950-51

EARL TORGESON
first baseman
1950-52

SAM JETHROE
outfielder
1950-52

WILLARD MARSHALL
outfielder 1950-52

ROY HARTSFIELD
second baseman
1950-52

DAVE COLE
pitcher
1950-53

Boston/Milwaukee Braves (continued)

WALKER COOPER
catcher 1950-53

SID GORDON
third base, outfield
1950-53

WARREN SPAHN
pitcher 1950-59-

MAX SURKONT
pitcher 1950-53

VERN BICKFORD
pitcher 1950-53

DEL CRANDALL
catcher
1950, 1953-59-

SIBBY SISTI
utility
1950-54

LUIS OLMO
third base, outfield
1950-51

Boston/Milwaukee Braves (continued)

ERNIE JOHNSON
pitcher
1950, 1952-58

GEORGE ESTOCK
pitcher 1951

LUIS MARQUEZ
outfielder 1951

DICK DONOVAN
pitcher 1951-52

EBBA ST. CLAIRE
catcher 1951-53

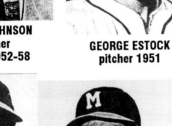

JOHNNY LOGAN
shortstop 1951-59–

LEW BURDETTE
pitcher 1951-59–

CHET NICHOLS
pitcher 1951-56

PHIL PAINE
pitcher
1951, 1954-57

BOB THORPE
outfielder
1951-53

JIM WILSON
pitcher 1951-54

Boston/Milwaukee Braves (continued)

BILLY REED
second baseman
1952

JACK DANIELS
outfielder
1952

JACK CUSICK
shortstop, third base
1952

SHELDON JONES
pitcher 1952

EDDIE MATHEWS
third baseman
1952-59-

PETE WHISENANT
outfielder 1952

GEORGE CROWE
first baseman
1952-53, 1955

VIRGIL JESTER
pitcher 1952-53

BILLY KLAUS
shortstop
1952-53

JACK DITTMER
second baseman
1952-56

MEL ROACH
utility
1953-54, 1957-59-

GENE CONLEY
pitcher 1952, 1954-58

JOE ADCOCK
first base, outfield
1953-59-

Boston/Milwaukee Braves (continued)

JIM PENDLETON
utility 1953-56

DAVE JOLLY
pitcher
1953-57

BILLY BRUTON
outfielder
1953-59-

ANDY PAFKO
outfielder
1953-59

HARRY HANEBRINK
utility 1953, 1957-58

DON LIDDLE
pitcher
1953

BOB BUHL
pitcher
1953-59-

JOEY JAY
pitcher
1953-55, 1957-59-

GEORGE METKOVICH
first base, outfield
1954

ROY SMALLEY
infielder 1954

SAM CALDERONE
catcher 1954

Boston/Milwaukee Braves (continued)

CHARLEY WHITE
catcher 1954-55

BOBBY THOMSON
outfield, third base
1954-57

RAY CRONE
pitcher
1954-57

DANNY O'CONNELL
infielder 1954-57

ROBERTO VARGAS
pitcher 1955

BOB ROSELLI
catcher
1955-56, 1958

EARL HERSH
outfielder
1956

HANK AARON
outfielder
1954-59-

HUMBERTO
ROBINSON
pitcher
1955-56, 1958

CHUCK TANNER
outfielder
1955-57

DEL RICE
catcher
1955-59

BOB TROWBRIDGE
pitcher 1956-59

LOU SLEATER
pitcher 1956

RED MURFF
pitcher 1956-57

FELIX MANTILLA
utility 1956-59-

TAYLOR PHILLIPS
pitcher 1956-57

Boston/Milwaukee Braves (continued)

FRANK TORRE
first baseman
1956-59-

WES COVINGTON
outfielder
1956-59-

NIPPY JONES
first base, outfield
1957

BOB TAYLOR
catcher, outfield
1957-58

RED SCHOENDIENST
second baseman
1957-59-

JOE KOPPE
shortstop
1958

CARL SAWATSKI
catcher 1957-58

BOB HAZLE
outfielder
1957-58

JUAN PIZARRO
pitcher 1957-59-

JOHN DEMERIT
outfielder 1957-59-

DON McMAHON
pitcher 1957-59-

EDDIE HAAS
outfielder
1958

Boston/Milwaukee Braves (continued)

CASEY WISE
infielder
1958-59

BOB RUSH
pitcher
1958-59-

CARLTON WILLEY
pitcher 1958-59-

LEE MAYE
outfielder
1959-

JOE MORGAN
second baseman
1959

MICKEY VERNON
first base, outfield
1959

BOBBY AVILA
second baseman
1959

RAY BOONE
first baseman
1959-

AL SPANGLER
outfielder 1959-

STAN LOPATA
catcher, first base
1959-

CHUCK COTTIER
second baseman
1959-

JOHNNY O'BRIEN
second baseman 1959

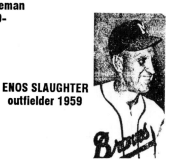

ENOS SLAUGHTER
outfielder 1959

BOB GIGGIE
pitcher 1959-

Brooklyn/Los Angeles Dodgers 1950-59

FRONT OFFICE:

BRANCH RICKEY
president/gen. mgr.
1950

WALTER O'MALLEY
president 1951-59

FRESCO THOMPSON
VP 1951-59

BUZZY BAVASI
VP, gen. mgr.
1951-59-

FIELD MANAGERS:

BURT SHOTTON
1950

CHUCK DRESSEN
1951-53

WALTER ALSTON
1954-59

COACHES:

JAKE PITLER 1950-57
CLYDE SUKEFORTH 1950-51
MILT STOCK 1950
COOKIE LAVAGETTO 1951-53
BILLY HERMAN 1952-57
TED LYONS 1954
JOE BECKER 1955-59
GREG MULLEAVY 1957-59
CHUCK DRESSEN 1958-59
RUBE WALKER 1958
PEEWEE REESE 1959

TRAINER: HAROLD WENDLER

THE PLAYERS:

JACK BANTA
pitcher 1950

REX BARNEY
pitcher 1950

BILLY LOES
pitcher
1950, 1952-56

WAYNE BELARDI
first baseman
1950-51, 1953-54

JOE LANDRUM
pitcher
1950, 1952

Brooklyn/Los Angeles Dodgers (continued)

GENE HERMANSKI
outfielder 1950-51

JOE HATTEN
pitcher 1950-51

TOMMY BROWN
outfielder 1950-51

EDDIE MIKSIS
infielder
1950-51

GEORGE SHUBA
outfielder
1950, 1952-55

DON NEWCOMBE
pitcher 1950-58

JACKIE ROBINSON
utility 1950-56

BRUCE EDWARDS
catcher 1950-51

CAL ABRAMS
outfielder
1950-52

PREACHER ROE
pitcher 1950-54

CHRIS VAN CUYK
pitcher 1950-52

ERV PALICA
pitcher
1950-51, 53-54

DAN BANKHEAD
pitcher 1950-51

Brooklyn/Los Angeles Dodgers (continued)

ROY CAMPANELLA
catcher 1950-57

BILLY COX
infielder
1950-55

BUD PODBIELAN
pitcher 1950-52

CARL FURILLO
outfielder
1950-59-

RALPH BRANCA
pitcher 1950-53, 1956

JIM RUSSELL
outfielder
1950-51

PEEWEE REESE
shortstop, third base
1950-58

BOBBY MORGAN
infielder 1950, 1952-53

GIL HODGES
first base, utility
1950-59-

DUKE SNIDER
outfielder
1950-59-

Brooklyn/Los Angeles Dodgers (continued)

CLEM LABINE
pitcher 1950-59-

DICK WILLIAMS
utility 1951-54, 1956

CARL ERSKINE
pitcher 1950-59

HANK EDWARDS
outfielder 1951

ROCKY BRIDGES
infielder
1951-52

DON THOMPSON
outfielder
1951, 1953-54

PHIL HAUGSTAD
pitcher 1951

RUBE WALKER
catcher 1951-58

**WAYNE
TERWILLIGER**
infielder 1951

JOHNNY SCHMITZ
pitcher 1951-52

ANDY PAFKO
outfield, third base
1951-52

CLYDE KING
pitcher 1951-52

Brooklyn/Los Angeles Dodgers (continued)

RAY MOORE
pitcher
1952-53

TOMMY HOLMES
outfielder 1952

**JOHNNY
RUTHERFORD**
pitcher 1952

JOE BLACK
pitcher
1952-55

BILL ANTONELLO
outfielder 1953

JIM GILLIAM
utility
1953-59–

SANDY AMOROS
outfielder
1952, 1954-57, 1959–

ROCKY NELSON
first baseman
1952, 1956

BEN WADE
pitcher
1952-54

JIM HUGHES
pitcher
1952-56

RUSS MEYER
pitcher
1953-55

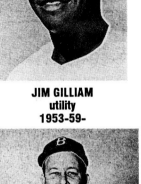

**HOMER
"DIXIE" HOWELL**
catcher
1953, 1955-56

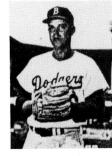

KEN LEHMAN
pitcher 1952, 1956-57

RON NEGRAY
pitcher 1952, 1958

BOB MILLIKEN
pitcher 1953-54

JOHNNY PODRES
pitcher 1953-59–

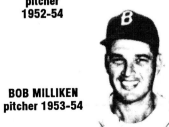

Brooklyn/Los Angeles Dodgers (continued)

PETE WOJEY
pitcher 1954

KARL SPOONER
pitcher 1954-55

TOM LASORDA
pitcher 1954-55

WALT MORYN
outfielder
1954-55

DON ZIMMER
infielder
1954-59

ED ROEBUCK
pitcher 1955-58

**CHARLES
"TIM" THOMPSON**
catcher 1954

DON HOAK
third baseman
1954-55

ROGER CRAIG
pitcher 1955-59-

SANDY KOUFAX
pitcher 1955-59-

DON DRYSDALE
pitcher 1956-59-

DON DEMETER
outfielder
1956, 1958-59-

FRANK KELLERT
first baseman
1955

DON BESSENT
pitcher 1955-58

**CHICO
FERNANDEZ**
shortstop
1956

SAL MAGLIE
pitcher
1956-57

RANDY JACKSON
third baseman
1956-58

GINO CIMOLI
outfielder
1956-58

CHARLEY NEAL
infielder
1956-59-

Brooklyn/Los Angeles Dodgers (continued)

RENE VALDES
pitcher 1957

JOHN ROSEBORO
catcher 1957-59-

JIM GENTILE
first baseman
1957-58

FRED KIPP
pitcher 1957-59

DON MILES
outfielder
1958

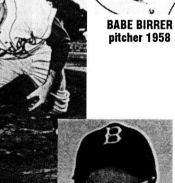

STEVE BILKO
first baseman
1958

ELMER VALO
outfielder
1957-58

JOE PIGNATANO
catcher 1957-59-

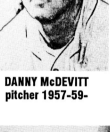

DANNY McDEVITT
pitcher 1957-59-

BOB KENNEDY
utility 1957

NORM LARKER
first base, outfield
1958-59-

BABE BIRRER
pitcher 1958

JACKIE COLLUM
pitcher 1957-58

**BOBBY
GIALLOMBARDO**
pitcher 1958

EARL ROBINSON
third baseman
1958

Brooklyn/Los Angeles Dodgers (continued)

BOB LILLIS
infielder
1958-59-

JOHNNY KLIPPSTEIN
pitcher 1958-59

RON FAIRLY
outfielder
1958-59-

LARRY SHERRY
pitcher 1958-59-

SOLLY DRAKE
outfielder
1959

FRANK HOWARD
outfielder
1958-59-

STAN WILLIAMS
pitcher 1958-59-

WALLY MOON
first base, outfield
1959-

RIP REPULSKI
outfielder 1959-

JIM BAXES
third baseman
1959

DICK GRAY
third baseman
1958-59

ART FOWLER
pitcher 1959-

CHUCK CHURN
pitcher 1959

CHUCK ESSEGIAN
outfielder 1959-

MAURY WILLS
shortstop 1959-

GENE SNYDER
pitcher 1959

Chicago Cubs 1950-59

FRONT OFFICE:

PHILIP K. WRIGLEY
president 1950-59

JIM GALLAGHER
bus. mgr. 1950-56

WID MATHEWS
personnel dir.
1950-56

CLARENCE ROWLAND
exec. VP 1955-59

JOHN HOLLAND
VP 1956-59

CHARLEY GRIMM
vice president
1957-59

FIELD MANAGERS:

FRANKIE FRISCH
1950-51

PHIL CAVARETTA
1951-53

STAN HACK
1954-56

BOB SCHEFFING
1957-59

COACHES:

BILL BAKER 1950
VIRGIL "SPUD" DAVIS 1950-53
ROY JOHNSON 1950-53
CHARLEY ROOT 1951-53
RAY BLADES 1953-56
BOB SCHEFFING 1954-55
DUTCH LEONARD 1954-56
PEPPER MARTIN 1956
FRED FITZSIMMONS 1957-59
RAY MUELLER 1957
GEORGE MYATT 1957-59
ROGERS HORNSBY 1958-59
ELVIN TAPPE 1959

TRAINERS:

ANDY LOTSHAW
AL SCHUENEMAN

THE PLAYERS:

EMIL VERBAN
utility 1950

HARRY CHITI
catcher
1950-52, 1955-56

HANK EDWARDS
outfielder 1950

DOYLE LADE
pitcher 1950

**JOHNNY
VANDER MEER**
pitcher 1950

Chicago Cubs (continued)

BOB SCHEFFING
catcher 1950

BILL VOISELLE
pitcher 1950

BOB BORKOWSKI
first base, outfield
1950-51

WAYNE
TERWILLIGER
utility
1950-51

CARMEN MAURO
outfielder 1950-51

RUBE WALKER
catcher 1950-51

HANK SAUER
outfielder
1950-55

WALT DUBIEL
pitcher 1950-52

ANDY PAFKO
outfielder
1950-51

MICKEY OWEN
catcher 1950-51

FRANK HILLER
pitcher 1950-51

JOHNNY SCHMITZ
pitcher 1950-51

ROY SMALLEY
shortstop 1950-53

Chicago Cubs (continued)

RON NORTHEY
outfielder
1950, 1952

PHIL CAVARETTA
first base, outfield
1950-53
(manager 1951-53)

DUTCH LEONARD
pitcher 1950-53

PAUL MINNER
pitcher 1950-56

BOB RUSH
pitcher
1950-57

RANDY JACKSON
third baseman
1950-55

PRESTON WARD
first base, outfield
1950, 1953

CARL SAWATSKI
catcher 1950, 1953

JOHNNY KLIPPSTEIN
pitcher 1950-54

WARREN HACKER
pitcher 1950-56

CHUCK CONNORS
first baseman 1951

HAL JEFFCOAT
outfielder, pitcher
1950-55

BILL SERENA
second, third base
1950-54

BOB RAMAZZOTTI
infielder 1950-53

JACK CUSICK
shortstop 1951

SMOKEY BURGESS
catcher 1951

Chicago Cubs (continued)

CAL McLISH
pitcher
1951

FRED RICHARDS
first baseman
1951

JOE HATTEN
pitcher 1951-52

BOB KELLY
pitcher 1951-53

BRUCE EDWARDS
catcher, infielder
1951-52, 1954

GENE HERMANSKI
outfielder 1951-53

BOB SCHULTZ
pitcher 1951-53

FRANKIE
BAUMHOLTZ
outfielder
1951-55

EDDIE MIKSIS
utility 1951-56

DEE FONDY
first baseman
1951-57

TURK LOWN
pitcher
1951-58

TOMMY BROWN
utility 1952-53

JOHN PRAMESA
catcher 1952

BOB ADDIS
outfielder
1952-53

LEON BRINKOPF
shortstop 1952

WILLIE RAMSDELL
pitcher 1952

TOBY ATWELL
catcher 1952-53

DON ELSTON
pitcher
1953, 1957-59-

DUKE SIMPSON
pitcher 1953

GEORGE
METKOVITCH
first base,
outfield
1953

SHELDON JONES
pitcher 1953

Chicago Cubs (continued)

DALE TALBOT
outfielder
1953-54

JOE GARAGIOLA
catcher 1953-54

RALPH KINER
outfielder
1953-54

JIM WILLIS
pitcher 1953-54

ERNIE BANKS
shortstop
1953-59-

CLYDE McCULLOUGH
catcher
1953-56

JIM BROSNAN
pitcher 1954, 1956-58

HAL RICE
outfielder
1954

STEVE BILKO
first baseman
1954

WALKER COOPER
catcher 1954-55

BILL TREMEL
pitcher 1954-56

JIM DAVIS
pitcher
1954-56

VERN MORGAN
third baseman
1954-55

GENE BAKER
second baseman
1953-57

HOWIE POLLET
pitcher 1953-55

BUBBA CHURCH
pitcher 1953-55

DAVE COLE
pitcher
1954

DON ROBERTSON
outfielder 1954

ELVIN TAPPE
catcher
1954-56, 1958

Chicago Cubs (continued)

JIM FANNING
catcher 1954-57

LLOYD MERRIMAN
outfielder 1955

HARRY PERKOWSKI
pitcher 1955

GALE WADE
outfielder
1955-56

JIM KING
outfielder
1955-56

SAM JONES
pitcher 1955-56

JIM BOLGER
third base,
outfield
1955, 1957-58

BOB SPEAKE
first base,
outfield
1955, 1957

TED TAPPE
outfielder
1955

JOHN ANDRE
pitcher 1955

HY COHEN
pitcher 1955

SOLLY DRAKE
outfielder
1956

DON HOAK
third baseman
1956

MONTE IRVIN
outfielder 1956

ED WINCENIAK
infielder
1956-57

PETE WHISENANT
outfielder 1956

HOBIE LANDRITH
catcher 1956

FRANK KELLERT
first baseman
1956

DON KAISER
pitcher 1955-57

DAVE HILLMAN
pitcher 1955-59

RUSS MEYER
pitcher 1956

VITO
VALENTINETTI
pitcher 1956-57

JOHNNY BRIGGS
pitcher 1956-58

JERRY KINDALL
infielder 1956-58

WALT MORYN
outfielder
1956-59-

MOE
DRABOWSKY
pitcher
1956-59-

Chicago Cubs (continued)

CHARLIE SILVERA
catcher 1957

JACKIE COLLUM
pitcher 1957

EDDIE HAAS
outfielder
1957

CASEY WISE
infielder 1957

DICK LITTLEFIELD
pitcher 1957

TOM POHOLSKY
pitcher 1957

BOBBY MORGAN
infielder 1957-58

CHUCK TANNER
outfielder
1957-58

**BOBBY
DEL GRECO**
outfielder
1957

JACK LITTRELL
infielder 1957

FRANK ERNAGA
outfielder 1957-58

ED MAYER
pitcher 1957-58

LEE WALLS
outfielder
1957-59

JOHN GORYL
infielder 1957-59

BOBBY ADAMS
infielder 1957-59

BOB WILL
outfielder
1957-58

CAL NEEMAN
catcher 1957-59-

GLEN HOBBIE
pitcher 1957-59-

DALE LONG
first baseman
1957-59

DICK DROTT
pitcher 1957-59-

BOB ANDERSON
pitcher 1957-59-

**ELMER
SINGLETON**
pitcher
1957-59

Chicago Cubs (continued)

MARCELINO SOLIS
pitcher 1958

DOLAN NICHOLS
pitcher 1958

HERSH FREEMAN
pitcher 1958

GENE FODGE
pitcher 1958

TONY TAYLOR
infielder 1958-59-

SAMMY TAYLOR
catcher 1958-59-

BOBBY THOMSON
third base, outfield
1958-59

ART SCHULT
first base,
outfield
1959-

MOE THACKER
catcher 1958

LOU JACKSON
outfielder 1958-59

JIM MARSHALL
first base, outfield
1958-59

BILLY WILLIAMS
outfielder 1959-

IRV NOREN
first base,
outfield
1959-

GEORGE ALTMAN
outfielder 1959-

BILL HENRY
pitcher 1958-59

JOHN BUZHARDT
pitcher 1958-59

ALVIN DARK
infielder 1958-59

TAYLOR PHILLIPS
pitcher 1958-59

EARL AVERILL JR.
utility 1959-

ART CECCARELLI
pitcher 1959-

Chicago White Sox 1950-59

FRONT OFFICE:

GRACE COMISKEY
president 1950-56

CHUCK COMISKEY
VP 1950-59

FRANK LANE
gen. mgr. 1950-55

JOHN RIGNEY
VP 1956-59

BILL VEECK
president
1959

HANK GREENBERG
VP 1959

FIELD MANAGERS:

JACK ONSLOW
1950

RED CORRIDEN
1950

PAUL RICHARDS
1951-54

MARTY MARION
1954-56

AL LOPEZ
1957-59

COACHES:

RAY BERRES 1950-59
BUSTER MILLS 1950
RED CORRIDEN 1950
JIMMY ADAIR 1951-52
ROGER "DOC" CRAMER 1951-53
LUMAN HARRIS 1951-54
MARTY MARION 1954
GEORGE MYATT 1955-56
DEL WILBER 1955-56

DON GUTTERIDGE 1955-59
TONY CUCCINELLO 1957-59
JOHNNY COONEY 1957-59

TRAINERS:

MUSH ESLER
ED FROELICH

THE PLAYERS:

JOHNNY OSTROWSKI
outfielder
1950

JERRY SCALA
outfielder 1950

MARV RICKERT
first base, outfield
1950

Chicago White Sox (continued)

MICKEY HAEFNER
pitcher 1950

BILL WIGHT
pitcher 1950

BOB KUZAVA
pitcher 1950

HERB ADAMS
outfielder 1950

MYRON W.
"MIKE" McCORMICK
outfielder 1950

EDDIE MALONE
catcher 1950

RAY SCARBOROUGH
pitcher 1950

LUKE APPLING
infielder 1950

CASS MICHAELS
second baseman
1950, 1954

EDDIE ROBINSON
first baseman
1950-52

BILL WILSON
outfielder
1950, 1953-54

CHICO
CARRASQUEL
shortstop
1950-55

PHIL MASI
catcher 1950-52

JOE KIRRENE
third baseman
1950, 1954

GORDON
GOLDSBERRY
first base, outfield
1950-51

GUS NIARHOS
catcher 1950-51

HANK MAJESKI
third baseman
1950-51

Chicago White Sox (continued)

NELSON FOX
second baseman
1950-59-

DAVE PHILLEY
outfield, first base
1950-51, 1956-57

GUS ZERNIAL
outfielder
1950-51

FLOYD BAKER
infielder
1950-51

BOB CAIN
pitcher
1950-51, 1954

KEN HOLCOMBE
pitcher 1950-52

RANDY GUMPERT
pitcher 1950-51

BILLY PIERCE
pitcher 1950-59-

JIM BUSBY
outfielder
1950-52, 1955

HOWIE JUDSON
pitcher 1950-52

LUIS ALOMA
pitcher 1950-53

LOU KRETLOW
pitcher 1950-53

MARV ROTBLATT
pitcher 1950-51

DON LENHARDT
first base, outfield
1951

DICK LITTLEFIELD
pitcher 1951

Chicago White Sox (continued)

MINNIE MINOSO
infield, outfield
1951-57

BERT HAAS
utility 1951

BOB DILLINGER
third baseman
1951

AL ZARILLA
outfielder
1951-52

HAL "SKINNY" BROWN
pitcher 1951-52

BUD STEWART
outfielder
1951-54

JOE DEMAESTRI
infielder 1951

PAUL LEHNER
outfielder 1951

BUD SHEELY
catcher 1951-53

HARRY DORISH
pitcher 1951-55

HECTOR RODRIGUEZ
third baseman
1952

RAY COLEMAN
outfielder 1951-52

SAUL ROGOVIN
pitcher 1951-53

BOB BOYD
first base, outfield
1951, 1953-54

JOE DOBSON
pitcher 1951-53

RED WILSON
catcher 1951-54

BILL KENNEDY
pitcher 1952

Chicago White Sox (continued)

MARV GRISSOM
pitcher 1952

CHUCK STOBBS
pitcher 1952

LEO THOMAS
third baseman
1952

WILLIE MIRANDA
infielder 1952

SHERMAN LOLLAR
catcher 1952-59-

JIM RIVERA
outfielder
1952-59-

SAM DENTE
utility 1952-53

ROCKY KRSNICH
third baseman
1952-53

SAM MELE
first base,
outfield
1952-53

TOM WRIGHT
outfielder
1952-53

BOB ELLIOTT
third base, outfield
1953

GENE BEARDEN
pitcher 1953

TOMMY BYRNE
pitcher 1953

**SAMMY
ESPOSITO**
infielder
1952, 1955-59-

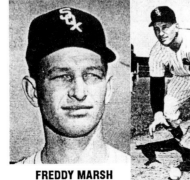

FREDDY MARSH
utility 1953-54

SANDY CONSUEGRA
pitcher 1953-56

CONNIE JOHNSON
pitcher 1953, 1955-56

BOB KEEGAN
pitcher 1953-58

Chicago White Sox (continued)

MIKE FORNIELES
pitcher 1953-56

FERRIS FAIN
first baseman
1953-54

VIRGIL TRUCKS
pitcher 1953-55

DICK STRAHS
pitcher 1954

MORRIE MARTIN
pitcher 1954-56

WILLARD MARSHALL
outfielder 1954-55

DON JOHNSON
pitcher 1954

MATT BATTS
catcher
1954

PHIL CAVARETTA
first base, outfield
1954-55

JACK HARSHMAN
pitcher, first base
1954-57

VERN STEPHENS
shortstop, third base
1953, 1955

**CARL
SAWATSKI**
catcher
1954

RON JACKSON
first baseman
1954-59

JOHNNY GROTH
outfielder
1954-55

GEORGE KELL
third baseman
1954-56

ED McGHEE
outfielder
1954-55

STAN JOK
third base, outfield
1954-55

Chicago White Sox (continued)

BOBBY ADAMS
infielder 1955

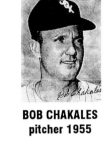

BOB CHAKALES
pitcher 1955

CLINT COURTNEY
catcher 1955

DICK DONOVAN
pitcher 1955-59-

LUIS APARICIO
shortstop 1956-59-

JIM BRIDEWESER
infielder 1955-56

EARL BATTEY
catcher 1955-59

RON NORTHEY
outfielder
1955-57

LES MOSS
catcher
1955-58

HOWIE POLLET
pitcher 1956

FRED HATFIELD
infielder 1956-57

BOB NIEMAN
outfielder
1955-56

BOB KENNEDY
utility 1955-57

HARRY BYRD
pitcher 1955-56

WALT DROPO
first baseman
1955-58

**MILLARD
"DIXIE" HOWELL**
pitcher 1955-58

ELLIS KINDER
pitcher 1956-57

Chicago White Sox (continued)

JIM DELSING
outfielder
1956

LARRY DOBY
outfielder
1956-57, 1959

BUBBA PHILLIPS
third base, outfield
1956-59

GERRY STALEY
pitcher 1956-59-

DON RUDOLPH
pitcher 1957-59

JIM LANDIS
outfielder
1957-59-

JOE DAHLKE
pitcher
1956

JIM McDONALD
pitcher 1956-58

JIM WILSON
pitcher 1956-58

TED BEARD
outfielder
1957-58

BARRY LATMAN
pitcher 1957-59

TITO FRANCONA
outfielder 1958

JIM DERRINGTON
pitcher 1956-57

PAUL LAPALME
pitcher 1956-57

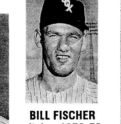

BILL FISCHER
pitcher 1956-58

EARL TORGESON
first baseman
1957-59-

TOM QUALTERS
pitcher 1958

RAY BOONE
first baseman
1958

BILLY GOODMAN
infielder 1958-59-

Chicago White Sox (continued)

EARLY WYNN
pitcher 1958-59-

BOB SHAW
pitcher
1958-59-

RAY MOORE
pitcher
1958-59-

TURK LOWN
pitcher 1958-59-

HARRY SIMPSON
first base, outfield
1959

JOHN ROMANO
catcher 1958-59

**JOHNNY
CALLISON**
outfielder
1958-59

AL SMITH
third base,
outfield
1958-59-

KEN McBRIDE
pitcher 1959-

TED KLUSZEWSKI
first baseman
1959-

DEL ENNIS
outfielder
1959

NORM CASH
outfield,
first base
1958-59

DON MUELLER
outfielder 1958-59

JIM McANANY
outfielder 1958-59-

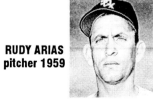

RUDY ARIAS
pitcher 1959

Cincinnati Reds 1950-59

FRONT OFFICE:

POWELL CROSLEY JR.
owner/president 1950-59

WARREN GILES
gen. mgr. 1950-51

GABE PAUL
gen. mgr. 1952-59

FIELD MANAGERS:

LUKE SEWELL
1950-52

ROGERS HORNSBY
1952-53

BUSTER MILLS
1953 (8 games)

JIMMY DYKES
1958

MAYO SMITH
1959

BIRDIE TEBBETTS
1954-58

FRED HUTCHINSON
1959

COACHES:

TONY CUCCINELLO 1950-51	DICK BARTELL 1954-55
GUS MANCUSO 1950	TOM FERRICK 1954-58
PHIL PAGE 1950-53	JIMMY DYKES 1955-58
DANNY LITWHILER 1951	FRANK McCORMICK 1956-57
TOMMY BRIDGES 1951	JOHNNY RIDDLE 1958
BEN CHAPMAN 1952	ELLIS "COT" DEAL 1959
EARLE BRUCKER 1952	WALLY MOSES 1959
BUSTER MILLS 1953	REGGIE OTERO 1959
FORD GARRISON 1953	

TRAINER: WAYNE ANDERSON

THE PLAYERS:

RON NORTHEY
outfielder 1950

PEANUTS LOWREY
utility 1950

BOBBY ADAMS
infielder 1950-55

JOHNNY HETKI
pitcher 1950

HOWIE FOX
pitcher 1950-51

Cincinnati Reds (continued)

BOB USHER
outfielder 1950-51

JOHNNY PRAMESA
catcher
1950-51

KENT PETERSON
pitcher 1950-51

LLOYD MERRIMAN
outfielder
1950-51, 1954

JOE ADCOCK
first base,
outfield
1950-52

GRADY HATTON
utility 1950-54

TED KLUSZEWSKI
first baseman 1950-57

BOB SCHEFFING
catcher 1950-51

DANNY LITWHILER
outfielder 1950-51

WILLIE RAMSDELL
pitcher 1950-51

CONNIE RYAN
utility 1950-51, 1954

ED ERAUTT
pitcher
1950-51, 1953

VIRGIL STALLCUP
shortstop 1950-52

HOMER "DIXIE" HOWELL
catcher
1950-52

SAMMY MEEKS
infielder 1950-51

JIM BOLGER
outfielder 1950-51, 1954

KEN RAFFENSBERGER
pitcher 1950-54

JOHN WYROSTEK
first base, outfield
1950-52

BUD BYERLY
pitcher 1950-52

HOBIE LANDRITH
catcher 1950-55

TED TAPPE
pinch-hitter
1950-51

Cincinnati Reds (continued)

EWELL BLACKWELL
pitcher 1950-52

HERM
WEHMEIER
pitcher
1950-54

HARRY PERKOWSKI
pitcher 1950-54

ROY McMILLAN
shortstop 1951-59-

HANK EDWARDS
outfielder 1951-52

WALLY WESTLAKE
outfielder 1952

FRANK SMITH
pitcher
1950-54, 1956

WALLY POST
outfielder
1951-57

EDDIE
PELLAGRINI
infielder
1952

CAL ABRAMS
outfielder 1952

JOE ROSSI
catcher 1952

WILLARD MARSHALL
outfielder 1952-53

BARNEY McCOSKY
outfielder 1951

ED BLAKE
pitcher
1951-53

NILES JORDAN
pitcher 1952

FRANK HILLER
pitcher 1952

BUBBA CHURCH
pitcher 1952-53

BOB BORKOWSKI
first base, outfield
1952-55

ANDY SEMINICK
catcher 1952-55

Cincinnati Reds (continued)

JOHNNY TEMPLE
second base, utility
1952-59

BUD PODBIELAN
pitcher 1952-57

JOE NUXHALL
pitcher 1952-59-

HOWIE JUDSON
pitcher 1953-54

ED BAILEY
catcher 1953-59-

GUS BELL
outfielder
1953-59-

JIM GREENGRASS
outfielder 1952-55

GEORGE LERCHEN
outfielder 1953

BOB MARQUIS
outfielder 1953

BOB KELLY
pitcher 1953, 1958

**JACKIE
COLLUM**
pitcher
1953-55

MOE SAVRANSKY
pitcher 1954

ROCKY BRIDGES
infielder 1953-57

CLYDE KING
pitcher 1953

FRED BACZEWSKI
pitcher 1953-55

NINO ESCALERA
utility 1954

KARL DREWS
pitcher 1954

**JERRY
LANE**
pitcher
1954-55

**CORKY
VALENTINE**
pitcher
1954-55

Cincinnati Reds (continued)

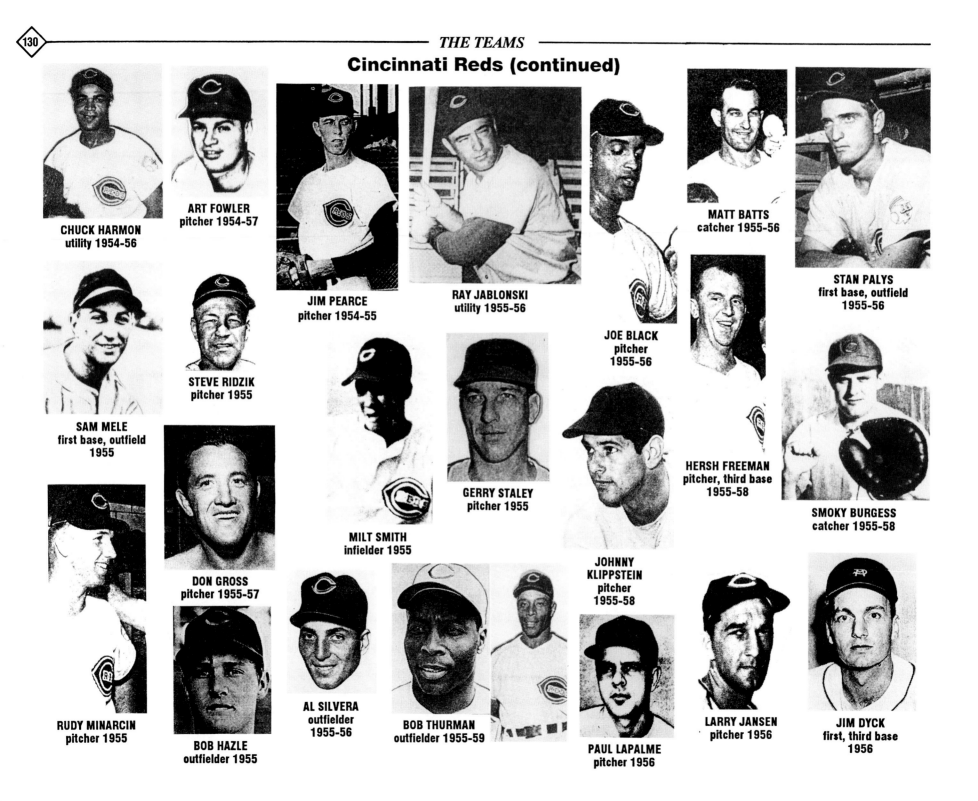

CHUCK HARMON
utility 1954-56

ART FOWLER
pitcher 1954-57

JIM PEARCE
pitcher 1954-55

RAY JABLONSKI
utility 1955-56

MATT BATTS
catcher 1955-56

STAN PALYS
first base, outfield
1955-56

SAM MELE
first base, outfield
1955

STEVE RIDZIK
pitcher 1955

JOE BLACK
pitcher
1955-56

HERSH FREEMAN
pitcher, third base
1955-58

MILT SMITH
infielder 1955

GERRY STALEY
pitcher 1955

SMOKY BURGESS
catcher 1955-58

DON GROSS
pitcher 1955-57

**JOHNNY
KLIPPSTEIN**
pitcher
1955-58

RUDY MINARCIN
pitcher 1955

BOB HAZLE
outfielder 1955

AL SILVERA
outfielder
1955-56

BOB THURMAN
outfielder 1955-59

PAUL LAPALME
pitcher 1956

LARRY JANSEN
pitcher 1956

JIM DYCK
first, third base
1956

Cincinnati Reds (continued)

BILL KENNEDY
pitcher 1956-57

ALEX GRAMMAS
infielder 1956-58

GEORGE CROWE
first baseman
1956-58

BROOKS LAWRENCE
pitcher 1956-59-

FRANK ROBINSON
outfielder, infielder
1956-59-

CLAUDE OSTEEN
pitcher 1957, 1959

ART SCHULT
outfielder
1956-57

TOM ACKER
pitcher 1956-59

WARREN HACKER
pitcher 1957

DON HOAK
infielder 1957-58

RAUL SANCHEZ
pitcher 1957

JERRY LYNCH
outfielder
1957-59-

HAL JEFFCOAT
pitcher, outfielder
1956-59

VICENTE AMOR
pitcher 1957

DUTCH DOTTERER
catcher 1957-59-

JOE TAYLOR
outfielder 1957

CHARLIE RABE
pitcher 1957-58

PETE WHISENANT
outfielder 1957-59-

BOBBY HENRICH
utility 1957-59

JAY HOOK
pitcher 1957-59-

Cincinnati Reds (continued)

EDDIE MIKSIS utility 1958

ALEX KELLNER pitcher 1958

JIM FRIDLEY outfielder 1958

STEVE BILKO first baseman 1958

HARVEY HADDIX pitcher 1958

VADA PINSON outfielder 1958-59-

DON NEWCOMBE pitcher 1958-59-

DEE FONDY first baseman 1958

WALT DROPO first baseman 1958-59

JIM O'TOOLE pitcher 1958-59-

WILLARD SCHMIDT pitcher 1958-59

WHITEY LOCKMAN utility 1959-

DREW "BUDDY" GILBERT outfielder 1959

JIM BROSNAN pitcher 1959-

ORLANDO PENA pitcher 1958-59-

BOB PURKEY pitcher 1958-59-

FRANK THOMAS utility 1959

WILLIE JONES third baseman 1959-

EDDIE KASKO infielder 1959-

JOHNNY POWERS outfielder 1959

BOB MABE pitcher 1959

LUIS ARROYO pitcher 1959

JIM PENDLETON utility 1959

Cleveland Indians 1950-59

FRONT OFFICE:

ELLIS RYAN
president
1950-52

MYRON WILSON JR.
president 1953-59

HANK GREENBERG
gen. mgr. 1950-57

FRANK LANE
gen. mgr. 1958-59

FIELD MANAGERS:

AL LOPEZ
1951-56

LOU BOUDREAU
1950

KIRBY FARRELL
1957

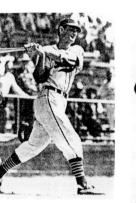

BOBBY BRAGAN
1958

JOE GORDON
1958-59

COACHES:

MEL HARDER 1950-59	BILL LOBE 1951-56
AL SIMMONS 1950-51	TONY CUCCINELLO 1952-56
MUDDY RUEL 1950	RED KRESS 1953-59
OSCAR MELILLO 1950	EDDIE STANKY 1957-58
JAKE FLOWERS 1951-52	JO-JO WHITE 1958-59

TRAINER:
WALLY BOCK

THE PLAYERS:

SAM ZOLDAK
pitcher 1950

ALLIE CLARK
outfielder
1950-51

HERB CONYERS
first baseman
1950

MARINO PIERETTI
pitcher 1950

GENE BEARDEN
pitcher 1950

Cleveland Indians (continued)

JOE GORDON
second baseman
1950

LOU BOUDREAU
infielder 1950
(manager 1950)

JOHN BERARDINO
infielder 1950, 1952

JESSE FLORES
pitcher 1950

THURMAN TUCKER
outfielder 1950-51

AL BENTON
pitcher 1950

RAY MURRAY
catcher 1950-51

AL ABER
pitcher
1950, 1953

DICK ROZEK
pitcher 1950-52

MICKEY VERNON
first baseman
1950, 1958

LARRY DOBY
outfielder
1950-55

MIKE GARCIA
pitcher 1950-59

RAY BOONE
infielder
1950-53

DICK WEIK
pitcher
1950, 1953

Cleveland Indians (continued)

BOB FELLER
pitcher 1950-56

BOB KENNEDY
third base, outfield
1950-54

LUKE EASTER
first baseman
1950-54

BOB LEMON
pitcher 1950-58

JIM HEGAN
catcher 1950-57

AL ROSEN
third base, infield
1950-56

STEVE GROMEK
pitcher 1950-53

DALE MITCHELL
outfield, first base
1950-56

EARLY WYNN
pitcher 1950-57

JIM LEMON
outfield,
first base
1950, 1953

MILT NIELSEN
outfielder 1951

BOBBY AVILA
second baseman
1950-58

Cleveland Indians (continued)

**CLARENCE
MADDERN**
outfield
1951

MERRILL COMBS
infielder 1951-52

BIRDIE TEBBETTS
catcher 1951-52

HAL NARAGON
catcher 1951, 1954-59

DAVE POPE
outfielder
1952, 1954-56

JIM FRIDLEY
outfielder
1952

SAM CHAPMAN
first base, outfield
1951

GEORGE ZUVERINK
pitcher 1951-52

HARRY SIMPSON
first base, outfield
1951-53, 1955

LOU BRISSIE
pitcher 1951-53

**SNUFFY
STIRNWEISS**
infielder
1951-52

TED WILKS
pitcher
1952-53

MICKEY HARRIS
pitcher 1952

PETE REISER
outfielder 1952

HANK MAJESKI
infielder
1952-55

JERRY FAHR
pitcher 1951

SAM JONES
pitcher
1951-52

BARNEY McCOSKY
outfielder 1951-53

BOB CHAKALES
pitcher 1951-54

BILL GLYNN
first base, outfield
1952-54

JOE TIPTON
catcher
1952-53

WALLY WESTLAKE
outfielder 1952-55

Cleveland Indians (continued)

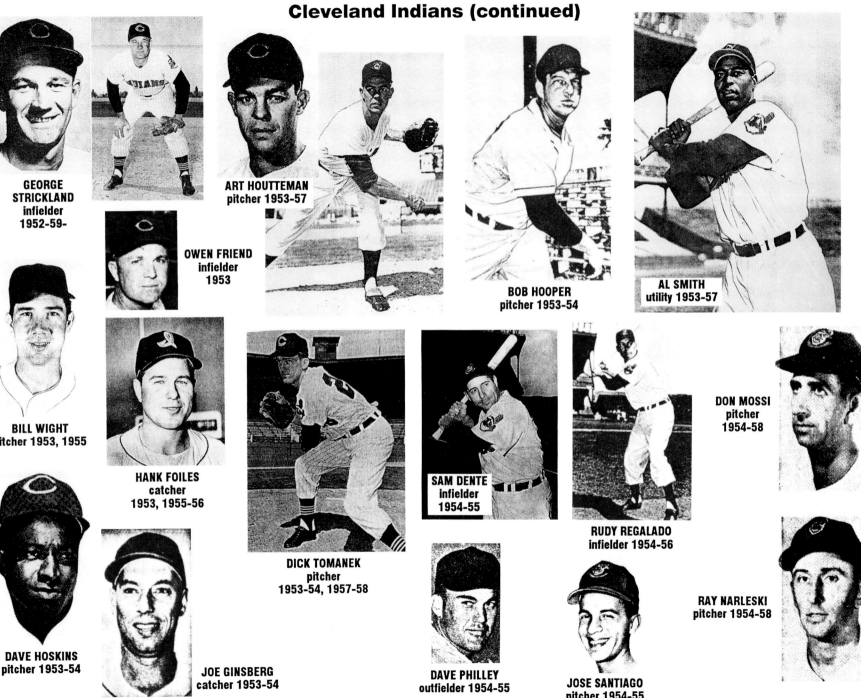

GEORGE STRICKLAND
infielder
1952-59-

OWEN FRIEND
infielder
1953

ART HOUTTEMAN
pitcher 1953-57

BOB HOOPER
pitcher 1953-54

AL SMITH
utility 1953-57

BILL WIGHT
pitcher 1953, 1955

HANK FOILES
catcher
1953, 1955-56

DICK TOMANEK
pitcher
1953-54, 1957-58

SAM DENTE
infielder
1954-55

RUDY REGALADO
infielder 1954-56

DON MOSSI
pitcher
1954-58

DAVE HOSKINS
pitcher 1953-54

JOE GINSBERG
catcher 1953-54

DAVE PHILLEY
outfielder 1954-55

JOSE SANTIAGO
pitcher 1954-55

RAY NARLESKI
pitcher 1954-58

Cleveland Indians (continued)

VIC WERTZ
first base,
outfield
1954-58

RALPH KINER
outfielder 1955

SAL MAGLIE
pitcher
1955-56

GENE WOODLING
outfielder 1955-57

HERB SCORE
pitcher
1955-59

HAL NEWHOUSER
pitcher 1954-55

FERRIS FAIN
first baseman
1955

JOE ALTOBELLI
first base, outfield
1955, 1957

BUD DALEY
pitcher
1955-57

ROCKY COLAVITO
outfielder
1955-59

SAM MELE
first base,
outfield
1956

STU LOCKLIN
outfielder
1955-56

HOOT EVERS
outfielder
1955-56

BOBBY YOUNG
infielder
1955-56

HANK AGUIRRE
pitcher 1955-57

BILLY HARRELL
utility 1955, 1957-58

KENNY KUHN
infielder
1955-57

JOE CAFFIE
outfielder
1956-57

Cleveland Indians (continued)

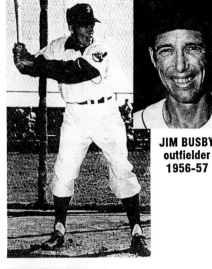

JIM BUSBY
outfielder
1956-57

PRESTON WARD
utility 1956-58

DICK WILLIAMS
third base, outfield
1957

LARRY RAINES
utility 1957-58

ROGER MARIS
outfielder
1957-58

MINNIE MINOSO
outfielder, infielder
1951, 1958-59

CHICO CARRASQUEL
shortstop, third base
1956-58

JOHN GRAY
pitcher 1957

VITO VALENTINETTI
pitcher 1957

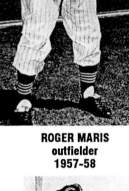

HOYT WILHELM
pitcher 1957-58

RUSS NIXON
catcher
1957-59-

BILLY HUNTER
shortstop,
third base
1958

JAY PORTER
catcher, infielder
1958

EARL AVERILL JR.
catcher, third base
1956, 1958

CAL McLISH
pitcher
1956-59

STAN PITULA
pitcher
1957

DICK BROWN
catcher 1957-59

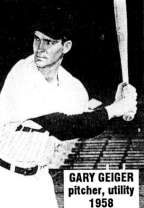

GARY GEIGER
pitcher, utility
1958

MORRIE MARTIN
pitcher 1958

HAL WOODESHICK
pitcher 1958

Cleveland Indians (continued)

VIC POWER
utility 1958-59-

BOB KELLY
pitcher 1958

RANDY JACKSON
third baseman
1958-59

GARY BELL
pitcher 1958-59-

DON FERRARESE
pitcher 1958-59

GENE LEEK
infielder
1959

ELMER VALO
outfielder 1959

WOODY HELD
utility 1958-59-

BILLY MORAN
shortstop,
second base
1958-59

DICK BRODOWSKI
pitcher 1958-59

JIM
"MUDCAT" GRANT
pitcher 1958-59-

CARROLL HARDY
outfielder 1958-59-

TITO FRANCONA
first base, outfield
1959-

JACK HARSHMAN
pitcher 1959-

Cleveland Indians (continued)

AL CICOTTE
pitcher 1959

BILLY MARTIN
second, third base
1959

JIM PIERSALL
third base, outfield
1959-

JIM PERRY
pitcher 1959-

JIM BOLGER
outfielder
1959

RAY WEBSTER
infielder 1959

ED FITZGERALD
catcher 1959

GRANNY HAMNER
infielder 1959

**ROBERT W.
"RIVERBOAT" SMITH**
pitcher 1959

BOBBY LOCKE
pitcher 1959-

JIM BAXES
infielder
1959

CHUCK TANNER
outfielder 1959-

Detroit Tigers 1950-59

FRONT OFFICE:

WALTER O. BRIGGS SR.
president 1950-51

W. O. "SPIKE" BRIGGS
president 1952-56
gen. mgr. 1957

JOHN FETZER
owner/chairman
1956-59

FRED KNORR
president
1956-57

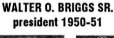

HARVEY HANSEN
president 1958-59

MUDDY RUEL
gen. mgr.
1954-56

BILLY EVANS
gen. mgr. 1950-51

CHARLEY GEHRINGER
VP/gen. mgr. 1951-53

JOHN McHALE
gen. mgr. 1958

RICK FERRELL
gen. mgr. 1959

FIELD MANAGERS:

RED ROLFE
1950-52

FRED
HUTCHINSON
1952-54

BUCKY HARRIS
1955-56

JACK TIGHE
1957-58

BILL NORMAN
1958-59

JIMMY DYKES
1959

COACHES:

DICK BARTELL 1950-52
RICK FERRELL 1950-53
TED LYONS 1950-53
BOB SWIFT 1953-54
SCHOOLBOY ROWE 1954-55
JOHNNY HOPP 1954
JOE GORDON 1954, 1956
BILLY HITCHCOCK 1955-59

JACK TIGHE 1955-56
WILLIS HUDLIN 1957-59
DON LUND 1957-58
TOMMY HENRICH 1958-59

TRAINER:
JACK HOMEL

THE PLAYERS:

EDDIE LAKE
shortstop, third base
1950

CHARLIE KELLER
outfielder 1950-51

HANK BOROWY
pitcher 1950-51

PAUL CALVERT
pitcher 1950-51

DON KOLLOWAY
first, second base
1950-52

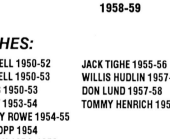

Detroit Tigers (continued)

JOHNNY GROTH
outfielder
1950-52, 1957-59-

TED GRAY
pitcher
1950-54

BOB SWIFT
catcher 1950-53

SAUL ROGOVIN
pitcher 1950-51

ART HOUTTEMAN
pitcher 1950-53

JERRY PRIDDY
second baseman
1950-53

DICK
KRYHOSKI
first baseman
1950-51

MARLIN STUART
pitcher 1950-52

AARON ROBINSON
catcher 1950-51

NEIL BERRY
infielder 1950-52

RAY HERBERT
pitcher 1950-54

JOHNNY LIPON
shortstop
1950-52

PAT MULLIN
outfielder 1950-53

Detroit Tigers (continued)

HAL NEWHOUSER
pitcher 1950-53

JOE GINSBERG
catcher 1950-53

VIC WERTZ
outfielder
1950-52

HOOT EVERS
outfielder
1950-52, 1954

FRANK HOUSE
catcher
1950-51, 1954-57

GEORGE KELL
third baseman
1950-52

PAUL
"DIZZY" TROUT
pitcher
1950-52

HAL WHITE
pitcher 1950-52

VIRGIL TRUCKS
pitcher 1950-52, 1956

Detroit Tigers (continued)

FRED HUTCHINSON
pitcher 1950-53
(manager 1952-54)

DICK MARLOWE
pitcher 1951-56

STEVE SOUCHOCK
utility 1951-55

GEORGE LERCHEN
outfielder 1952

DON LUND
outfielder
1952-54

EARL JOHNSON
pitcher 1951

BOB CAIN
pitcher
1951

AL FEDEROFF
second base, shortstop
1951-52

JOHNNY HOPP
first base, outfield
1952

CLIFF MAPES
outfielder
1952

WALT DROPO
first baseman
1952-54

GENE BEARDEN
pitcher 1951

WAYNE McLELAND
pitcher 1951-52

RUSS SULLIVAN
outfielder 1951-53

DON LENHARDT
outfielder 1952

DICK LITTLEFIELD
pitcher 1952

DAVE MADISON
pitcher 1952-53

BILL WIGHT
pitcher 1952-53

Detroit Tigers (continued)

NED GARVER
pitcher 1952-56

HARVEY KUENN
shortstop, utility
1952-59

MILT JORDAN
pitcher 1953

BILLY HITCHCOCK
infielder 1953

FRED HATFIELD
infielder 1952-56

JOHNNY PESKY
infielder 1952-54

JIM DELSING
outfielder 1952-56

BILL TUTTLE
outfielder
1952, 1954-57

JOHNNY BUCHA
catcher 1953

OWEN FRIEND
second baseman
1953

HAL ERICKSON
pitcher 1953

MATT BATTS
catcher 1952-54

BUD BLACK
pitcher
1952, 1955-56

BILLY HOEFT
pitcher 1952-59

RAY
SCARBOROUGH
pitcher 1953

FRANK CARSWELL
outfielder 1953

EARL HARRIST
pitcher 1953

BOB NIEMAN
outfielder
1953-54

Detroit Tigers (continued)

STEVE GROMEK
pitcher 1953-57

AL ABER
pitcher
1953-57

RALPH BRANCA
pitcher 1953-54

ROBERT G.
"BOB" MILLER
pitcher
1953-56

RENO BERTOIA
infielder, 1953-58

AL KALINE
outfielder
1953-59-

PAUL FOYTACK
pitcher 1953, 1955-59-

DICK WEIK
pitcher 1953-54

RAY BOONE
infielder
1953-58

WAYNE BELARDI
first baseman
1954-56

CHARLIE KRESS
first base, outfield
1954

GEORGE
ZUVERINK
pitcher
1954-55

Detroit Tigers (continued)

FRANK LARY
pitcher 1954-59-

RED WILSON
catcher
1954-59-

JACK PHILLIPS
utility 1955-57

RON SAMFORD
infielder
1955, 1957

JIM BUNNING
pitcher 1955-59-

FRANK BOLLING
second baseman
1954-59-

FERRIS FAIN
first baseman
1955

EARL TORGESON
first baseman 1955-57

JOE COLEMAN SR.
pitcher 1955

CHARLEY MAXWELL
outfield, first base
1955-59-

DUKE MAAS
pitcher
1955-57

JIM SMALL
outfielder
1955-57

J. W. "JAY" PORTER
catcher, utility
1955-57

BABE BIRRER
pitcher 1955

HARRY MALMBERG
second baseman 1955

LEO CRISTANTE
pitcher 1955

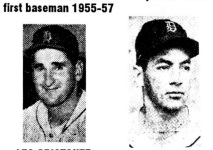

BUBBA PHILLIPS
third base, outfield
1955

Detroit Tigers (continued)

JIM BRIDEWESER
infielder
1956

BOB KENNEDY
third base, outfield
1956

CHARLIE LAU
catcher
1956, 1958-59

EDDIE ROBINSON
first baseman 1957

DON LEE
pitcher
1957-58

BOBO OSBORNE
first base, outfield
1957-59-

VITO VALENTINETTI
pitcher
1958

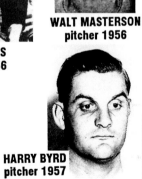

BUDDY HICKS
infielder 1956

WALT MASTERSON
pitcher 1956

JIM FINIGAN
second, third base
1957

HERM WEHMEIER
pitcher 1958

GEORGE SPENCER
pitcher 1958

COOT VEAL
shortstop
1958-59

MILT BOLLING
infielder 1958

JOE PRESKO
pitcher 1958

DAVE PHILLEY
utility 1957

HARRY BYRD
pitcher 1957

JACK DITTMER
infielder 1957

BOB SHAW
pitcher
1957-58

LOU SLEATER
pitcher 1957-58

STEVE BOROS
infielder
1957-58

BILL TAYLOR
outfielder
1957-58

HERB MOFORD
pitcher 1958

AL CICOTTE
pitcher 1958

LOU SKIZAS
third base, outfield
1958

Detroit Tigers (continued)

HANK AGUIRRE
pitcher 1958-59-

BILL FISCHER
pitcher 1958

OSSIE VIRGIL
third baseman
1958

JIM HEGAN
catcher 1958

EDDIE YOST
third baseman
1959

DON MOSSI
pitcher
1959-

TITO FRANCONA
first base, outfield
1958

BILLY MARTIN
shortstop, third base
1958

GAIL HARRIS
first baseman
1958-59-

TOM MORGAN
pitcher 1958-59-

GEORGE SUSCE
pitcher 1958-59

TED LEPCIO
infielder 1959

ROBERT G.
"BOB" SMITH
pitcher
1959

RAY NARLESKI
pitcher 1959

BOB HAZLE
outfielder
1958

GUS ZERNIAL
first base, outfield
1958-59

NEIL CHRISLEY
outfielder 1959-

BARNEY SCHULTZ
pitcher 1959

ROCKY BRIDGES
infielder 1959

LARRY DOBY
first base, outfield
1959

JERRY DAVIE
pitcher 1959

LOU BERBERET
catcher 1959-

PETE BURNSIDE
pitcher 1959-

DAVE SISLER
pitcher 1959-

New York/San Francisco Giants 1950-59

FRONT OFFICE:

HORACE STONEHAM
president 1950-59

CHUB FEENEY
VP/gen. mgr. 1950-59

FIELD MANAGERS:

LEO DUROCHER
1950-55

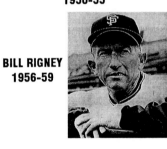

BILL RIGNEY
1956-59

COACHES:

FRED FITZSIMMONS 1950-55
HERMAN FRANKS 1950-55, 1958-59
FRANK SCHELLENBACK 1950-55
LARRY JANSEN 1954
DAVEY WILLIAMS 1956-57
BUCKY WALTERS 1956-57
RAY MUELLER 1956
TOMMY HENRICH 1957
WES WESTRUM 1958-59
NICK TESTA 1958
SALTY PARKER 1958-59
HANK SAUER 1959

TRAINER: FRANK BOWMAN

THE PLAYERS:

KIRBY HIGBE
pitcher 1950

ANDY HANSEN
pitcher 1950

RUDY RUFER
shortstop
1950

TOOKIE GILBERT
first baseman
1950, 1953

EDDIE STANKY
second baseman
1950-51

JACK HARSHMAN
first base, pitcher
1950, 1952

ALVIN DARK
shortstop
1950-56

New York/San Francisco Giants (continued)

ROY WEATHERLY
outfielder 1950

JACK LOHRKE
infielder 1950-51

SHELDON JONES
pitcher 1950-51

CLINT HARTUNG
pitcher, outfielder
1950-52

BILL RIGNEY
infielder 1950-53
(manager 1956-59-)

MONTE IRVIN
infield, outfield
1950-55

DON MUELLER
outfielder
1950-57

SPIDER JORGENSEN
third base, outfield
1950-51

JACK MAGUIRE
first base, outfield
1950-51

SAL YVARS
catcher
1950-53

MONTE KENNEDY
pitcher 1950-53

JACK KRAMER
pitcher 1950-51

SAM CALDERONE
catcher 1950, 1953

GEORGE SPENCER
pitcher 1950-55

DAVE KOSLO
pitcher 1950-53

HANK THOMPSON
infield, outfield
1950-56

New York/San Francisco Giants (continued)

WHITEY LOCKMAN
first base, outfield
1950-58

BOBBY THOMSON
third base, outfield
1950-53, 1957

SAL MAGLIE
pitcher 1950-55

LARRY JANSEN
pitcher 1950-54

WES WESTRUM
catcher 1950-57

JIM HEARN
pitcher
1950-56

**ALEX
KONIKOWSKI**
pitcher
1951, 1954

AL GETTEL
pitcher
1951

WILLIE MAYS
outfielder
1951-52, 1954-59-

ROGER BOWMAN
pitcher 1951-52

ARTIE WILSON
infielder 1951

**GEORGE
BAMBERGER**
pitcher
1951-52

RAY NOBLE
catcher 1951-53

AL CORWIN
pitcher
1951-55

DAVEY WILLIAMS
second baseman
1951-55

CHUCK DIERING
outfielder 1952

New York/San Francisco Giants (continued)

BOB ELLIOTT
third base, outfield
1952

HAL GREGG
pitcher 1952

BILL CONNELLY
pitcher 1952-53

HOYT WILHELM
pitcher 1952-56

GEORGE WILSON
first base, outfield
1952-53, 1956

DARYL SPENCER
infielder
1952-53, 1956-59

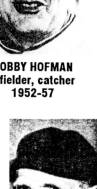

BOBBY HOFMAN
infielder, catcher
1952-57

MAX LANIER
pitcher 1952-53

DUSTY RHODES
outfielder
1952-57, 1959

FRANK HILLER
pitcher 1953

MARV GRISSOM
pitcher 1953-58

AL WORTHINGTON
pitcher 1953-59

RON SAMFORD
second baseman
1954

MARIO PICONE
pitcher
1952, 1954

RAY KATT
catcher
1952-57

RUBEN GOMEZ
pitcher, outfield
1953-58

HOOT EVERS
outfielder
1954

EBBA ST. CLAIRE
catcher 1954

BOB LENNON
outfielder 1954, 1956

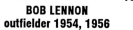

PAUL GIEL
pitcher
1954-55, 1958

New York/San Francisco Giants (continued)

BILLY GARDNER
infielder 1954-55

DON LIDDLE
pitcher 1954-56

JOE AMALFITANO
infielder
1954-55

WINDY McCALL
pitcher 1954-57

RAY MONZANT
pitcher 1954-58

JOHNNY ANTONELLI
pitcher
1954-59-

FOSTER CASTLEMAN
utility
1954-57

BILL TAYLOR
outfielder 1954-57

SID GORDON
third base, outfield
1955

GAIL HARRIS
first baseman
1955-57

DICK LITTLEFIELD
pitcher
1956

BILL SARNI
catcher
1956

STEVE RIDZIK
pitcher 1956-57

WAYNE TERWILLIGER
infielder
1955-56

PETE BURNSIDE
pitcher 1955, 1957-58

MAX SURKONT
pitcher 1956-57

RED SCHOENDIENST
second baseman 1956-57

OSSIE VIRGIL
utility 1956-57

JOE MARGONERI
pitcher 1956-57

BILL WHITE
first base, outfield
1956, 1958

New York/San Francisco Giants (continued)

JACKIE BRANDT
outfielder, utility
1956, 1958-59

ED BRESSOUD
infielder
1956-59-

**MICHAEL
"MIKE" McCORMICK**
pitcher 1956-59-

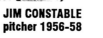

JIM CONSTABLE
pitcher 1956-58

JIM DAVIS
pitcher 1957

ANDRE RODGERS
shortstop 1957-59-

VALMY THOMAS
catcher 1957-58

RAY CRONE
pitcher
1957-58

DANNY O'CONNELL
infielder 1957-59

RAY JABLONSKI
utility 1957-58

HANK SAUER
outfielder
1957-59

GORDON JONES
pitcher 1957-59

STU MILLER
pitcher 1957-59-

DON JOHNSON
pitcher 1958

DON TAUSSIG
outfielder 1958

CURT BARCLAY
pitcher 1957-59

JIM FINIGAN
second, third base
1958

JIM KING
outfielder
1958

BOB SPEAKE
outfielder 1958-59

New York/San Francisco Giants (continued)

JIM DAVENPORT
shortstop, third base
1958-59-

ORLANDO CEPEDA
first base, outfield
1958-59-

DOM ZANNI
pitcher 1958-59

FELIPE ALOU
outfielder 1958-59-

WILLIE KIRKLAND
outfielder 1958-59-

WILLIE McCOVEY
first baseman 1959-

BOB SCHMIDT
catcher 1958-59-

LEON WAGNER
outfielder 1958-59

SAM JONES
pitcher 1959-

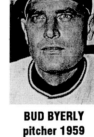

JOSE PAGAN
infielder 1959-

BUD BYERLY
pitcher 1959

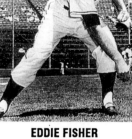

EDDIE FISHER
pitcher 1959-

JOE SHIPLEY
pitcher 1958-59-

HOBIE LANDRITH
catcher 1959-

JACK SANFORD
pitcher 1959-

JIM HEGAN
catcher 1959

New York Yankees 1950-59

FRONT OFFICE:

DAN TOPPING
president/co-owner
1950-59

DEL WEBB
co-owner
1950-59

GEORGE WEISS
gen. mgr. 1950-59

FIELD MANAGER:

CASEY STENGEL
1950-59

COACHES:

FRANK CROSETTI 1950-59
BILL DICKEY 1950-57
JIM TURNER 1950-59
TOMMY HENRICH 1951
RALPH HOUK 1954, 1958-59

TRAINER:

GUS MAUCH

THE PLAYERS:

TOMMY HENRICH
first baseman
1950

JOE PAGE
pitcher
1950

JOE DIMAGGIO
outfielder
1950-51

CLIFF MAPES
outfielder 1950-51

BILLY JOHNSON
third, first base
1950-51

FRED SANFORD
pitcher 1950-51

TOM FERRICK
pitcher 1950-51

JOE OSTROWSKI
pitcher 1950-52

JOHNNY HOPP
first base, outfield
1950-52

New York Yankees (continued)

JACKIE JENSEN
outfielder 1950-52

VIC RASCHI
pitcher 1950-53

ED "WHITEY" FORD
pitcher 1950, 1953-59-

TOMMY BYRNE
pitcher
1950-51, 1954-57

JOHNNY MIZE
first baseman
1950-53

GENE WOODLING
outfielder 1950-54

JOE COLLINS
first base,
outfield
1950-57

PHIL RIZZUTO
shortstop, second base
1950-56

RALPH HOUK
catcher 1950-54

BOBBY BROWN
third baseman
1950-52, 1954

ALLIE REYNOLDS
pitcher 1950-54

CHARLIE SILVERA
catcher 1950-56

New York Yankees (continued)

BILLY MARTIN
infielder
1950-53, 1955-57

JERRY COLEMAN
infielder 1950-57

ED LOPAT
pitcher
1950-55

HANK BAUER
outfielder
1950-59

YOGI BERRA
catcher 1950-59-

JACK KRAMER
pitcher 1951

MICKEY MANTLE
outfield, infield
1951-59-

FRANK SHEA
pitcher 1951

JOHNNY SAIN
pitcher 1951-55

JIM BRIDEWESER
infielder 1951-53

**STUBBY
OVERMIRE**
pitcher
1951

BOB WIESLER
pitcher
1951, 1954-55

BOBBY HOGUE
pitcher 1951-52

BOB KUZAVA
pitcher 1951-54

TOM MORGAN
pitcher
1951-52, 1954-56

New York Yankees (continued)

ART SCHALLOCK
pitcher 1951-55

GIL McDOUGALD
infielder 1951-59-

BOB CERV
outfielder
1951-56

KAL SEGRIST
infielder
1952

BILL MILLER
pitcher 1952-54

EWELL BLACKWELL
pitcher 1952-53

ANDY CAREY
third base, utility
1952-59-

JIM McDONALD
pitcher 1952-54

RAY SCARBOROUGH
pitcher 1952-53

WILLIE MIRANDA
infielder 1953-54

IRV NOREN
first base,
outfield
1952-56

LOREN BABE
third baseman
1952-53

TOM GORMAN
pitcher 1952-54

DON BOLLWEG
first baseman
1953

BILL RENNA
outfielder
1953

STEVE KRALY
pitcher 1953

GUS TRIANDOS
catcher 1953-54

MARLIN STUART
pitcher 1954

HARRY BYRD
pitcher 1954

FRANK LEJA
first baseman
1954-55

LOU BERBERET
catcher 1954-55

New York Yankees (continued)

EDDIE ROBINSON
first base
1954-56

BOB GRIM
pitcher
1954-58

JIM KONSTANTY
pitcher 1954-56

BILL SKOWRON
first base, infield
1954-59-

ELSTON HOWARD
catcher, utility
1955-59-

ENOS SLAUGHTER
outfielder
1954-55, 1956-59

WOODY HELD
infielder
1954, 1957

BILLY HUNTER
shortstop 1955-56

TOMMY CARROLL
shortstop, third base
1955-56

MARV
THRONEBERRY
first base, outfield
1955, 1958-59

RIP COLEMAN
pitcher 1955-56

BOBBY RICHARDSON
infielder 1955-59-

TOM STURDIVANT
pitcher 1955-59

DON LARSEN
pitcher
1955-59

BOB TURLEY
pitcher
1955-59-

JOHNNY KUCKS
pitcher 1955-59

JOHN BLANCHARD
catcher, utility
1955, 1959-

MICKEY
McDERMOTT
pitcher
1956

New York Yankees (continued)

JIM COATES
pitcher
1956, 1959-

RALPH TERRY
pitcher
1956-57, 1959-

NORM SIEBERN
outfield, first base
1956, 1958-59

JERRY LUMPE
infielder 1956-59

AL CICOTTE
pitcher 1957

SAL MAGLIE
pitcher 1957-58

ZEKE BELLA
outfield,
first base
1957

TONY KUBEK
utility 1957-59-

DARREL JOHNSON
catcher 1957-58

HARRY SIMPSON
first base, outfield
1957-58

ART DITMAR
pitcher
1957-59-

BOBBY SHANTZ
pitcher 1957-59-

RYNE DUREN
pitcher 1957-59-

GARY BLAYLOCK
pitcher 1959

CLETE BOYER
third base, shortstop
1959-

ZACK MONROE
pitcher 1958-59

FRITZ BRICKELL
infielder 1958-59

VIRGIL TRUCKS
pitcher 1958

DUKE MAAS
pitcher
1958-59-

JIM PISONI
outfielder
1959-

HECTOR LOPEZ
third base, outfield
1959-

ELI GRBA
pitcher
1959-

Philadelphia/Kansas City Athletics 1950-59

FRONT OFFICE:

CONNIE MACK
president
1950-54

ROY MACK
VP 1950-54

ART EHLERS
gen. mgr. 1951-53

ARNOLD JOHNSON
president 1955-59

PARKE CARROLL
VP/gen. mgr. 1955-59

FIELD MANAGERS:

CONNIE MACK
1950

JIMMY DYKES
1951-53

EDDIE JOOST
1954

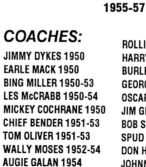

LOU BOUDREAU
1955-57

HARRY CRAFT
1957-59

TRAINERS:

ED SCHWARTZ
JAMES TADLEY

COACHES:

JIMMY DYKES 1950	ROLLIE HEMSLEY 1954
EARLE MACK 1950	HARRY CRAFT 1955-57
BING MILLER 1950-53	BURLEIGH GRIMES 1955
LES McCRABB 1950-54	GEORGE SUSCE 1955-56
MICKEY COCHRANE 1950	OSCAR MELILLO 1955-56
CHIEF BENDER 1951-53	JIM GLEESON 1957
TOM OLIVER 1951-53	BOB SWIFT 1957-59
WALLY MOSES 1952-54	SPUD CHANDLER 1957-58
AUGIE GALAN 1954	DON HEFFNER 1958
	JOHNNY SAIN 1959

THE PLAYERS:

BOB DILLINGER
third baseman 1950

MIKE GUERRA
catcher 1950

**BOB
WELLMAN**
outfielder
1950

Philadelphia/Kansas City Athletics (continued)

JOE MURRAY
pitcher 1950

LOU BRISSIE
pitcher 1950-51

SAM CHAPMAN
outfielder 1950-51

BARNEY McCOSKY
outfielder 1950-51

FERRIS FAIN
first baseman
1950-52

PAUL LEHNER
outfielder 1950-51

ALEX KELLNER
pitcher 1950-58

HANK WYSE
pitcher 1950-51

KERMIT WAHL
infielder 1950-51

JOE TIPTON
catcher 1950-52

JOHN KUCAB
pitcher 1950-52

WALLY MOSES
outfielder 1950-51

ELMER VALO
outfielder
1950-56

DICK FOWLER
pitcher 1950-52

**BILLY
HITCHCOCK**
infielder
1950-52

HARRY BYRD
pitcher
1950, 1952-53

BOB HOOPER
pitcher 1950-52

MOE BURTSCHY
pitcher
1950-51, 1954-56

JOE COLEMAN SR.
pitcher 1950-53

EDDIE JOOST
shortstop
1950-54
(manager 1954)

Philadelphia/Kansas City Athletics (continued)

BOBBY SHANTZ
pitcher 1950-56

CARL SCHEIB
pitcher 1950-54

PETE SUDER
infielder 1950-55

JOE ASTROTH
catcher 1950-56

GUS ZERNIAL
outfield, first base
1951-57

LOU LIMMER
first baseman
1951, 1954

HANK MAJESKI
third base 1951-52

MORRIE MARTIN
pitcher 1951-54

LOU KLEIN
second baseman
1951

SAM ZOLDAK
pitcher 1951-52

**EVERETT
"SKEETER" KELL**
second baseman
1952

HAL BEVAN
third baseman
1952, 1955

ED WRIGHT
pitcher 1952

DAVE PHILLEY
third base, outfield
1951-53

RAY MURRAY
catcher 1951-53

ALLIE CLARK
infield, outfield
1951-53

**SHERRY
ROBERTSON**
utility 1952

JACK LITTRELL
infielder
1952, 1954-55

BOBO NEWSOM
pitcher 1952-53

Philadelphia/Kansas City Athletics (continued)

KITE THOMAS
outfielder 1952-53

TOM HAMILTON
first base, outfield
1952-53

CHARLIE BISHOP
pitcher 1952-55

MARION FRICANO
pitcher
1952-55

BOB TRICE
pitcher 1953-55

FRANK FANOVICH
pitcher 1953

CASS MICHAELS
second baseman
1952-53

WALT KELLNER
pitcher 1952-53

CARMEN MAURO
third base, outfield
1953

NEAL WATLINGTON
catcher
1953

BILL HARRINGTON
pitcher
1953, 1955-56

DICK ROZEK
pitcher 1953-54

AL SIMA
pitcher
1954

ED McGHEE
outfielder
1953-54

EDDIE ROBINSON
first baseman
1953, 1956

BILLY SHANTZ
catcher 1954-55

JOHN GRAY
pitcher 1954-55

JIM ROBERTSON
catcher 1954-55

BILL WILSON
outfielder, pitcher
1954-55

TOM GIORDANO
second base
1953

LOREN BABE
infielder
1953

JOE DEMAESTRI
shortstop, infielder
1953-59

OZZIE VAN BRABANT
pitcher 1954-55

SONNY DIXON
pitcher 1954-55

LEROY WHEAT
pitcher
1954-55

Philadelphia/Kansas City Athletics (continued)

DON BOLLWEG
first baseman
1954-55

JIM FINIGAN
infielder
1954-56

SPOOK JACOBS
second baseman
1954-56

VIC POWER
infield, outfield
1954-58

JOHNNY SAIN
pitcher 1955

ENOS SLAUGHTER
outfielder 1955-56

CLETE BOYER
infielder
1955-57

BILL RENNA
outfielder
1954-56

ART DITMAR
pitcher 1954-56

ARNOLD PORTOCARRERO
pitcher 1954-57

JOE TAYLOR
outfielder
1954

JERRY SCHYPINSKI
infielder 1955

WALT CRADDOCK
pitcher 1955-56, 1958

HARRY SIMPSON
first base, outfield
1955-57, 1958-59

HECTOR LOPEZ
utility 1955-59

VIC RASCHI
pitcher
1955

DICK KRYHOSKI
first baseman
1955

GUS KERIAZAKOS
pitcher 1955

ART CECCARELLI
pitcher
1955-56

LOU SLEATER
pitcher 1955

RAY HERBERT
pitcher 1955, 1958-59-

TOM GORMAN
pitcher 1955-59

CLOYD BOYER
pitcher 1955

GLENN COX
pitcher 1955-58

Philadelphia/Kansas City Athletics (continued)

JOE GINSBERG
catcher 1956

TOM LASORDA
pitcher
1956

RANCE PLESS
infielder
1956

JOSE SANTIAGO
pitcher 1956

LOU KRETLOW
pitcher 1956

JACK CRIMIAN
pitcher 1956

AL PILARCIK
outfielder
1956

JACK McMAHAN
pitcher 1956

TROY HERRIAGE
pitcher 1956

MIKE BAXES
shortstop, second base
1956, 1958

JOHNNY GROTH
outfielder
1956-57

TIM THOMPSON
catcher 1956-57

**HAROLD W.
"HAL" SMITH**
catcher 1956-59

BILLY MARTIN
infielder 1957

JIM PISONI
outfielder
1956-57

LOU SKIZAS
outfielder,
third base
1956-57

WALLY BURNETTE
pitcher 1956-58

IRV NOREN
first base,
outfield
1957

TOM MORGAN
pitcher 1957

RYNE DUREN
pitcher 1957

GENE HOST
pitcher 1957

Philadelphia/Kansas City Athletics (continued)

MICKEY McDERMOTT
pitcher,
first base
1957

RIP COLEMAN
pitcher 1957, 1959

NED GARVER
pitcher 1957-59-

RALPH TERRY
pitcher 1957-59

VIRGIL TRUCKS
pitcher 1957-58

BOB CERV
outfielder
1957-59-

BOB MARTYN
outfielder
1957-59

JACK URBAN
pitcher 1957-58

BILLY HUNTER
infielder 1957-58

MILT GRAFF
second baseman
1957-58

WOODY HELD
utility 1957-58

DUKE MAAS
pitcher 1958

BOB DAVIS
pitcher 1958

BILL TUTTLE
outfielder
1958-59-

CHICO CARRASQUEL
shortstop,
third base
1958

BOB GRIM
pitcher
1958-59

ROGER MARIS
outfielder
1958-59

PRESTON WARD
utility 1958-59

KENT HADLEY
first baseman
1958-59

HARRY CHITI
catcher 1958-59-

BUD DALEY
pitcher 1958-59-

Philadelphia/Kansas City Athletics (continued)

FRANK HOUSE
catcher 1958-59

DICK TOMANEK
pitcher 1958-59

WHITEY HERZOG
first base, outfield
1958-59-

HOWIE REED
pitcher 1958-59-

LOU KLIMCHOCK
second baseman
1958-59-

JOHN TSITOURIS
pitcher 1958-59-

MURRY DICKSON
pitcher 1958, 1959

DICK WILLIAMS
utility 1959-

RUSS MEYER
pitcher 1959

JOHNNY KUCKS
pitcher 1959-

**WAYNE
TERWILLIGER**
infielder
1959-

RUSS SNYDER
outfielder 1959-

RAY BOONE
first, third base
1959

JOE MORGAN
third baseman
1959

RAY JABLONSKI
third baseman 1959-

JERRY LUMPE
infielder 1959-

TOM STURDIVANT
pitcher 1959

ZEKE BELLA
first base, outfield
1959

AL GRUNWALD
pitcher 1959

Philadelphia Phillies 1950-59

FRONT OFFICE:

BOB CARPENTER
president 1950-59

L. WISTER RANDOLPH
VP 1950-54

ROY HAMEY
gen. mgr. 1954-58

JOHN QUINN
VP/gen. mgr. 1959

FIELD MANAGERS:

EDDIE SAWYER
1950-52, 1958-59

STEVE O'NEILL
1952-54

TERRY MOORE
1954

MAYO SMITH
1955-58

COACHES:

BENNY BENGOUGH 1950-58
CY PERKINS 1950-54
DUSTY COOKE 1950-52
GEORGE EARNSHAW 1950
MAJE McDONNELL 1951-57
EDDIE MAYO 1952-54
EARL COMBS 1954
WALLY MOSES 1955-58
WHITLOW WYATT 1955-57

ANDY SEMINICK 1957-58
KEN SILVESTRI 1959
JOHNNY RIDDLE 1959
TOM FERRICK 1959
DICK CARTER 1959

TRAINER:

FRANK WEICHEO

THE PLAYERS:

BLIX DONNELLY
pitcher 1950

PAUL STUFFEL
pitcher 1950, 1952-53

MIKE GOLIAT
second baseman
1950-51

MILO CANDINI
pitcher 1950-51

DICK SISLER
outfielder 1950-51

WILLIE JONES
third baseman
1950-59

Philadelphia Phillies (continued)

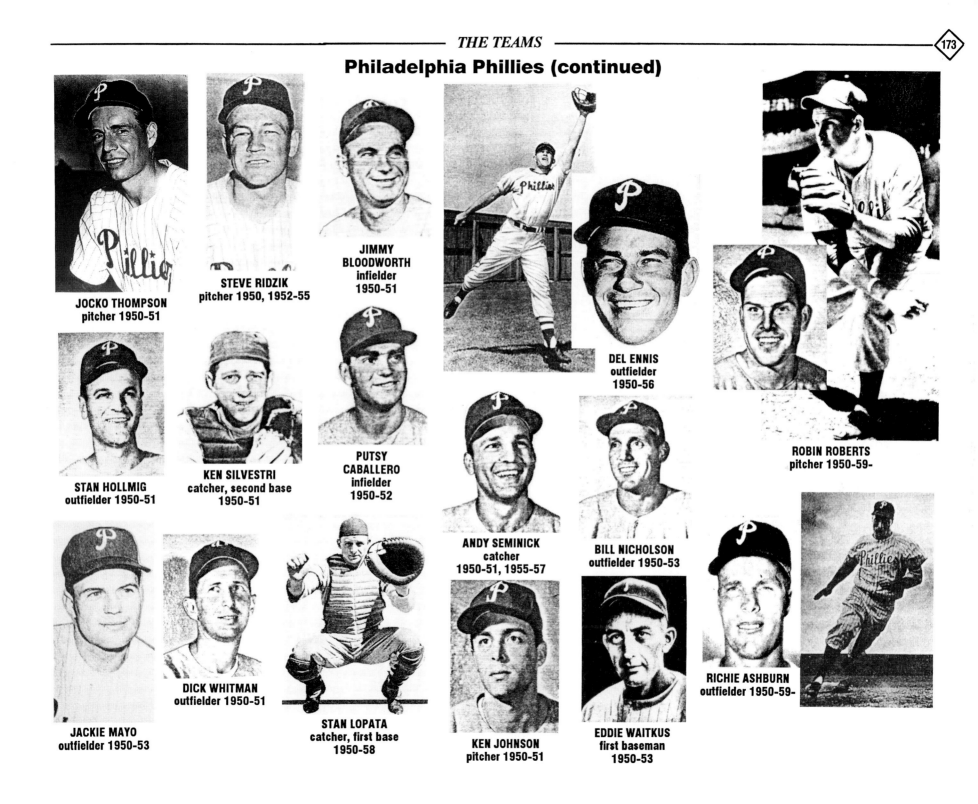

JOCKO THOMPSON
pitcher 1950-51

STEVE RIDZIK
pitcher 1950, 1952-55

JIMMY BLOODWORTH
infielder
1950-51

DEL ENNIS
outfielder
1950-56

ROBIN ROBERTS
pitcher 1950-59-

STAN HOLLMIG
outfielder 1950-51

KEN SILVESTRI
catcher, second base
1950-51

PUTSY CABALLERO
infielder
1950-52

ANDY SEMINICK
catcher
1950-51, 1955-57

BILL NICHOLSON
outfielder 1950-53

JACKIE MAYO
outfielder 1950-53

DICK WHITMAN
outfielder 1950-51

STAN LOPATA
catcher, first base
1950-58

KEN JOHNSON
pitcher 1950-51

EDDIE WAITKUS
first baseman
1950-53

RICHIE ASHBURN
outfielder 1950-59-

Philadelphia Phillies (continued)

JIM KONSTANTY
pitcher 1950-54

CURT SIMMONS
pitcher
1950, 1952-59-

KEN
HEINTZELMAN
pitcher
1950-52

GRANNY HAMNER
shortstop, infield
1950-59

RUSS MEYER
pitcher 1950-52

NILES JORDAN
pitcher 1951

LEO CRISTANTE
pitcher 1951

TOMMY BROWN
utility 1951-52

ANDY HANSEN
pitcher 1951-53

MEL CLARK
outfielder
1951-55

BUBBA CHURCH
pitcher 1950-52

ROBERT J.
"BOB" MILLER
pitcher
1950-58

EDDIE
PELLAGRINI
infielder 1951

DEL WILBER
catcher 1951-52

DICK YOUNG
second baseman
1951-52

KARL DREWS
pitcher 1951-54

HOWIE FOX
pitcher 1952

NIPPY JONES
first baseman
1952

Philadelphia Phillies (continued)

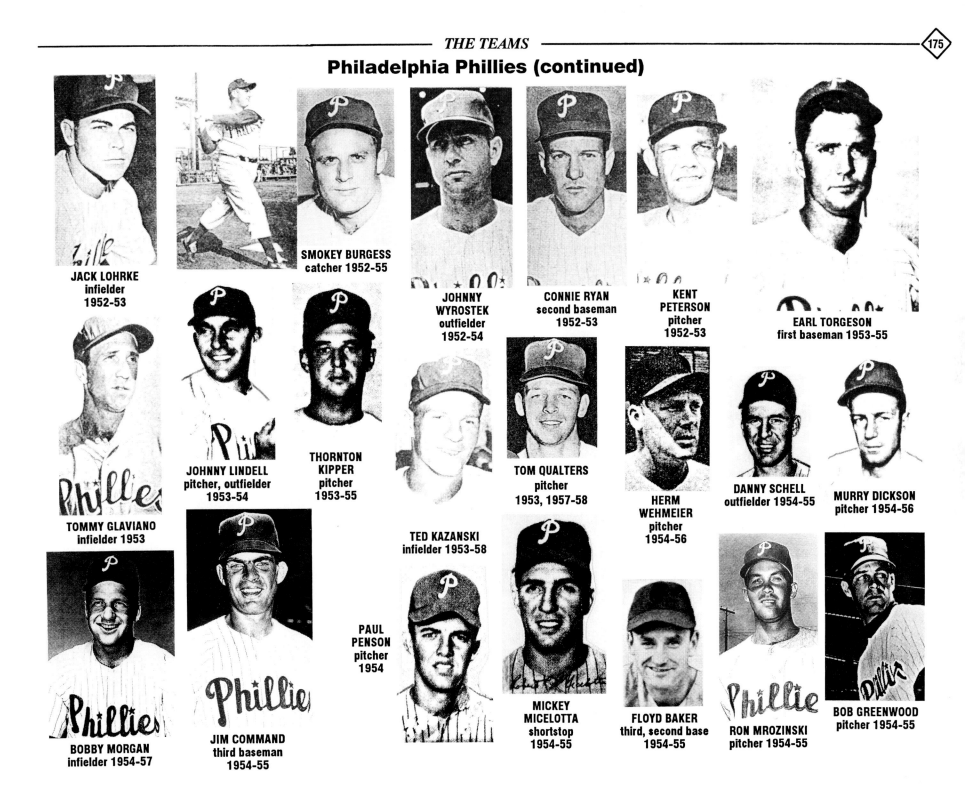

JACK LOHRKE
infielder
1952-53

SMOKEY BURGESS
catcher 1952-55

**JOHNNY
WYROSTEK**
outfielder
1952-54

CONNIE RYAN
second baseman
1952-53

**KENT
PETERSON**
pitcher
1952-53

EARL TORGESON
first baseman 1953-55

TOMMY GLAVIANO
infielder 1953

JOHNNY LINDELL
pitcher, outfielder
1953-54

**THORNTON
KIPPER**
pitcher
1953-55

TED KAZANSKI
infielder 1953-58

TOM QUALTERS
pitcher
1953, 1957-58

**HERM
WEHMEIER**
pitcher
1954-56

DANNY SCHELL
outfielder 1954-55

MURRY DICKSON
pitcher 1954-56

BOBBY MORGAN
infielder 1954-57

JIM COMMAND
third baseman
1954-55

**PAUL
PENSON**
pitcher
1954

**MICKEY
MICELOTTA**
shortstop
1954-55

FLOYD BAKER
third, second base
1954-55

RON MROZINSKI
pitcher 1954-55

BOB GREENWOOD
pitcher 1954-55

Philadelphia Phillies (continued)

BOB KUZAVA
pitcher 1955

JACK MEYER
pitcher 1955-59-

LYNN LOVENGUTH
pitcher 1955

PEANUTS LOWREY
utility 1955

JIM GREENGRASS
third base, outfield
1955-56

SAUL ROGOVIN
pitcher 1955-57

RON NEGRAY
pitcher 1955-56

GLEN GORBOUS
outfielder 1955-57

MARV BLAYLOCK
first base, outfield
1955-57

ROY SMALLEY
shortstop 1955-58

BOB BOWMAN
outfielder, pitcher
1955-59

JIM OWENS
pitcher
1955-56, 1958-59-

BEN FLOWERS
pitcher 1956

DUANE PILLETTE
pitcher 1956

HARVEY HADDIX
pitcher 1956-57

ELMER VALO
outfielder 1956

STU MILLER
pitcher 1956

**FRANKIE
BAUMHOLTZ**
outfielder
1956-57

Philadelphia Phillies (continued)

JOE LONNETT
catcher 1956-59

JACK SANFORD
pitcher 1956-58

MACK BURK
catcher 1956, 1958

ED BOUCHEE
first baseman
1956-59-

SOLLY HEMUS
infielder 1956-58

DICK FARRELL
pitcher 1956-59-

CHUCK HARMON
utility 1957

RON NORTHEY
pinch-hitter
1957

RIP REPULSKI
outfielder 1957-58

WARREN HACKER
pitcher 1957-58

**CHICO
FERNANDEZ**
shortstop
1957-59

DON CARDWELL
pitcher 1957-59-

JIM HEARN
pitcher 1957-59

SETH MOREHEAD
pitcher 1957-59

HARRY ANDERSON
first base, outfield
1957-59-

BOBBY YOUNG
second baseman
1958

PANCHO HERRERA
first, third baseman
1958

Philadelphia Phillies (continued)

CHUCK ESSEGIAN
outfielder 1958

CARL SAWATSKI
catcher 1958-59

WALLY POST
outfielder
1958-59-

RAY SEMPROCH
pitcher 1958-59

CHRIS SHORT
pitcher 1959-

DAVE PHILLEY
first base, outfield
1958-59-

JIM HEGAN
catcher
1958-59

SPARKY ANDERSON
second baseman 1959

SOLLY DRAKE
outfielder 1959

GENE FREESE
second, third base
1959

RUBEN GOMEZ
pitcher 1959-

VALMY THOMAS
catcher 1959

JOE KOPPE
infielder 1959-

GENE CONLEY
pitcher 1959-

JIM BOLGER
outfielder
1959

TAYLOR PHILLIPS
pitcher
1959-

HUMBERTO ROBINSON
pitcher 1959-

HARRY HANEBRINK
utility 1959

Pittsburgh Pirates 1950-59

FRONT OFFICE:

FRANK McKINNEY
president 1950

JOHN GALBREATH
president 1951-59

BRANCH RICKEY
VP 1951-55
chairman 1956-59

ROY HAMEY
gen. mgr. 1950

TOM JOHNSON
VP 1955-59

JOE L. BROWN
gen. mgr. 1956-59

FIELD MANAGERS:

BILLY MEYER
1950-52

FRED HANEY
1953-55

BOBBY BRAGAN
1956-57

DANNY MURTAUGH
1957-59

COACHES:

HONUS WAGNER 1950-51
BILL POSEDEL 1950-53
JOHNNY RIDDLE 1950
GOLDIE HOLT 1950
BABE HERMAN 1951
MILT STOCK 1951-52
SAM NARRON 1952-59
CLYDE SUKEFORTH 1952-57
JOHN FITZPATRICK 1953-56
DANNY MURTAUGH 1956-57

LEN LEVY 1957-59
BILL BURWELL 1958-59
JIMMY DYKES 1959

TRAINER:

CHARLES JORGENSEN

THE PLAYERS:

VIC LOMBARDI
pitcher 1950

JOHNNY HOPP
first base, outfield
1950

WOODY MAIN
pitcher
1950, 1952-53

DALE COOGAN
first baseman
1950

HANK BOROWY
pitcher 1950

NANNY FERNANDEZ
third baseman 1950

Pittsburgh Pirates (continued)

JOHN BERARDINO
infielder 1950

BOB CHESNES
pitcher 1950

RALPH KINER
outfielder 1950-53

WALLY WESTLAKE
outfield, third base
1950-51

VERN LAW
pitcher
1950-51, 1954-59-

GUS BELL
outfielder
1950-52

BILL PIERRO
pitcher 1950

STAN ROJEK
second base, shortstop
1950-51

JUNIOR WALSH
pitcher 1950-51

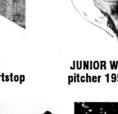

CLIFF CHAMBERS
pitcher 1950-51

MEL QUEEN
pitcher 1950-52

EARL TURNER
catcher 1950

RAY MUELLER
catcher 1950

ED STEVENS
first baseman
1950

**BOB
DILLINGER**
third baseman
1950-51

HANK SCHENZ
infielder 1950-51

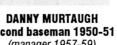

DANNY MURTAUGH
second baseman 1950-51
(manager 1957-59)

**BILL
MACDONALD**
pitcher
1950, 1953

Pittsburgh Pirates (continued)

TED BEARD
outfielder
1950-52

BILL WERLE
pitcher 1950-52

**ED
FITZGERALD**
catcher
1950-53

DANNY O'CONNELL
infielder 1950, 1953

JACK PHILLIPS
first base, utility
1950-52

TOM SAFFELL
outfielder
1950-51, 1955

CLYDE McCULLOUGH
catcher 1950-52

BILL KOSKI
pitcher 1951

MURRY DICKSON
pitcher 1950-53

PETE REISER
third base, outfield
1951

TED WILKS
pitcher
1951-52

JOE MUIR
pitcher
1951-52

**GEORGE
STRICKLAND**
infielder
1950-52

PETE CASTIGLIONE
utility 1950-53

DINO RESTELLI
outfielder 1951

MONTY BASGALL
second baseman 1951

JACK MERSON
second, third base
1951-52

DON CARLSEN
pitcher 1951-52

Pittsburgh Pirates (continued)

JOE GARAGIOLA
catcher 1951-53

BILL HOWERTON
third base, outfield
1951-52

ERV DUSAK
utility 1951-52

DICK SMITH
infielder
1951-55

FRANK THOMAS
outfielder, utility
1951-58

PAUL PETTIT
pitcher 1951, 1953

**GEORGE
METKOVICH**
first base, outfield
1951-53

HOWIE POLLET
pitcher
1951-53, 1956

BOB FRIEND
pitcher 1951-59-

DICK COLE
infielder
1951, 1953-56

JIM WAUGH
pitcher 1952-53

CLEM KOSHOREK
infielder 1952-53

HARRY FISHER
pitcher 1951-52

ROCKY NELSON
first base, outfield
1951, 1959-

DALE LONG
first baseman
1951, 1955-57

PAUL LAPALME
pitcher 1951-54

RON NECCIAI
pitcher 1952

CAL HOGUE
pitcher 1952-54

TONY BARTIROME
first baseman 1952

Pittsburgh Pirates (continued)

RON KLINE
pitcher
1952, 1955-59

BRANDY DAVIS
outfielder 1952-53

GEORGE MUNGER
pitcher 1952, 1956

DICK HALL
utility, pitcher
1952-57, 1959

BILL BELL
pitcher
1952, 1955

LEE WALLS
outfielder
1952, 1956-57

DICK GROAT
shortstop
1952, 1955-59-

BOBBY DEL GRECO
outfielder,
third base
1952, 1956

GENE HERMANSKI
outfielder
1953

BOB HALL
pitcher 1953

CARLOS BERNIER
outfielder 1953

MIKE SANDLOCK
catcher 1953

BOB SCHULTZ
pitcher 1953

JOHNNY LINDELL
pitcher, first base
1953

HAL RICE
outfielder
1953-54

JOHNNY HETKI
pitcher 1953-54

VIC JANOWICZ
catcher, utility
1953-54

CAL ABRAMS
outfielder
1953-54

ED PELLAGRINI
infielder 1953-54

PAUL SMITH
first base, outfield
1953, 1957-58

ELROY FACE
pitcher
1953, 1955-59-

FELIPE MONTEMAYOR
outfielder
1953, 1955

ROGER BOWMAN
pitcher 1953, 1955

Pittsburgh Pirates (continued)

JOHNNY O'BRIEN
infielder, pitcher
1953, 1955-58

EDDIE O'BRIEN
shortstop, utility
1953, 1955-58

NICK KOBACK
catcher
1953-55

JACK SHEPARD
catcher 1953-56

TOBY ATWELL
catcher 1953-56

PRESTON WARD
utility 1953-56

GAIR ALLIE
infielder 1954

BOB SKINNER
infield, outfield
1954, 1956-59-

GAIL HENLEY
outfielder
1954

WALKER COOPER
catcher 1954

GEORGE
O'DONNELL
pitcher 1954

CURT ROBERTS
second baseman
1954-56

JAKE THIES
pitcher 1954-55

SID GORDON
third base, outfield
1954-55

MAX SURKONT
pitcher 1954-56

JERRY LYNCH
outfield, catcher
1954-56

BILL HALL
catcher
1954, 1956, 1958

NELLIE KING
pitcher 1954-57

LAURIN PEPPER
pitcher 1954-57

BOB PURKEY
pitcher 1954-57

DICK LITTLEFIELD
pitcher 1954-56

GEORGE FREESE
third baseman 1955

BEN WADE
pitcher 1955

LINO DONOSO
pitcher 1955-56

Pittsburgh Pirates (continued)

FRED WATERS
pitcher 1955-56

RED SWANSON
pitcher 1955-57

HARDY PETERSON
catcher 1955, 1957-59

ROBERTO CLEMENTE
outfielder 1955-59-

BILL VIRDON
outfielder 1956-59-

BILL MAZEROSKI
second baseman
1956-59-

ROMAN MEJIAS
outfielder
1955, 1957-59-

GENE FREESE
infielder 1955-58

JOHNNY POWERS
outfielder 1955-58

CHOLLY NARANJO
pitcher 1956

LUIS ARROYO
pitcher 1956-57

DANNY KRAVITZ
catcher 1956-59-

HANK FOILES
catcher 1956-59

BUDDY PRITCHARD
utility 1957

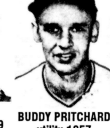

DICK RAND
catcher 1957

GENE BAKER
infielder 1957-58

**WHAMMY
DOUGLAS**
pitcher
1957

DEE FONDY
first baseman
1957

JIM PENDLETON
utility 1957-58

Pittsburgh Pirates (continued)

BENNIE DANIELS
pitcher 1957-59-

GEORGE WITT
pitcher 1957-59-

ROBERT G. "BOB" SMITH
pitcher 1957-59

KEN HAMLIN
shortstop 1957, 1959

GEORGE PEREZ
pitcher 1958

R. C. STEVENS
first baseman 1958-59-

DICK STUART
first baseman 1958-59-

DON WILLIAMS
pitcher 1958-59

TED KLUSZEWSKI
first baseman 1958-59

BOB PORTERFIELD
pitcher 1958-59

DICK SCHOFIELD
utility 1958-59-

DON GROSS
pitcher 1958-59-

CURT RAYDON
pitcher 1958

HARRY BRIGHT
utility 1958-59-

RON BLACKBURN
pitcher 1958-59

SMOKY BURGESS
catcher 1959-

AL JACKSON
pitcher 1959

DON HOAK
third baseman 1959-

JOE CHRISTOPHER
outfielder 1959-

FREDDIE GREEN
pitcher 1959-

HARVEY HADDIX
pitcher 1959-

PAUL GIEL
pitcher 1959

St. Louis Browns 1950-53

FRONT OFFICE:

WM. O. DEWITT
president/gen. mgr.
1950-51
VP 1952-53

CHARLES DEWITT
VP 1950-51

BILL VEECK
president
1951-53

RUDIE SCHAFFER
gen. mgr. 1952-53

FIELD MANAGERS:

ZACK TAYLOR
1950-51

ROGERS HORNSBY
1952

MARTY MARION
1952-53

COACHES:

JACK TOBIN 1950-51
RALPH WINEGARNER 1950-51
EARLE BRUCKER 1950-51
BOB SCHEFFING 1952-53
BILL NORMAN 1952-53
MARTY MARION 1952

TRAINER:

BOB BAUMAN

THE PLAYERS:

OWEN FRIEND
infielder 1950

CUDDLES MARSHALL
pitcher 1950

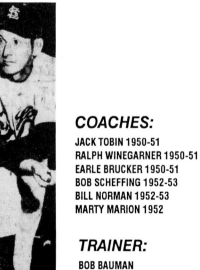

FRANK GUSTINE
third baseman 1950

JOE OSTROWSKI
pitcher
1950

BILL SOMMERS
second, third base
1950

TOMMY FINE
pitcher 1950

St. Louis Browns (continued)

AL WIDMAR
pitcher 1950-51

KEN WOOD
outfielder
1950-51

DICK STARR
pitcher 1950-51

TOM UPTON
infielder 1950-51

DON LENHARDT
utility 1950-51

**SNUFFY
STIRNWEISS**
infielder 1950

HARRY DORISH
pitcher 1950

DICK KOKOS
outfielder
1950, 1953

BILLY DEMARS
infielder 1950-51

BILL KENNEDY
pitcher 1950-51

DON JOHNSON
pitcher 1950-51

DUANE PILLETTE
pitcher 1950-53

JACK BRUNER
pitcher 1950

TOM FERRICK
pitcher 1950

SID SHACHT
pitcher
1950-51

SHERM LOLLAR
catcher 1950-51

LOU KRETLOW
pitcher 1950, 1953

RAY COLEMAN
outfielder
1950-52

St. Louis Browns (continued)

NED GARVER
pitcher, outfield
1950-52

CLIFF FANNIN
pitcher 1950-52

LEO THOMAS
infielder 1950, 1952

LES MOSS
catcher
1950-53

**STUBBY
OVERMIRE**
pitcher
1950-52

JIM DELSING
outfielder
1950-52

LOU SLEATER
pitcher 1950-52

HANK ARFT
first baseman
1950-52

ROY SIEVERS
third base, outfield,
first base
1950-53

PAUL LEHNER
outfielder
1951

JOHNNY BERO
infielder 1951

JOE LUTZ
first baseman
1951

DALE LONG
first base, outfield
1951

JACK MAGUIRE
utility 1951

DUKE MARKELL
pitcher 1951

JIM SUCHECKI
pitcher 1951

CLIFF MAPES
outfielder 1951

JOHN BERARDINO
utility 1951

St. Louis Browns (continued)

BEN TAYLOR
first baseman 1951

JIM McDONALD
pitcher 1951

EDDIE GAEDEL
pinch-hitter 1951
(one at-bat)

SATCHEL PAIGE
pitcher 1951-53

TOMMY BYRNE
pitcher 1951-52

IRV MEDLINGER
pitcher 1951

FRED SANFORD
pitcher 1951

FRANK SAUCIER
outfielder 1951

BOBBY YOUNG
second baseman
1951-53

BOBBY HOGUE
pitcher 1951-52

BOB TURLEY
pitcher 1951, 1953

BOB MAHONEY
pitcher 1951-52

FRED MARSH
infielder 1951-52

EARL RAPP
outfielder 1951-52

BILL JENNINGS
shortstop 1951

MATT BATTS
catcher 1951

JIM DYCK
third base, outfield
1951-53

EARL HARRIST
pitcher 1952

BOB NIEMAN
outfielder 1951-52

TOM WRIGHT
outfielder 1952

St. Louis Browns (continued)

JIM RIVERA
outfielder 1952

KEN HOLCOMBE
pitcher 1952

GENE BEARDEN
pitcher 1952

JOE DEMAESTRI
infielder 1952

AL ZARILLA
outfielder 1952

VIC WERTZ
outfielder
1952-53

DARRELL JOHNSON
catcher 1952

**GORDON
GOLDSBERRY**
first base, outfield
1952

CASS MICHAELS
infielder 1952

GEORGE SCHMEES
first base, outfield
1952

MARTY MARION
shortstop, third base
1952-53
(manager 1952-53)

**J. W.
"JAY" PORTER**
third base,
outfield
1952

DAVE MADISON
pitcher 1952

DICK KRYHOSKI
first baseman
1952-53

WILLIE MIRANDA
shortstop, third base
1952-53

DICK LITTLEFIELD
pitcher 1952-53

MARLIN STUART
pitcher 1952-53

St. Louis Browns (continued)

CLINT COURTNEY
catcher 1952-53

BOB CAIN
pitcher
1952-53

HANK EDWARDS
outfielder 1953

NEIL BERRY
infielder 1953

VIRGIL TRUCKS
pitcher 1953

MIKE BLYZKA
pitcher 1953

BOB ELLIOTT
third baseman 1953

VERN STEPHENS
third baseman 1953

JOHNNY GROTH
outfielder 1953

BOBO HOLLOMAN
pitcher 1953

DON LARSEN
pitcher, outfielder
1953

HARRY BRECHEEN
pitcher 1953

MAX LANIER
pitcher 1953

BILLY HUNTER
shortstop 1953

HAL WHITE
pitcher 1953

St. Louis Cardinals 1950-59

FRONT OFFICE:

FRED SAIGH
president
1950-52

WM. WALSINGHAM JR.
VP 1950-53

RICHARD MEYER
gen. mgr. 1954-55

AUGUST A. BUSCH
president 1953-59

FRANK LANE
gen. mgr. 1956-57

BING DEVINE
gen. mgr. 1958-59

FIELD MANAGERS:

EDDIE DYER
1950

MARTY MARION
1951

EDDIE STANKY
1952-55

HARRY WALKER
1955

**FRED
HUTCHINSON**
1956-58

STAN HACK
1958
(10 games)

SOLLY HEMUS
1959

COACHES:

TERRY MOORE 1950-52, 1956-58
TONY KAUFMANN 1950
RAY BLADES ?-1951-?
MIKE RYBA 1951-54
JOHNNY RIDDLE 1952-55
DIXIE WALKER 1953-55   HARRY WALKER 1959
BILL POSEDEL 1954-57   HOWIE POLLET 1959
LOU KAHN 1955   JOHNNY KEANE 1959
JOHNNY HOPP 1956   RAY KATT 1959
STAN HACK 1957-58
AL HOLLINGSWORTH 1957-58

TRAINER: H. J. "DOC" WEAVER

THE PLAYERS:

FRED MARTIN
pitcher 1950

JOHNNY LINDELL
outfielder 1950

St. Louis Cardinals (continued)

JOHNNY BUCHA
catcher 1950

MARTY MARION
shortstop 1950

JOE GARAGIOLA
catcher 1950-51

BILL HOWERTON
outfielder 1950-51

STAN MUSIAL
first base, outfield
1950-59-

AL PAPAI
pitcher
1950

CHUCK DIERING
outfielder 1950-51

TED WILKS
pitcher 1950-51

NIPPY JONES
first baseman
1950-51

HOWIE POLLET
pitcher 1950-51

EDDIE MILLER
shortstop, second base
1950

ERV DUSAK
pitcher,
outfielder
1950-51

MAX LANIER
pitcher 1950-51

HARRY BRECHEEN
pitcher 1950-52

CLOYD BOYER
pitcher 1950-52

St. Louis Cardinals (continued)

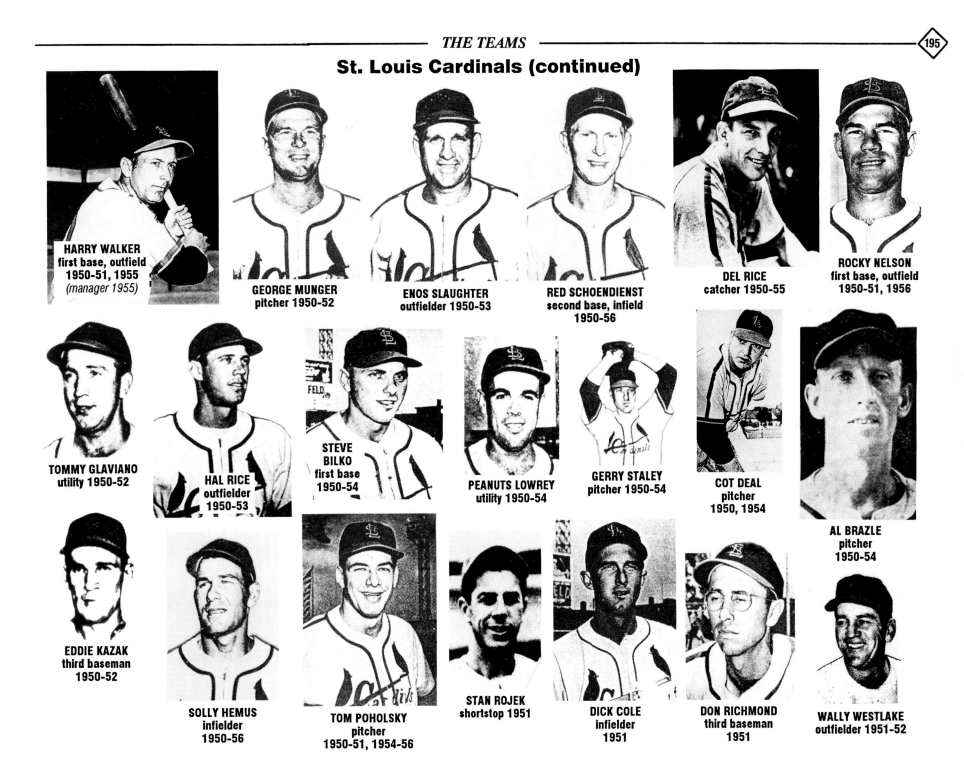

HARRY WALKER
first base, outfield
1950-51, 1955
(manager 1955)

GEORGE MUNGER
pitcher 1950-52

ENOS SLAUGHTER
outfielder 1950-53

RED SCHOENDIENST
second base, infield
1950-56

DEL RICE
catcher 1950-55

ROCKY NELSON
first base, outfield
1950-51, 1956

TOMMY GLAVIANO
utility 1950-52

HAL RICE
outfielder
1950-53

STEVE BILKO
first base
1950-54

PEANUTS LOWREY
utility 1950-54

GERRY STALEY
pitcher 1950-54

COT DEAL
pitcher
1950, 1954

AL BRAZLE
pitcher
1950-54

EDDIE KAZAK
third baseman
1950-52

SOLLY HEMUS
infielder
1950-56

TOM POHOLSKY
pitcher
1950-51, 1954-56

STAN ROJEK
shortstop 1951

DICK COLE
infielder
1951

DON RICHMOND
third baseman
1951

WALLY WESTLAKE
outfielder 1951-52

St. Louis Cardinals (continued)

JACK CRIMIAN
pitcher 1951-52

BILL SARNI
catcher
1951-52, 1954-56

BILLY JOHNSON
third baseman
1951-53

EDDIE STANKY
second base
1952-53
(manager 1952-55)

WILMER MIZELL
pitcher 1952-53, 1956-59

LES FUSSELMAN
catcher
1952-53

WILLARD SCHMIDT
pitcher
1952-53, 1955-57

CLIFF CHAMBERS
pitcher
1951-53

JACKIE COLLUM
pitcher 1951-53, 1956

VERN BENSON
third base, outfield
1951-53

LARRY MIGGINS
first base, outfield
1952

BILL WERLE
pitcher 1952

HARVEY HADDIX
pitcher 1952-56

BOBBY TIEFENAUR
pitcher
1952, 1955

DICK BOKELMANN
pitcher
1951-53

JOE PRESKO
pitcher 1951-54

VIRGIL STALLCUP
shortstop 1952-53

EDDIE YUHAS
pitcher
1952-53

ED ERAUTT
pitcher 1953

SAL YVARS
catcher
1953-54

HAL WHITE
pitcher 1953-54

MIKE CLARK
pitcher 1952-53

STU MILLER
pitcher
1952-54, 1956

DICK SISLER
first baseman
1952-53

St. Louis Cardinals (continued)

PETE CASTIGLIONE
infielder 1953-54

RAY JABLONSKI
utility 1953-54, 1959

RIP REPULSKI
outfielder
1953-56

DICK SCHOFIELD
shortstop 1953-58

HARRY ELLIOTT
outfielder
1953, 1955

VIC RASCHI
pitcher 1954-55

WALLY MOON
outfield, first base
1954-58

ROYCE LINT
pitcher 1954

RALPH BEARD
pitcher 1954

TOM BURGESS
outfielder 1954

**BROOKS
LAWRENCE**
pitcher
1954-55

MEL WRIGHT
pitcher 1954-55

GORDON JONES
pitcher 1954-56

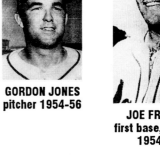

JOE FRAZIER
first base, outfield
1954-56

**JOE
CUNNINGHAM**
first base,
outfield
1954, 1956-59-

ALEX GRAMMAS
shortstop, third base
1954-56, 1959-

TOM ALSTON
first baseman
1954-57

PETE WHISENANT
outfielder 1955

NELS BURBRINK
catcher 1955

**BOBBY
STEPHENSON**
infielder 1955

LUIS ARROYO
pitcher 1955

**KEN
BOYER**
third base,
utility
1955-59-

St. Louis Cardinals (continued)

BARNEY SCHULTZ
pitcher 1955

FLOYD WOOLDRIDGE
pitcher 1955

AL GETTEL
pitcher 1955

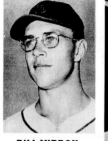

JOHNNY MACKINSON
pitcher 1955

FRANK SMITH
pitcher 1955

BEN FLOWERS
pitcher 1955-56

BILL VIRDON
outfielder
1955-56

DON BLASINGAME
second base, infield
1955-59

LARRY JACKSON
pitcher
1955-59-

LINDY McDANIEL
pitcher 1955-59-

PAUL LAPALME
pitcher 1955-56

WHITEY LOCKMAN
first base, outfield
1956

BOBBY MORGAN
infielder 1956

CHARLIE PEETE
outfielder 1956

GRADY HATTON
infielder 1956

HANK SAUER
outfielder 1956

MAX SURKONT
pitcher 1956

ELLIS KINDER
pitcher 1956

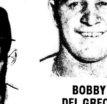

JIM KONSTANTY
pitcher 1956

DON LIDDLE
pitcher 1956

BOBBY DEL GRECO
outfielder
1956

CHUCK HARMON
utility 1956-57

RAY KATT
catcher
1956, 1958-59

St. Louis Cardinals (continued)

BOB
BLAYLOCK
pitcher
1956, 1959

MURRY DICKSON
pitcher 1956-57

WALKER COOPER
catcher 1956-57

ALVIN DARK
shortstop, third base
1956-58

HERM WEHMEIER
pitcher 1956-58

HAROLD R.
"HAL" SMITH
catcher
1956-59-

JIM DAVIS
pitcher 1957

LLOYD MERRITT
pitcher 1957

DON LASSETTER
outfielder 1957

JIMMY KING
outfielder 1957

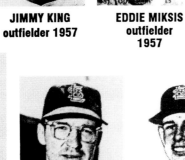

EDDIE MIKSIS
outfielder
1957

LYNN LOVENGUTH
pitcher 1957

HOYT WILHELM
pitcher 1957

HOBIE LANDRITH
catcher 1957-58

BILLY MUFFET
pitcher 1957-58

DEL ENNIS
outfielder
1957-58

SAM JONES
pitcher
1957-58

EDDIE KASKO
infielder 1957-58

VON McDANIEL
pitcher 1957-58

MORRIE MARTIN
pitcher 1957-58

FRANK BARNES
pitcher 1957-58

TOM CHENEY
pitcher
1957, 1959

IRV NOREN
outfielder
1957-59

BOBBY GENE
SMITH
outfielder
1957-59-

GENE GREEN
catcher, outfield
1957-59

St. Louis Cardinals (continued)

**ROBERT L.
"BOB" MILLER**
pitcher
1957, 1959-

PHIL PAINE
pitcher 1958

RUBEN AMARO
infielder 1958

SAL MAGLIE
pitcher 1958

NELS CHITTUM
pitcher 1958

JIM BROSNAN
pitcher 1958-59

ELLIS BURTON
outfielder
1958

BEN VALENZUELA
third baseman
1958

BOB MABE
pitcher 1958

BILL WIGHT
pitcher 1958

CHUCK STOBBS
pitcher 1958

GENE FREESE
infielder 1958

JOE TAYLOR
outfielder 1958

CURT FLOOD
outfield, infield
1958-59-

LEE TATE
infielder
1958-59

PHIL CLARK
pitcher 1958-59

BILL SMITH
pitcher
1958-59

St. Louis Cardinals (continued)

CHUCK ESSEGIAN
outfielder 1959

GEORGE CROWE
first baseman
1959-

GINO CIMOLI
outfielder 1959

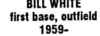

BILL WHITE
first base, outfield
1959-

HOWIE NUNN
pitcher 1959

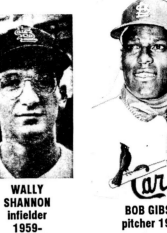

**WALLY
SHANNON**
infielder
1959-

BOB GIBSON
pitcher 1959-

ERNIE BROGLIO
pitcher 1959-

GENE OLIVER
catcher, utility
1959

BOB DULIBA
pitcher 1959-

DICK RICKETTS
pitcher 1959

HAL JEFFCOAT
pitcher 1959

J. W. "JAY" PORTER
catcher, first base
1959

GARY BLAYLOCK
pitcher 1959

MARSHALL BRIDGES
pitcher 1959-

DICK GRAY
utility 1959-

ALEX KELLNER
pitcher 1959

LEON CARMEL
outfielder 1959

Washington Senators 1950-59

FRONT OFFICE:

CLARK GRIFFITH
president 1950-55

CALVIN GRIFFITH
VP 1950-55
president 1956-59

WOOTTON YOUNG
VP 1951-57

JOE HAYNES
VP 1956-59

EUGENE YOUNG
VP 1957-59

FIELD MANAGERS:

CHUCK DRESSEN
1955-57

BUCKY HARRIS
1950-54

COOKIE LAVAGETTO
1957-59

COACHES:

NICK ALTROCK 1950-53
CLYDE MILAN 1950-52
GEORGE MYATT 1950-54
JOE FITZGERALD 1950-56
JOE HAYNES 1953-55
HIENIE MANUSH 1953-54
COOKIE LAVAGETTO 1955-57
ELLIS CLARY 1955-59
BILLY JURGES 1956-59
WALTER BECK 1957-59
SAM MELE 1959

TRAINER:

GEORGE LENTZ

THE PLAYERS:

RAY SCARBOROUGH
pitcher
1950

AL KOZAR
second baseman
1950

AL EVANS
catcher
1950

LLOYD HITTLE
pitcher 1950

STEVE NAGY
pitcher 1950

ED "BUD" STEWART
outfielder 1950

Washington Senators (continued)

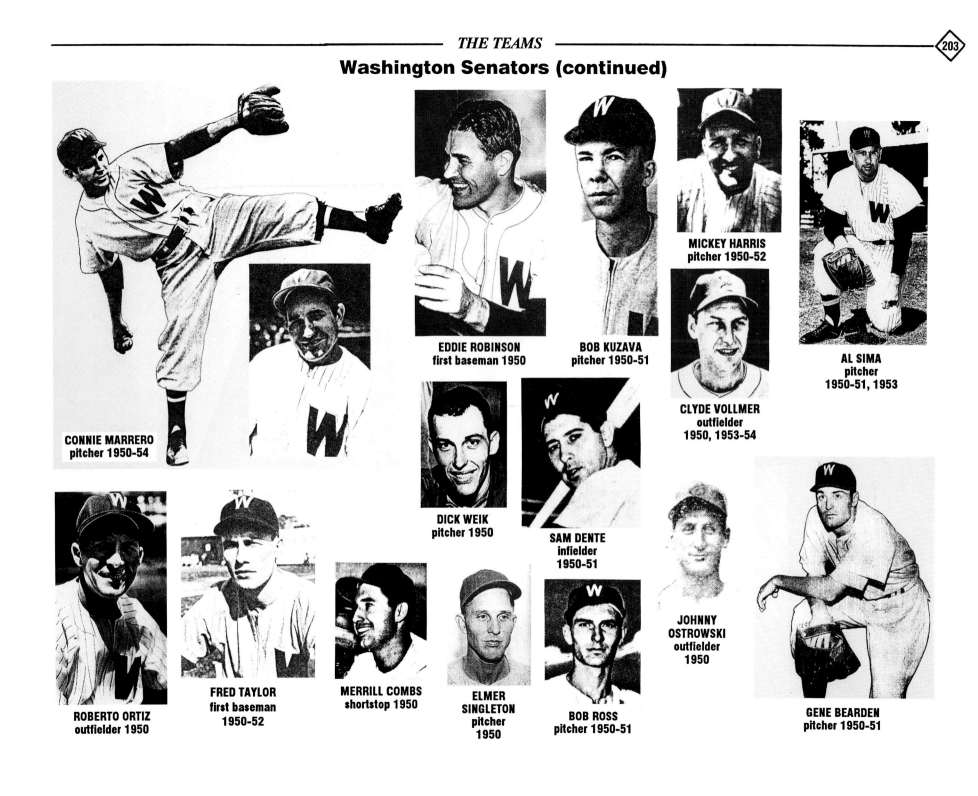

CONNIE MARRERO
pitcher 1950-54

EDDIE ROBINSON
first baseman 1950

BOB KUZAVA
pitcher 1950-51

MICKEY HARRIS
pitcher 1950-52

AL SIMA
pitcher
1950-51, 1953

CLYDE VOLLMER
outfielder
1950, 1953-54

DICK WEIK
pitcher 1950

SAM DENTE
infielder
1950-51

JOHNNY
OSTROWSKI
outfielder
1950

ROBERTO ORTIZ
outfielder 1950

FRED TAYLOR
first baseman
1950-52

MERRILL COMBS
shortstop 1950

ELMER
SINGLETON
pitcher
1950

BOB ROSS
pitcher 1950-51

GENE BEARDEN
pitcher 1950-51

Washington Senators (continued)

SID HUDSON
pitcher 1950-52

CASS MICHAELS
second baseman
1950-52

IRV NOREN
first base, outfield
1950-52

SHERRY ROBERTSON
utility 1950-52

JOE HAYNES
pitcher 1950-52

GIL COAN
outfielder
1950-53

SAM MELE
first base, outfield
1950-52

JULIO MORENO
pitcher 1950-53

EDDIE YOST
third base, utility
1950-58

WILLIE MIRANDA
infielder 1951

MICKEY VERNON
first baseman
1950-55

MICKEY GRASSO
catcher 1950-53

SANDY CONSUEGRA
pitcher
1950-53

MIKE GUERRA
catcher 1951

DAN PORTER
outfielder
1951

JIM PEARCE
pitcher 1950, 1953

DICK STARR
pitcher 1951

FRED SANFORD
pitcher 1951

Washington Senators (continued)

BOB PORTERFIELD
pitcher 1951-55

TOM FERRICK
pitcher 1951-52

CLYDE KLUTTZ
catcher 1951-52

FRANK CAMPOS
outfielder
1951-53

PETE RUNNELS
utility 1951-57

BOBO NEWSOM
pitcher 1952

MYRON "MIKE" McCORMICK
outfielder 1951

RANDY GUMPERT
pitcher 1952

EARL RAPP
outfielder 1952

ARCHIE WILSON
outfielder 1952

FLOYD BAKER
infielder 1952-53

DON JOHNSON
pitcher 1951-52

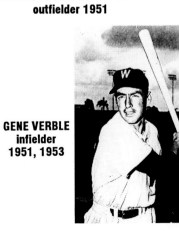

GENE VERBLE
infielder
1951, 1953

MIKE FORNIELES
pitcher 1952

LOU SLEATER
pitcher 1952

WALT MASTERSON
pitcher
1952-53

Washington Senators (continued)

KEN WOOD
outfielder
1952-53

MEL HODERLEIN
infielder 1952-54

FRANK SHEA
pitcher 1952-55

BUNKY STEWART
pitcher 1952-56

JERRY LANE
pitcher 1953

JACKIE JENSEN
outfielder 1952-53

JOHNNY SCHMITZ
pitcher 1953-55

JIM BUSBY
outfielder
1952-55

JERRY SNYDER
infielder 1952-58

LES PEDEN
catcher 1953

KITE THOMAS
catcher, outfield
1953

BOB OLDIS
catcher
1953-55

TOMMY BYRNE
pitcher 1953

**WAYNE
TERWILLIGER**
infielder
1953-54

TONY ROIG
infielder
1953, 1955-56

SONNY DIXON
pitcher 1953-54

DEAN STONE
pitcher 1953-57

ED FITZGERALD
catcher 1953-59

Washington Senators (continued)

CHUCK STOBBS
pitcher 1953-59-

JOHNNY PESKY
infielder 1954

GUS KERIAZAKOS
pitcher
1954

LEROY DIETZEL
infielder 1954

CAMILO PASCUAL
pitcher 1954-59-

HARMON KILLEBREW
infield, outfield 1954-59-

JOE TIPTON
catcher
1954

JESS LEVAN
utility 1954-55

STEVE KORCHEK
catcher
1954-55, 1958-59

ROY SIEVERS
first base, outfield
1954-59

TOM WRIGHT
outfielder
1954-56

JIM LEMON
outfielder
1954-59-

CARLOS PAULA
outfielder 1954-56

MICKEY McDERMOTT
pitcher
1954-55

TOMMY UMPHLETT
first base, outfield
1954-55

Washington Senators (continued)

JOHNNY GROTH
outfielder 1955

JUAN DELIS
utility 1955

BOBBY KLINE
pitcher, infielder
1955

BRUCE EDWARDS
catcher, third base
1955

PEDRO RAMOS
pitcher 1955-59-

ERNIE ORAVETZ
outfielder 1955-56

TED ABERNATHY
pitcher 1955-57

DICK HYDE
pitcher
1955, 1957-59-

BOB CHAKALES
pitcher 1955-57

JULIO BECQUER
first baseman
1955, 1957-59-

LYLE LUTTRELL
shortstop 1956-57

**JERRY
SCHOONMAKER**
outfielder
1955, 1957

**JOSE
VALDIVIALSO**
shortstop
1955-56, 1959-

CLINT COURTNEY
catcher 1955-59

CONNIE GROB
pitcher 1956

KARL OLSON
outfielder
1956-57

**EVELIO
HERNANDEZ**
pitcher
1956-57

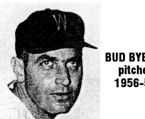

BUD BYERLY
pitcher
1956-58

Washington Senators (continued)

BOB WIESLER
pitcher 1956-58

WHITEY HERZOG
first base, outfield
1956-58

HERB PLEWS
infielder
1956-59

HAL GRIGGS
pitcher
1956-59

TEX CLEVENGER
pitcher 1956-59-

BOB USHER
outfielder
1957

MILT BOLLING
infielder 1957

GARLAND SHIFFLETT
pitcher
1957

LOU BERBERET
catcher 1957-58

ART SCHULT
first base, outfield
1957

JIM HEISE
pitcher
1957

RUSS KEMMERER
pitcher 1957-59-

NEIL CHRISLEY
outfield, third base
1957-58

ROCKY BRIDGES
infielder 1957-58

RALPH LUMENTI
pitcher 1957-59

FAYE THRONEBERRY
outfielder
1957-59-

AL CICOTTE
pitcher 1958

JIM CONSTABLE
pitcher 1958

OSSIE ALVAREZ
infielder 1958

BOBBY MALKMUS
infielder 1958-59

Washington Senators (continued)

BOB ALLISON
outfielder
1958-59-

VITO VALENTINETTI
pitcher
1958-59

BILL FISCHER
pitcher 1958-59-

JOHN SCHAIVE
second baseman
1958-59

KEN ASPROMONTE
utility 1958-59-

NORM ZAUCHIN
first baseman
1958-59

JOHN ROMONOSKY
pitcher
1958-59

RENO BERTOIA
infielder 1959-

HAL WOODESHICK
pitcher 1959-

HAL NARAGON
catcher 1959-

ZOILO VERSALLES
shortstop 1959-

LENNY GREEN
outfielder
1959-

ALBIE PEARSON
outfielder
1958-59

BILLY CONSOLO
infielder 1959-

JIM KAAT
pitcher 1959-

RON SAMFORD
infielder 1959

J. W. "JAY" PORTER
catcher, first base
1959

American League Uniforms 1950-59

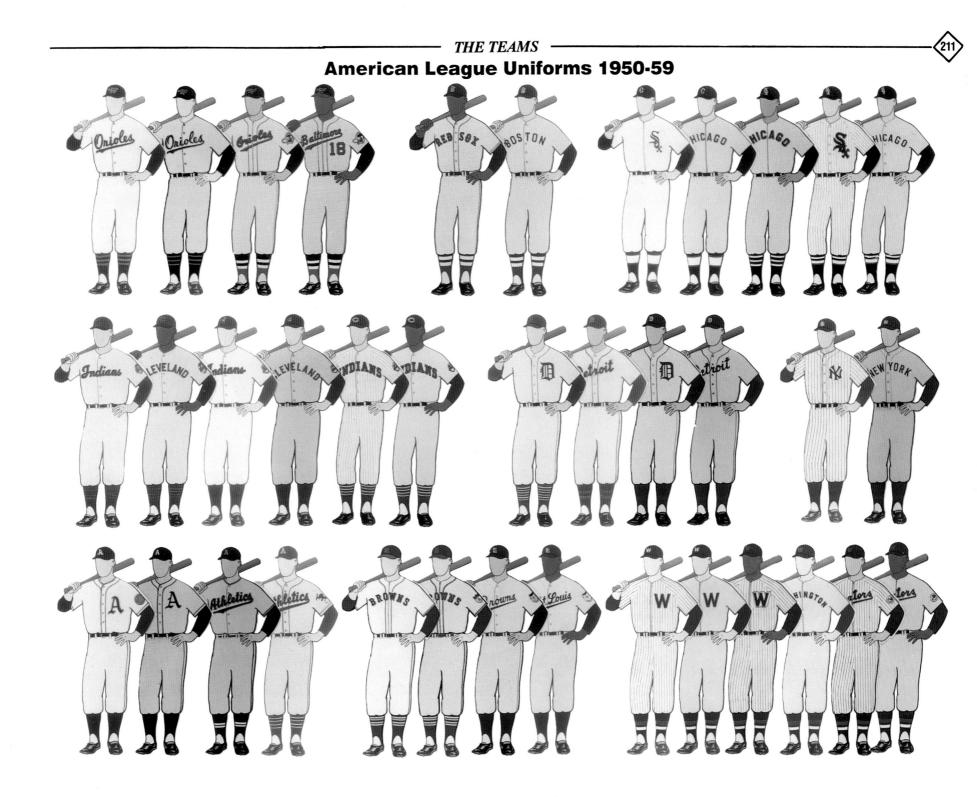

THE TEAMS
National League Uniforms 1950-59

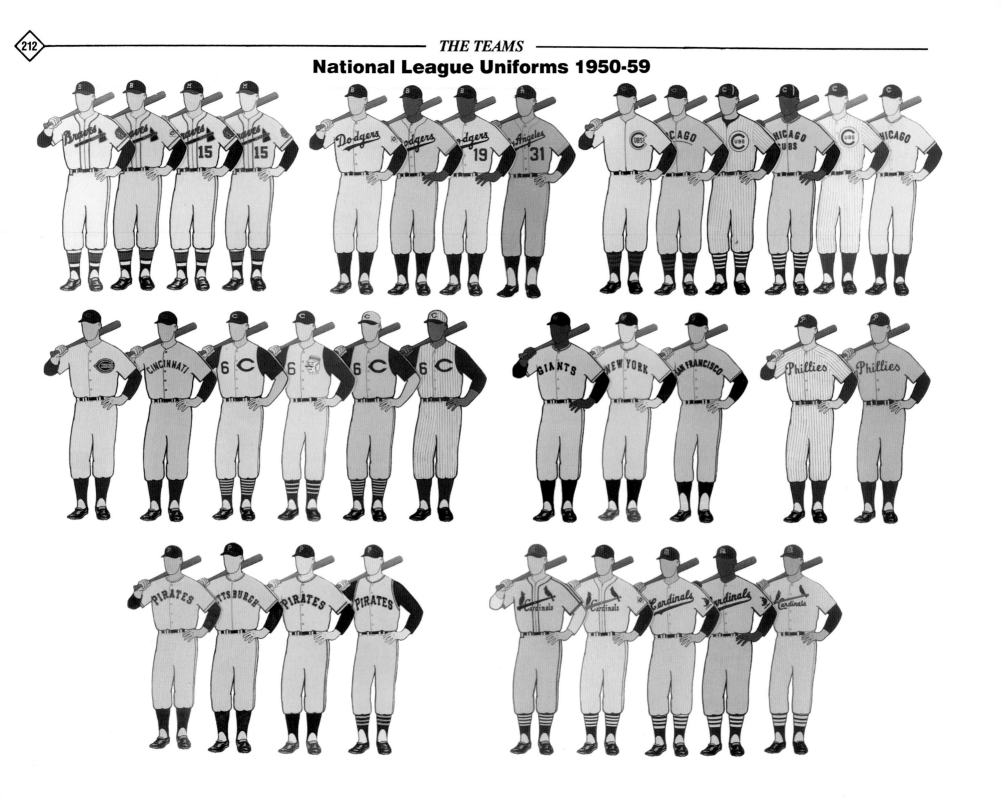

THE SEASONS

1950

The first year of the new decade saw a significant milestone for the American League. The league itself was entering its 50th season as a major league, but more remarkable was Connie Mack's 50th year at the helm of the Philadelphia Athletics. The team observed Mack's golden anniversary by wearing extra gold trimmings plus a commemorative patch on their sleeves. Mack announced that he would retire from managing at season's end and devote his remaining years to front office affairs. Another old veteran of the American League, Bucky Harris, was back for his third tenure as manager of the Washington Senators. The honeymoon was apparently over for Commissioner Happy Chandler at year's end as major league owners failed to renew his contract with a 3/4 majority vote. Chandler refused to resign and persevered under duress well into 1951, but his days were clearly numbered (a curious parallel to the more recent dilemma of Commissioner Fay Vincent).

In Chicago, Jack Onslow was replaced by Red Corriden after a miserable 8-20 start by the White Sox. In June, veteran manager Joe McCarthy resigned from the Red Sox job for health reasons and was succeeded by Steve O'Neill. For the first time since the war years, no inductee was selected for Cooperstown's Hall of Fame. Two Hall of Famers passed on in 1950—Kiki Cuyler in February and Grover Alexander in November. 1950 would be the last year in Brooklyn for club president Branch Rickey and also for Frank McKinney as owner/president of the Pittsburgh Pirates. Ted Williams established a record high in salaries with a new $125,000 contract for 1950. The Pirates also set a high mark in signing bonuses with a reported $100,000 to young pitcher Paul Pettit. Major League total attendance fell off almost 3 million from 1949, an ominous sign of future troubles.

Network broadcasting of major league games began to make an impact as the new decade began. The Dumont television network was offering New York games to a far flung audience and the major national TV networks were contemplating future plans to offer selected Saturday games to a national audience. The Mutual Radio Network had established its "game of the day" broadcasts in 1949 and would return with Al Helfer at the mike. Another newcomer to national radio coverage of big league baseball was the maverick Liberty Broadcasting System, featuring owner/-announcer Gordon McLendon. McLendon's specialty was in recreating games convincingly and informatively via teletype reports, but he was also a gifted play-by-play broadcaster.

The Cards' Red Schoendienst hit a dramatic 14th inning HR to give the NL a victory in the 1950 All-Star game at Chicago's Comiskey Park.

Red Sox Manager Joe McCarthy retired in June, ending a 25-year career as a major league pilot.

Popular White Sox veteran Luke Appling made 1950 his final season. He's shown here holding Tiger baserunner Pat Mullin at first base.

For A's Owner/Manager Connie Mack, 1950 was to be his 50th and last year as field boss. Tributes came from every corner of the U.S.A. With Commissioner Happy Chandler looking on, he tosses out the customary first ball at the All-Star game in Chicago.

The Braves' Vern Bickford turned in 1950's only no-hitter.

Young Dodger slugger Gil Hodges hit four homers at Ebbets Field on August 31.

Detroit outfielder Hoot Evers in the locker room after a sensational ninth inning inside-the-park HR that beat the Yanks on June 23. The see-saw battle set a record total of 11 HRs by both clubs.

The 1950 season provided some fresh contenders in the races of both leagues. In the American League, the Detroit Tigers were blessed with career years from some of their veterans and led the league for most of the summer. But the talented Yankees, sparked by rookies Whitey Ford and Billy Martin, finally won out. The Philadelphia Phillies, who had not won a pennant since 1915, held off a late surge by Brooklyn and copped the flag on the last day of the season, thanks to a clutch home run by Dick Sisler vs. the Dodgers in the 10th inning. The Phils' blend of exciting young stars captured the imagination of fans everywhere and they were dubbed the "Whiz Kids" by the baseball writers. In keeping with their new winning image, the Phillies introduced a brand new uniform set with all-red trimmings and red pinstripes at home. Reliever Jim Konstanty proved to be the key ingredient of the team's success and was rewarded with MVP honors for the NL. Phil Rizzuto was the AL's MVP winner. The top rookies in each league were both from Boston—Walt Dropo and Sam Jethroe. Dropo shared the top RBI total (144) with teammate Vern Stephens as the Red Sox produced a .302 team batting average. Bob Lemon of Cleveland and the Braves' Warren Spahn were the top moundsmen, leading their respective leagues in both wins and strikeouts. Ralph Kiner once again led the majors in homers with 47. Billy Goodman (.354) and Stan Musial (.346) were the batting champs for 1950.

The All-Star game returned to its baptismal site at Chicago's Comiskey Park and Red Schoendienst gave the NL a 14-inning victory with a home run off Bob Feller. In Detroit on June 23, the Tigers and Yanks hit a record 11 home runs in a 10-9 thriller that went to Detroit on an inside the park blast by Hoot Evers in the ninth. Gil Hodges hit four home runs in a game at Ebbets Field on August 31. The Braves' Vern Bickford tossed the season's only no-hitter, beating Brooklyn 7-0 at Braves Field on August 11.

The Yankees managed to sweep the upstart "Whiz Kids" in four straight in the Fall Classic, but it was a tight pitching duel all the way and with a little luck it could have been a toss-up series. The Phillies lost pitching ace Curt Simmons to military service and manager Eddie Sawyer gambled in the opening game by starting reliever Jim Konstanty. Vic Raschi countered Konstanty's five-hit performance with a superb two-hitter and a 1-0 Yankee victory. Joe DiMaggio homered off Robin Roberts in the tenth inning of game two to give the Phils another heartbreaking loss, 2-1. Rookie Whitey Ford finished it off with a 5-2 victory in the final game to give the New Yorkers their third world championship in four years.

Phillies' hurler Jim Konstanty helped the surprising "Whiz Kids" of 1950 to their first flag in 35 years. He was voted league MVP for his efforts.

The 1950 edition of the Detroit Tigers, after stubbornly clinging to first place most of the summer, collapsed at season's end. In a crucial late-season game at Cleveland, catcher Aaron Robinson (on the far right) walks away from sliding Bob Lemon (the winning run), believing he had made a force-out. This eerie afternoon contest was played out with the lights turned on because of semi-darkness from the haze of Canadian forest fires in the north.

Rookie pitcher Whitey Ford helped the Yanks to their second straight pennant with a 9-1 record.

The great Joe DiMaggio makes a circus catch of a long drive by the Phils' Del Ennis in game 2 of the 1950 World Series.

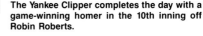

The Yankee Clipper completes the day with a game-winning homer in the 10th inning off Robin Roberts.

A dejected Dick Sisler wonders what went wrong after a four-game sweep by the New Yorkers in the '50 Fall Classic.

1951

HIT RECORDS OF 1951

TENNESSEE WALTZ *Patti Page*
MY HEART CRIES FOR YOU *Guy Mitchell/Mitch Miller*
IF *Perry Como*
TRULY, TRULY FAIR *Guy Mitchell*
MOCKIN' BIRD HILL *Les Paul & Mary Ford/Patti Page*
HOW HIGH THE MOON *Les Paul & Mary Ford*
MISTER AND MISSISSIPPI *Patti Page*
ROSE, ROSE I LOVE YOU *Frankie Laine*
TOO YOUNG *Nat King Cole*
COME ON-A MY HOUSE *Rosemary Clooney*
BECAUSE OF YOU *Tony Bennett*
SIN *Eddy Howard/Four Aces*
COLD, COLD HEART *Tony Bennett*
HEY, GOOD LOOKIN' *Hank Williams*

It was an anniversary year for both major leagues as 1951 marked the NL's 75th season and the AL's 50th. Sleeve patches were worn by all players to commemorate the occasions. Long-time National League President Ford Frick replaced the embattled Happy Chandler as high commissioner of baseball in mid-summer. Cincinnati's Warren Giles, a candidate for the commissioner's post, was shortly named to succeed Frick as NL president. Gabe Paul of the Reds organization was then named to fill the GM vacancy in Cincinnati. Walter O'Malley succeeded Branch Rickey as Brooklyn's chief executive after Rickey had teamed up with new owner John Galbreath to run the Pirates operation. Bill Veeck, baseball's P.T. Barnum, resurfaced as new owner of the hapless St. Louis Browns. A Tiger legend, taciturn Charley Gehringer, replaced Billy Evans as general manager of the floundering Detroit club. Organized baseball was once again placed under the legislative microscope by a congressional committee hearing which concentrated on the reserve clause and the farm systems. The Pacific Coast League, arguing its case for independent major league status, was designated as OPEN classification. Television coverage of big league baseball on a full coast-to-coast basis became a reality with the coverage of the NL playoffs and World Series over the network's new transcontinental transmission equipment.

No less than seven new field managers debuted in 1951: Senor Al Lopez in Cleveland, veteran Jimmy Dykes replacing Connie Mack in Philadelphia, Chuck Dressen in Brooklyn, Marty Marion with the Cardinals, and Paul Richards with the White Sox. Two popular veteran players replaced veteran NL field bosses later in the season—Tommy Holmes in Boston and Phil Cavaretta in Chicago. 1951 was to be the final season for Boston's Bobby Doerr and the fabled Yankee Clipper Joe DiMaggio, but future Yankee stars Mickey Mantle and Gil McDougald made solid contributions to another winning season. Another sparkling rookie made his presence felt across town at the Polo Grounds—the Giants' "Say Hey" kid, Willie Mays.

The Yanks' Allie Reynolds produced the rare feat of two no-hitters in 1951, while Bob Feller added his third career no-hitter. Pittsburgh's Cliff Chambers also did the trick on May 6. Bill Veeck was pulling out all stops in an effort to salvage the Browns operation. He signed the ageless Satchel Paige and presented the most celebrated publicity stunt in baseball history by inserting Midget Eddie Gaedel into a game with Detroit. The city of Detroit was celebrating its 250th birthday and was awarded the All-Star game out of turn to add to the festivities. The National Leaguers spoiled the day with an 8-3 victory, but hometown heroes Wertz and Kell homered to give the Motor City fans a lift. Detroit fans were demoralized by the inexplicable collapse of the 1950 contenders and the death of popular Tiger announcer Harry Heilmann the day before the All-Star classic. Another popular baseball announcer, St. Louis' Gabby Street, passed away in February. Other baseball notables who expired in 1951 were Eddie Collins in March and Shoeless Joe Jackson in December. Mel Ott and Jimmy Foxx were inducted in Cooperstown that summer and Heilmann's fatal bout with cancer assured him of nomination the following year.

Preparing for the most celebrated publicity stunt of the decade, Browns' Manager Zack Taylor suits up midget Eddie Gaedel for his pinch-hitting appearance in an August doubleheader vs. Detroit.

On July 1 vs. Detroit, Bob Feller hurled the third no-hitter of his great career.

Popular Tiger announcer Harry Heilmann, stricken with terminal cancer, made a few brief returns to the broadcast booth before his death in July. Shown here with Ty Tyson, who came out of retirement to fill in for Harry in 1951.

Yankee pitching ace Allie Reynolds made history with a pair of no-hit games in 1951. He is shown delivering the final pitch (to Ted Williams) of his second gem at Yankee Stadium on September 28.

Baseball's two premier backstops Yogi Berra and Roy Campanella capped outstanding seasons with MVP awards. The top rookies were Willie Mays and Gil McDougald. Rapid Robert Feller enjoyed his last really productive season, leading the league with 22 wins plus his no-hit gem. Stan Musial was once again baseball's top hitter with a .355 BA, while the Athletics' Ferris Fain took AL honors with a .344 mark. Gus "Ozark Ike" Zernial was traded from the White Sox to the Philadelphia A's early in the year and proceeded to lead the league in home runs (33) and RBIs (129). The surging "Go-Go" Chicago White Sox reawakened their South Side fans with their first winning season since the war years. Names like Billy Pierce, Nelson Fox, Jim Busby and Minnie Minoso plus the leadership of Paul Richards helped transform the Sox into a legitimate contender for the fifties.

But the real excitement of the 1951 season was saved for last. The most dramatic ending ever of any pennant race took place at New York's Polo Grounds on Oct. 3. Leo Durocher's Giants overcame a 13-1/2 game lead to tie Brooklyn at season's end to force a three-game playoff. The two clubs swapped wins and went into the rubber game with the Dodger's ace Don Newcombe slated to give the favored Dodgers the flag. Newk was in control for most of the game but weakened in the ninth. He yielded to Ralph Branca still holding a two-run lead with two men on. Bobby Thomson stepped into Branca's second pitch and delivered the "shot heard 'round the world"—a three-run homer into the lower left field stands that brought the Giants back from the dead and a World Series date with the Yankees.

The momentum of that dramatic finish propelled the Giants into a two-games-to-one lead in the Series, but once again the Yanks delivered for Casey Stengel by taking the last three games. The Bronx Bombers served notice to the Cinderella Giants in game five with a 13-1 trouncing and finished the job in the last game behind the clutch pitching of Vic Raschi. A disappointment for Giant fans, but even a World Series victory could not have upstaged the excitement of the "little miracle of Coogan's Bluff" a week earlier.

Giants' Manager Leo Durocher confers with his 1951 rookie sensation Willie Mays.

The explosion of euphoria that followed the "miracle of Coogan's Bluff" even upstaged the atomic bomb in the New York papers.

Bobby Thomson is mobbed by teammates as he crosses home plate to give the flag to the Giants on the last pitch of the 1951 NL playoffs.

Tiger outfielder Vic Wertz hits a mammoth home run in the fourth inning of the All-Star game at Detroit, won by the Nationals 8-3.

1951 was Joe D's final season, but rookie teammate Mickey Mantle arrived to carry on the tradition of superstars in the Yankee outfield.

DiMaggio finished out his "class" career in style, shown here scoring on a fourth-game homer in the '51 Series.

Manager Stengel celebrates the Series conquest of the Giants with Hank Bauer, who hit a base-clearing triple in the final game.

1952

SLOW POKE *Peewee King*
CRY *Johnny Ray*
WHEEL OF FORTUNE *Kay Starr*
PITTSBURGH, PA *Guy Mitchell/Mitch Miller*
BLUE TANGO *Leroy Anderson*
HIGH NOON *Tex Ritter/Frankie Laine*
A GUY IS A GUY *Doris Day*
KISS OF FIRE *Georgia Gibbs*
JAMBALAYA *Hank Williams*
HERE IN MY HEART *Al Martino*
WISH YOU WERE HERE *Eddie Fisher*
AUF WIEDERSEHN . . . *Vera Lynn*
HALF AS MUCH *Rosemary Clooney*

1952 saw some front office changes for major league clubs. The Perini family gained full control of the Boston Braves operation, setting the stage for the historic shift to Milwaukee the following year. Myron Wilson succeeded Ellis Ryan as Cleveland president late in the year. Former president Bill Dewitt was retained by Veeck as VP and was replaced as St. Louis Browns' GM by Rudie Schaffer. In Detroit, the death of owner Walter O. Briggs in January triggered a prolonged era of front office instability that produced some blockbuster trades and a last place finish for the first time in the history of the franchise. New faces for 1952 in the managerial ranks included Lou Boudreau (Red Sox), Rogers Hornsby (St. Louis Browns), Fred Hutchinson (Tigers), Eddie Stanky (Cardinals), Steve O'Neill (Phillies), and Charlie Grimm (Braves). The irascible Hornsby was soon replaced in St. Louis by Marty Marion and ended up with Cincinnati, replacing Luke Sewell there. Former player Frank Secory joined another former pitching star, Lon Warneke, on the National League umpire staff. The late Harry Heilmann and Paul Waner were named to baseball's Hall of Fame. The Korean War began to take its toll on major league rosters as many top players, including superstars Ted Williams and Willie Mays, were called into military service. At the same time, however, several departed players returned in 1952 such as Curt Simmons and Art Houtteman.

The Mutual Broadcasting System lured the incomparable Dizzy Dean from Yankee telecasts to join with Al Helfer, Gene Kirby, and Buddy Blattner in their "game of the day" radio broadcasts for 1952. Dean's folksy and grammatically horrendous delivery was an instant hit with most fans and Mutual's ratings soared whenever he was at the mike. The Liberty Broadcasting System, after filing a lawsuit against Major League

Baseball over legal rights to broadcast games, closed up shop in May.

A bumper crop of bonus players grabbed headlines in 1952 and forced enactment of a new bonus rule restricting wholesale "hoarding" of talent by wealthier clubs. Red Sox owner Tom Yawkey, who had opened his wallet to sign 17 highly-touted youngsters, was the principal target of the new ruling. Signing untried talent for enormous sums became risky business, but it paid dividends in Detroit and Pittsburgh, where Harvey Kuenn and Dick Groat had impressive major league debuts. Another rookie who attracted media attention was the Red Sox' Jim Piersall, whose celebrated antics turned out to be a symptom of mental disorder, for which he was hospitalized later during the 1952 season. Pitcher Virgil Trucks, despite a 5-19 WL record with the woeful Bengals, duplicated Allie Reynold's feat of '51 with a pair of no-hit games plus a near-perfect one-hitter. Brooklyn's Carl Erskine delivered the year's only other gem when he no-hit the Cubs on June 19. Workhorse Robin Roberts nearly became the first 30-game winner in 17 years, but fell short at 28 victories. Rookie Hoyt Wilhelm contributed 15 wins for the runner-up Giants and produced a league-leading 2.43 ERA. Little Bobby Shantz had a brilliant 24-7 year with the A's, while Allie Reynolds led the AL in strikeouts (160) and ERA (2.07). Ferris Fain and Stan Musial each reclaimed their batting championships, but Detroit's Walt Dropo got everyone's attention with a record-tying 12 consecutive hits.

Detroit's Virgil Trucks (left) embraces Vic Wertz, who hit a two-out homer in the ninth to give Trucks a 1-0 no-hit victory. It was the first of two for the Tiger hurler in 1952.

Cincinnati's Warren Giles was the new NL president, succeeding Ford Frick.

Wisconsin's Harvey Kuenn signed with Detroit for $55,000, one of many bonus players recruited during the early 1950s.

On May 21, the Brooklyn Dodgers posted 15 runs in one inning of a 19-1 rout of the Cincinnati Reds.

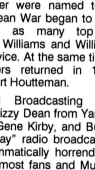

Two minor league pitching prospects of the Pirates, Ron Necciai and Bill Bell, got headlines with Bristol of the Appalachian League. Necciai struck out all 27 in a no-hitter, while Bell threw consecutive hitless games plus a later seven-inning gem. Both joined Pittsburgh at season's end.

The ageless Satchel Paige still pitched creditably for the hapless Brownies in 1952, winning 12 games and drawing decent crowds, a rarity for owner Bill Veeck. Shown here with catcher Clint Courtney.

The midsummer classic, the All-Star game, in Philadelphia's Shibe Park went to the National Leaguers for the third straight year by a rain-shortened 3-2 score. Most Valuable Player awards for the 1952 season went to pitcher Bobby Shantz of the Philadelphia A's and to Hank Sauer of the Chicago Cubs, with a league-leading 37 home runs and 121 RBIs. Rookie-of-the-Year honors went to A's hurler Harry Byrd and Dodger pitcher Joe Black. Black contributed 15 wins and a sterling 2.15 ERA to a balanced Brooklyn staff that helped the Dodgers wrest the flag from the cross-town Giants. The New York Yankees nosed out a pitching-rich Cleveland club (three 20-game winners) to capture their fourth straight pennant under Casey Stengel.

The Dodgers, as usual, provided stiff opposition for the Bronx Bombers, extending the series to a full seven games. But once again, in the end the championship was in Yankee hands. Dodger Manager Chuck Dressen surprised all by naming Rookie-of-the-Year Joe Black, a reliever, to start the series. Black, with better support than the ill-fated Konstanty in 1950, was up to the task and became the first black to record a World Series victory, a solid 4-2 route-going performance. It was a thrilling see-saw series that could have gone either way, but the New Yorkers once again captured the last two must-win games, highlighted by a game-saving spear of an infield fly by second baseman Billy Martin in game seven. For Brooklyn, it was "wait 'til next year" once again.

Jackie Robinson took Vic Raschi "downtown" on his first pitch of the 1952 All-Star contest in Philadelphia. The NL won a rain-shortened affair, 3-2.

On April 30, Ted Williams was feted on his final game before reporting for military duty in the Korean conflict. The war effort recruited a number of major league players in the early-mid '50s.

Brooklyn's rookie pitching star Joe Black posted a 15-4 record to help the Bums win the 1952 pennant. He also pitched and won the Series opener, the first black hurler to do so.

The Tigers' Walt Dropo tied Pinky Higgins' 1938 record of 12 consecutive hits in 1952.

Flatbush Avenue's "boys of summer" celebrate retrieving the '52 NL flag from the hated Giants on September 23 with a clinching victory over the Phils at Ebbets Field.

Aging slugger Johnny Mize is greeted by Yogi Berra after a circuit clout in the fourth game of the '52 World Series.

Yankee pitcher Bob Kuzava, who finished off Brooklyn in brilliant fashion to close out the finale of the 1952 Series, is mobbed by jubilant teammates and Casey Stengel (far left).

1953

After five decades of continuous stability in the geography of the major league alignment, the heretofore unthinkable occurred in 1953. Only a month before the season was to open, American League owners rejected Bill Veeck's plan to relocate his Browns to the beer capital and, with stunning swiftness, the National League then cleared the way for Braves owner Lou Perini to abandon Boston for the awaiting Milwaukee County Stadium. Pitiful attendance in recent years in the Hub made fellow owners supportive of the last-minute switch. The Wisconsin city welcomed the return of big league baseball with open arms and a brand new stadium. The reborn Milwaukee Braves found new life as they miraculously soared to a second place finish after floundering in seventh place the year before. Milwaukee fans responded in kind with 1.8 million paid admissions. Relocation of franchises and even expansion were suddenly greeted with enthusiasm by both leagues after the financial windfall of the Milwaukee experiment. In Pittsburgh, Branch Rickey issued a revolutionary all-fiberglass game cap that the Pirates continued to wear through the mid-fifties. The ABC-TV network and the Falstaff brewery inaugurated a televised Saturday "game of the week" program in an agreement with several American League clubs. Dizzy Dean and Buddy Blattner teamed up to describe the games, which were often "blacked out" in major league markets where there was a competing home date.

The Cleveland Indians had a new president, Myron Wilson, and in St. Louis millionaire brewer August Busch purchased the Cardinal franchise from Fred Saigh. Busch immediately set about to purchase Sportsman's Park from its previous landlord, the St. Louis Browns. Not even master merchandiser Bill Veeck could salvage the doomed Brownies, and the successful transplant of the Braves made the Browns a logical candidate for the same fate the following winter. In late September, Veeck's financial predicament finally ended with the announced sale of his Brownies to a Baltimore group, ending a 52-year residency in St. Louis. The only managerial changes for 1953 were in Pittsburgh, where Fred Haney replaced Billy Meyer, and in Cincinnati, where Rogers Hornsby was gone by season's end. Former big league stars Jess Burkett and Clyde Milan passed on in 1953. The Hall of Fame had a bumper crop of inductees, eight in all—Dizzy Dean, Al Simmons, Chief Bender, Bobby Wallace, Harry Wright, Ed Barrow, Bill Klem, and Tom Connolly.

Dizzy Dean and Buddy Blattner were the voices for ABC's nationally televised "game of the week" for 1953.

Milwaukee welcomed major league baseball with open arms and capacity crowds in their new County Stadium.

A young high school outfielding sensation from Baltimore celebrated the signing of a $35,000 bonus contract with Detroit. His parents, Mr. and Mrs. Kaline, were obviously delighted.

The St. Louis Cardinals were sold off early in the year by Fred Saigh (left) to beer baron August A. Busch Jr. The price tag was a reported $3,750,000.

Pitcher Bobo Holloman, in his first start for the St. Louis Browns, turned in a no-hit performance.

Al Simmons (left) and Dizzy Dean, 1953's nominees to baseball's Hall of Fame, show off their prized plaques.

Mickey Mantle added an early benchmark to his budding legend by propelling a mammoth 565 ft. homer out of Washington's Griffith Stadium early in the season. Bobo Holloman, a 28-year-old rookie with marginal credentials, registered a no-hit game for the St. Louis Browns on May 6 and after 1953, was never heard from again. On June 18, the Boston Red Sox scored a record 17 runs in one inning against Tiger pitchers. The Tigers signed an 18-year-old phenom off the Baltimore sandlots named Al Kaline and immediately put him in a Detroit uniform. A much-ballyhooed teenager, Frank Leja, was the center of a tampering controversy by several clubs and finally signed with the Yankees for a huge bonus. At Cincinnati on July 14, the National League All-Stars continued their winning streak against the AL with an easy 5-1 victory.

In the 1953 pennant races, the favored Yankees and Dodgers won easily, with Brooklyn amassing 105 victories, a franchise record. Roy Campanella and Carl Furillo led the assault with Campy slamming out 41 homers and a league leading 142 RBIs. Furillo's .344 BA led the majors. The league's MVP awards went to Campanella and Cleveland's Al Rosen, who had a career season with 43 HRs and 145 RBIs. The Braves' slugging third baseman Eddie Mathews ended Ralph Kiner's reign as home run king with 47 round-trippers. Teammate Warren Spahn had the majors' top ERA at 2.10 and tied Robin Roberts for most victories with 23. Washington's veteran first sacker Mickey Vernon was the AL leader with a .337 batting average. The top rookies were Detroit's Harvey Kuenn (.308 BA and 209 hits) and Dodger second baseman Junior Gilliam.

In the '53 Fall Classic, it was the same old story for the fifth year in succession as the invincible Yankee dreadnought vanquished the Brooklyns in six games. Stengel's marauders were sparked by pesky Billy Martin, who hit a record .500 in the series and drove in the final run in the ninth inning of game six. Carl Furillo had delivered a clutch two-run homer in the top of the ninth to tie the score and keep Dodger hopes alive, but Billy the Kid was literally on fire and was not to be denied.

Fiery Billy Martin had his finest hour in the '53 World Series, leading the Yankees to victory with his timely hitting and heads-up fielding.

Cleveland's Al Rosen had his finest year, barely missing a ''triple crown,'' and was named the AL's MVP.

Mickey Mantle (inset) hit one of the longest homers on record, clearing the distant left field bleachers at Griffith Stadium. It was unofficially measured at 565 feet.

Roy Campanella led the Dodgers to another pennant with 41 homers and a league-leading 142 RBIs. He was later chosen NL MVP for the second time.

A wiry shortstop named Ernie Banks joined the Cubs late in 1953 and gave Northside fans a badly needed hero.

Brooklyn right fielder Carl Furillo led the majors with a .344 BA and hit a clutch home run to keep Dodger hopes alive in the last game of the Series.

Martin is mobbed by jubilant New York mates after driving in the final winning run in game 6.

1954

The St. Louis Browns faded into history during the winter of 1953-54. A group of Baltimore investors headed by Clarence Miles and James Keelty had relieved Bill Veeck of the franchise and opened the 1954 season as the new Baltimore Orioles. The mammoth new Municipal Stadium, built to be shared with the football Colts, was packed with 46,000 fans on opening day to welcome big league baseball back to Baltimore. Vice President Nixon was on hand to throw out the ceremonial first ball. Later in the year, the similarly ailing Philadelphia Athletics franchise was sold by Connie Mack to one Arnold Johnson, whose first priority was to vacate Shibe Park for a fresh start in Kansas City in the coming year. Johnson was a wealthy industrialist who had already acquired ownership of Yankee Stadium and the Kansas City Park the year before, providing him with an influential role in the purchase of the Athletics franchise from the Macks. The complicated deal was finalized in November and work began immediately to enlarge the existing AAA facility, to be renamed Municipal Stadium.

Athletics' coach and pitching legend Chief Bender died in May. Other baseball notables who passed on in 1954 were Rabbit Maranville, Hugh Duffy, and sportswriter Grantland Rice. Maranville, Bill Terry, and Bill Dickey were 1954's Hall of Fame inductees. A young outfielder named Henry Aaron made a quiet debut with the Milwaukee Braves and hit a modest total of 13 home runs. Another freshman, Wally Moon of the

Cardinals, hit .304 and was given Rookie of the Year honors. The Yanks' 20-game winner Bob Grim was the AL's top rookie. Willie Mays made a spectacular return from Army service with an MVP season: 41 homers, 110 RBIs, and a league-leading .345 BA to lead the Giants to the NL flag. Catcher Yogi Berra of the second-place Yankees was the American League's MVP. Popular Cardinals veteran Enos Slaughter was traded to the New York Yankees just before opening day.

1954 saw a revolving door of managerial changes. Eddie Joost became the last pilot of the Athletics in Philadelphia, taking over for Jimmy Dykes, who accepted the helm of the new Baltimore club. Popular Cub veteran Stan Hack replaced another popular Cub veteran Phil Cavaretta at Wrigley Field. Birdie Tebbetts was Cincinnati's new man while the Dodgers promoted from within, naming the relatively unknown Walter Alston to manage the Brooklyn entry. Late in the season, Paul Richards announced his signing with Baltimore for 1955 and was replaced by Marty Marion. Terry Moore finished out the Phils' season, replacing Steve O'Neill. Veteran AL umpire Bill McGowan retired in mid-1954 after 30 years of service and then passed away in December. Another veteran arbiter, Bill Stewart, made 1954 the last of his 22 seasons in the National League. After several years of conducting Phillies' affairs without a general manager, owner Bob Carpenter hired Roy Hamey in that capacity.

The town of Baltimore celebrated its new major league identity with a gigantic street parade.

Vice-President Richard Nixon was on hand to throw out the first ball at the Orioles' opener.

Veteran coach Chief Bender, a pitching ace for Connie Mack's early century teams and a Hall of Famer, passed away in May 1954.

The Milwaukee Braves showcased a future legend, Henry Aaron, for the first time in 1954. He hit a modest .280 with 13 HRs.

The "Say-Hey Kid," Willie Mays, returned from the Army in 1954 and quickly established himself as a genuine NYC "folk hero," leading the Giants to the pennant with MVP stats. His "stick ball" ventures in the streets of Harlem further enhanced his fan worship.

The National League witnessed some awesome power hitting in 1954—Joe Adcock of the Braves hit four homers and a double in a July game at Ebbets Field and Stan Musial set a new ML record in May with five in a doubleheader vs. New York. Muscular Ted Kluszewski topped the majors with 49. A future home run champ named Banks played his first full season at shortstop for the lowly Cubs and hit a misleading total of only 19 homers.

Discounting post-season play, 1954 was a year that belonged to Cleveland. The Ohio city hosted the All-Star game and the American Leaguers finally ended their 50's drought with an 11-7 victory. Hometown heroes Al Rosen (with a pair) and Larry Doby contributed homers in this free-swinging affair. But the American League pennant race was also an all-Cleveland affair as the Indians amassed a league record of 111 wins to temporarily end the domination of the Yankees. Casey's troops actually cracked the 100-win circle for the first time under Stengel with 103, but still finished a full eight games off the pace of the tribe. Everything seemed to click for Al Lopez that summer—Bob Lemon and Early Wynn led a balanced pitching rotation that produced a staff ERA of 2.78. The relief tandem of Don Mossi and Ray Narleski were nearly flawless all season, saving game after game. Little Bobby Avila had a career year, leading the AL with a .341 BA. Larry Doby and Al Rosen provided the heavy artillery as the Indians led the league in round-trippers. Almost unnoticed because of the remarkable tribe's output, Leo Durocher's Giants unseated favored Brooklyn in the NL race.

But the seemingly unbeatable Indians were in for a rude awakening in the October classic. A spectacular game-saving catch by Willie Mays off a long drive by Vic Wertz in game one plus some pinch-hitting heroics by an unknown reserve named Dusty Rhodes propelled the underdog Giants to an unbelievable four-game sweep of the championship series. The Cleveland club and its loyal followers were devastated by what has to rank as one of the most stunning upsets in World Series history.

Willie Mays, about to make the most publicized catch in World Series history.

Indians' first baseman Vic Wertz hit .500 in a losing cause in the '54 Classic and was the victim of Mays' spectacular game-saving catch in game 1.

The Cardinals' own "folk hero," Stan Musial, electrified the baseball world with five HRs in a doubleheader—still a record. His peculiar batting stance was one of his trademarks.

Cleveland's incredible 111-win season under Al Lopez (center) was paced by 23-game winners Early Wynn (left) and Bob Lemon (right).

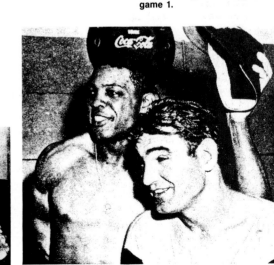

The big heroes of the Giants' Series sweep, Willie Mays and pinch-hitter Dusty Rhodes, celebrate their unlikely triumph.

Indians' second sacker Bobby Avila made a solid contribution to the team's record season with a .341 BA, tops in the league.

Jim Wilson of Milwaukee authored 1954's only no-hitter.

Joe Adcock tied a record with four round-trippers plus a double in one game.

Muscular Ted Kluszewski led the majors in 1954 with 49 HRs.

1955

HIT RECORDS OF 1955

MR. SANDMAN *Chordettes*
LET ME GO, LOVER *Joan Weber*
HEARTS OF STONE *Fontane Sisters*
MELODY OF LOVE *Four Aces, B. Vaughn, D. Carroll*
SINCERELY *McGuire Sisters*
CRAZY OTTO *Johnny Maddox*
BALLAD OF DAVY CROCKETT *Bill Hayes*
CHERRY PINK & APPLE BLOSSOM WHITE
  Perez Prado
UNCHAINED MELODY *Al Hibbler*
ROCK AROUND THE CLOCK *Bill Haley*
AIN'T THAT A SHAME *Pat Boone/Fats Domino*
YELLOW ROSE OF TEXAS *Mitch Miller*
LOVE IS A MANY SPLENDORED THING *Four Aces*
AUTUMN LEAVES *Roger Williams*

Another change in the map of ML baseball was in order for the season of 1955. Philadelphia lost its membership in the American League as the Athletics moved their operation to Kansas City. Ex-president Harry Truman was the guest of honor in the Missouri city as new manager Lou Boudreau's KC Athletics inaugurated the major league season in the western city. The phenomenal financial successes of franchise relocations gave other troubled owners needed ammunition to bargain for better deals with host cities. Brooklyn owner Walter O'Malley prophesied that 1957 would be the last year the Dodgers would play in Ebbets Field and made arrangements to play seven home games in Jersey City in 1956. The bonus player wars were in full swing as Baltimore invested 3/4 million dollars on a host of young phenoms, including one Brooks Robinson. Falstaff's "game of the week" telecasts switched over to CBS, but retained the popular Dizzy Dean and Buddy Blattner. GM Frank Lane feuded openly with VP Chuck Comiskey and finally left the White Sox organization to take a similar post with the St. Louis Cardinals. The legendary Branch Rickey reduced his role in the Pirates organization to adviser and Joe L. Brown succeeded him as GM. Clarence Miles resigned as Baltimore president late in the year, succeeded by James Keelty.

Pirates' immortal Honus Wagner, an active coach right up to 1951, died at age 80 in December.

Managerial changes were once again abundant— Paul Richards was the new GM/manager in Baltimore, Chuck Dressen resurfaced in Washington, newcomer Mayo Smith was the Phillies' new boss, Mike Higgins replaced Boudreau in Boston, and the ageless Bucky Harris returned to manage Detroit after a 22-year absence. Harry Walker replaced Eddie Stanky in St. Louis a month into the season. Giants pilot Leo Durocher announced his retirement at season's end to pursue a new career in television. The baseball writers selected Joe DiMaggio, Ted Lyons, Dazzy Vance, Gabby Hartnett, "Home Run" Baker, and Ray Schalk for enshrinement in the Hall of Fame. A trio of baseball immortals passed on later in the year—Cy Young, Honus Wagner, and Clark Griffith. Three veteran stars called it quits after the 1955 season: Ralph Kiner, Preacher Roe, and Allie Reynolds.

25-year-old Harry Agganis, already a sports legend in the Boston area, died unexpectedly in June. He had been off to a fine start with a .313 BA for the Bosox. A young Puerto Rican outfielder named Roberto Clemente made his debut in Pittsburgh, but the rookie sensation of the year was Cleveland's Herb Score. Score was destined to make Indians fans forget Bob Feller's achievements, as he fanned 245 and won 16. Detroit's Al Kaline, only two years out of high school, served notice that he was a potential superstar by winning the AL batting championship with a .340 mark. Sam Jones of the Cubs hurled the only no-hitter of the 1955 season. Milwaukee hosted the All-Star game as the National League resumed its winning ways, 6-5. Mickey Mantle and Stan Musial homered for their respective leagues. Musial's blast in the ninth settled the issue.

Kansas City fans line up for tickets at Municipal Stadium for the grand opening.

20-year-old outfielder Al Kaline topped the majors with a .340 BA in 1955.

Washington owner Clark Griffith, a legendary figure in American League history, passed away in October 1955.

Ex-President Harry Truman inaugurates American League baseball in Kansas City as A's Manager Boudreau and Tigers' boss Bucky Harris look on.

The Red Sox' Harry Agganis, the locally popular "Golden Greek," was mourned by all of New England after his untimely death at age 25.

"Trader" Frank Lane (left) was hired in 1955 by August Busch to improve the standing of his beloved St. Louis Cardinals.

Yogi Berra repeated as the AL's Most Valuable Player and his Brooklyn counterpart, Roy Campanella, was voted the award in the senior circuit. Wondrous Willie Mays hit a career-high 51 homers while his Brooklyn counterpart, Duke Snider, drove in a league-leading 136 runs to help the Bums to yet another NL championship. The Dodgers won easily, never out of first place from day one of the season. Milwaukee's improving Braves nosed out the reigning champion Giants for the runner-up spot. In the American League race, Casey Stengel's bombers reclaimed the flag from a still formidable Cleveland club. Marty Marion's version of the "Go-Go" White Sox made their first serious pennant challenge of the decade, winning 91 games with a close third place finish. Billy Pierce posted the decade's best ERA, a sparkling 1.97, and produced a club record of 33-1/3 consecutive shutout innings.

The 1955 World Series was a return to business as usual—Yankees vs. Dodgers. But, at long last it was Brooklyn's turn to rewrite the final outcome. After the first two games, it looked like the same tired scenario with the Yankees capturing both to take a 2-0 lead. But the Bums came storming back with three straight victories at Ebbets field to reclaim the advantage. Whitey Ford evened the series in game six with a four-hit 5-1 victory. But Johnny Podres, who had won game three, was magnificent in shutting down the New Yorkers without a run in the finale. The key play in game seven was a remarkable running catch by Sandy Amoros in the left field corner that converted a sure double by Berra into a double play instead. For the delirious fans of Flatbush, the beloved Bums were finally kings of the diamond—a fitting climax to the long history of big league baseball in Brooklyn.

Cub pitcher Sam Jones (center) savors his May 12 no-hit game, flanked by Manager Stan Hack (left) and catcher Clyde McCullough.

NL stars Gene Conley (left), Joe Nuxhall (center), and Stan Musial, who hit a game-winning HR, rejoice after victory in the midsummer classic at Milwaukee.

Like 1954, the 1955 Series also featured a spectacular game-saving catch—this time by Dodger left fielder Sandy Amoros off the bat of Yogi Berra in game 7.

Worth a second look, Amoros is about to snare Yogi's drive in the LF corner and then double up McDougald to preserve Podres' shutout victory.

Cleveland's Herb Score was the rookie pitching sensation of 1955 with 245 Ks.

Future Pirates' star Bob Clemente made his ML debut in '55.

Leo Durocher stepped down as Giants' skipper at season's end to pursue a career in TV.

Dodgers' (left to right) Labine, Gilliam, Snider, and Loes celebrate the clinching of the '55 flag. Brooklyn was on top from start to finish.

A delirious Roy Campanella tackles winning hurler Johnny Podres as the Bums win their first ever world championship.

1956

The year began with the final chapter of a legendary career as Connie Mack died at the age of 93 in February. Mack's death followed that of another AL legend, Clark Griffith, by a matter of months as the Washington club was now guided by adopted nephew Calvin Griffith. A pair of contemporary AL sluggers, Hank Greenberg and Joe Cronin, were named to join Cooperstown's Hall of Fame. Another Hall-of-Famer, Al Simmons, expired in May. The plight of the minor leagues was relieved considerably by the establishment of a $500,000 stabilization fund to offset the damaging financial effects of expanded TV-radio coverage of major league games. The majors also agreed to cut their early season rosters to make more players available to the minor league clubs. A new lucrative five-year TV-radio contract was signed with NBC and prime sponsor Gillette for broadcast rights on the All-Star games and World Series. A sweeping new pension program also went into effect for the players. Brooklyn's experiment with seven home games in Jersey City was financially successful and the Dodgers announced their intentions to repeat the trial in 1957. In another ominous move for the Brooklyn faithful, O'Malley purchased the LA PCL franchise from the Chicago Cubs, including their Coast League baseball park. The Detroit Tigers changed ownership at season's end—no longer associated with the Briggs estate.

A new and prestigious honor, the Cy Young Award, was established to designate the top pitcher in the major leagues and Brooklyn's 27-game winner Don Newcombe was a runaway choice. In Pittsburgh, Branch Rickey had vacated his GM role to become board chairman, and Joe L. Brown (son of famed comedian Joe E. Brown) assumed the duties of general manager. Long-time Chicago Cub executives Jim Gallagher and Wid Mathews were "history" in a monumental shake-up by owner Phil Wrigley in October. The Cardinals' new boss, GM Frank Lane, signed Freddie Hutchinson as field manager for 1956. Bill Rigney was the Giants' choice to succeed Leo Durocher. Other new field bosses for 1956 were Bobby Bragan in Pittsburgh and Fred Haney, who replaced Milwaukee's Charlie Grimm 46 games into the season.

The Cincinnati Reds re-established a novelty in uniform designs with a sleeveless vest, something the Cubs had tried in the early forties. In St. Louis, the Cardinals dared to present a uniform without the famous two-birds-on-a-bat feature that met with a mild outcry from traditionalists. Mutual Radio's "game of the day" was still alive and well, with Rex Barney and John McLean added to the announcing team. The TV "game of the week" telecasts were also well established, with Dizzy Dean and Buddy Blattner calling the plays. The annual All-Star classic at Washington's Griffith Stadium was once again an NL affair, 7-3. The decade's top sluggers Mays, Musial, Mantle, and Williams all homered to the delight of a national TV audience. The incomparable Williams' public image was severely tarnished by several "spitting" incidents (one wag referred to them as "great expectorations"), resulting in a record $5000 fine by owner Tom Yawkey. Cleveland outfielder Jim Busby accomplished a rare slugging feat in July with grand slam home runs in successive games.

A truly epic baseball career came to an end on February 8 when death took Connie Mack at age 93.

Joe Cronin is presented his plaque at Hall of Fame induction in Cooperstown. Commissioner Frick is the presenter.

Legends of baseball convened for Hall of Fame night in Baltimore on August 24. (Left to right): Cobb, Foxx, Vance, Waner, Speaker, Dickey, Ott, Home Run Baker, and Grove.

Dale Long of the Pirates homered in eight consecutive games—a record performance.

Slugger Hank Greenberg joined Cronin in membership to the "Hall" in 1956.

Red Sox lefty Mel Parnell no-hit the White Sox on July 14.

Mickey Mantle produced a legendary season—his 52 HRs, 130 RBIs, and .353 BA constituting a rare triple crown and a near-unanimous MVP award. Pittsburgh's Dale Long got headlines with a record streak of eight home runs in eight consecutive games. The much-improved Cincinnati Reds also displayed remarkable home run power with a record-tying season total of 221. In the MVP selection for the National League, Don Newcombe was the obvious choice with his impressive Cy Young Award credentials. Detroit's Frank Lary was the AL's top winner at 21-13, while Herb Score of the tribe once again posted an awesome 263 K's to go along with his 20 victories. Rookie-of-the-Year honors went to Cincinnati's Frank Robinson and the "Go-Go" Sox's fleet young shortstop Luis Aparicio. Hank Aaron's .328 average was tops in the National League while Duke Snider's 43 homers were the most in the NL.

Mickey Mantle became the decade's only triple crown winner with a spectacular MVP year.

Dodger ace Don Newcombe's 27 wins made him the first recipient of the new Cy Young Award in 1956.

In the pennant races, Brooklyn barely edged out the surging Braves and Reds. The acquisition of Sal Maglie from Cleveland probably gave them the edge as "the Barber" contributed 13 wins including a no-hit game along the way. Carl Erskine also tossed a no-hitter that summer, as did Boston's Mel Parnell in the junior circuit. Thanks to Mantle's incredible year, the Yankees cruised to another flag, winning by nine games over the perennial runner-ups, Cleveland. Even three 20-game winners (Wynn, Score, Lemon) could not propel the Tribe into serious contention.

With the monkey finally off their back after the 1955 series, the Dodgers were confident they could repeat as world champs and give the hated Yankees their second straight setback. They jumped off to a quick 2-0 game lead in the first two games at Ebbets but the New Yorkers found themselves at Yankee Stadium, sweeping the next three games there. In game five, Don Larsen pitched a PERFECT no-hit game—something never accomplished in the World Series before, indeed not at all in major league baseball since 1922. It was arguably the greatest hurling feat in the history of the game. It completely obscured the next game's clutch four-hit shutout by Clem Labine to even the series and a fine three-hit shutout by Johnny Kucks in the clincher. Larsen had apparently mesmerized the Dodger offense for the balance of the series and once again the cry of "Wait 'til next year!" emanated from Flatbush Avenue.

Dodgers' owner Walter O'Malley demonstrated his disenchantment with Ebbets Field in 1956 by scheduling seven home dates in nearby Jersey City's Roosevelt Stadium. The above scene is the first of such dates on April 19.

Yogi Berra crosses the plate after belting out only the fifth grand-slam in Series history.

Yankee hurler Don Larsen pitched the "game of games" with a sparkling PERFECT no-hitter against Brooklyn in game 5 of the 1956 World Series. His opening pitch to Junior Gilliam is depicted.

A familiar 1956 sight whenever the Cincinnati Reds were in action—Ed Bailey has just parked one of the record-tying 221 round-trippers hit by the Reds' wrecking crew of that summer.

1957

The year 1957 was sadly destined to be the final season for the NEW YORK Giants and BROOKLYN Dodgers. The dawning of the jet age, along with the financial success of previous franchise shifts, enticed owner Walter O'Malley to abandon his struggles with the borough bureaucrats and strike a deal with the beckoning West Coast metropolis of Los Angeles. He connived with Giants' owner Horace Stoneham, who had previously considered a move to Minneapolis, to make it a tandem leap with the Giants heading for San Francisco to perpetuate the Giant/Dodger rivalry. It was perhaps poetic justice that the two lame duck franchises failed to seriously contend for the pennant, which was Milwaukee's reward for record attendance there. Once again, major league baseball was scrutinized in a much-publicized congressional hearing in mid-summer without coming to any significant conclusions about the anti-trust status of the sport. The whole pattern of major league demographics was in a state of upheaval by this time. Air travel, even for short hops, was rapidly replacing slow and outmoded train travel. Overall attendance was back on the upswing, and receipts from network television were becoming a significant windfall for league treasuries. NBC-TV jumped into the "game of the week" competition with CBS and hired colorful Leo Durocher and veteran Lindsay Nelson to try to upstage Diz and Buddy. Times were definitely "a-changin'."

Sam Crawford and Joe McCarthy were 1957's Hall of Fame inductees. In Detroit, a new syndicate headed by John Fetzer and Fred Knorr had purchased the club from the Briggs family but retained "Spike" Briggs as general manager until his abrupt resignation in April. John McHale was elevated to fill the GM post vacated by Briggs. Veteran minor league manager and coach Jack Tighe was hired to replace Bucky Harris as Tiger pilot. Another unknown minor leaguer, Kerby Farrell, was elevated to the post of Cleveland manager to replace Senor Al Lopez, off to Chicago to pilot the White Sox for 1957. Cleveland GM Hank Greenberg, in a surprise move, was ousted late in the year. Bob Scheffing replaced Stan Hack as Cubs pilot and into the season, several more new managerial faces emerged—Cookie Lavagetto in Washington, Harry Craft in Kansas City, and Danny Murtaugh in Pittsburgh. Murtaugh replaced Bobby Bragan after a series of somewhat "childish" incidents performed on the field by the Bucs' pilot.

The season had just begun to warm up when young Cleveland pitching sensation Herb Score was struck in the eye by a vicious line drive off the bat of Gil McDougald. Herb was lost for the season, and sadly never regained the prowess achieved prior to the accident. The All-Star game was won by the American League, 6-5, at St. Louis' Busch Stadium (Sportsman's Park). Unfortunately, the midsummer classic was tainted by a balloting controversy that forced a redefinition of All-Star selections in subsequent seasons. Over-zealous Cincinnati followers lost all objectivity in the All-Star voting and deliberately "stuffed" the ballot boxes in an effort to present a nearly all-Reds lineup in the final tally. Commissioner Ford Frick interceded in the interests of fairness and negated some of the voting results.

Tribe pitching sensation Herb Score's career was derailed by a vicious line drive in early '57.

Phils' hurler Jack Sanford, with 19 wins and 188 Ks, was the NL's top rookie in '57.

Bob "Hurricane" Hazle was a late-summer sensation for the champion Braves.

A familiar sight, especially on Sundays, to Tiger fans in 1957—Charley Maxwell crossing the plate after another round-tripper.

Memories of "me 'n Paul" were rekindled in St. Louis with the pitching brothers act of Lindy (left) and Von (right) McDaniel—posing here with Dizzy Dean.

Giants' owner Horace Stoneham (left) confers with Dodgers' owner Peter O'Malley over their joint decision to abandon NYC and relocate to the West Coast in '58.

Mickey Mantle had another fine season at the plate, hitting .365 and winning the MVP award. But 38-year-old Ted Williams stole his thunder by posting a remarkable .388 batting average. Washington's Roy Sievers with 42 homers and 114 RBIs denied Mantle the other two elements of the triple crown. Williams' NL counterpart, Stan Musial, led his league again with a .351 mark, while young Henry Aaron established himself as a bona fide slugging star with 44 HRs and 132 RBIs. Bob Keegan of the White Sox delivered the season's only no-hitter on August 20. The Cardinals showcased an 18-year-old pitching marvel, Von McDaniel, who ultimately proved to be another "flash in the pan." The top rookies of 1957 were Yankee shortstop Tony Kubek and Phillies hurler Jack Sanford.

Another sensational rookie who made headlines in '57 was Bob "Hurricane" Hazle, who hit .403 in 41 games for the Milwaukee Braves to help them run away from the pack in the NL pennant race. Another key arrival in solidifying the Braves' pennant drive was second baseman Red Schoendienst, obtained from the Giants in an early season trade. The Yankees once again coasted to an AL flag, finishing eight games ahead of an upsurging White Sox club under Al Lopez. The Sox's Billy Pierce led the staff with 20-12, tying Detroit's Jim Bunning as the only AL 20-game winners.

For the first time in the decade, baseball's world championship was denied to New York fans as the Braves prevailed in an evenly fought seven-game series. Pitcher Lew Burdette was easily the MVP of the Fall Classic as he won three times, the final two being shutouts. It looked very much like a new order was in the making in the National League.

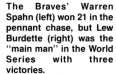

Ted's NL counterpart, Stan the Man, won his fourth batting title of the decade with a .351 mark.

The incomparable Ted Williams, at age 38, flirted once again with a .400 BA, finishing with a sensational .388.

Washington fans had their own slugging hero in Roy Sievers, who led the AL with 42 HRs and 114 RBIs. On a special night of tribute attended by VP Nixon, Roy is overcome with emotion.

The Braves' Warren Spahn (left) won 21 in the pennant chase, but Lew Burdette (right) was the "main man" in the World Series with three victories.

Frustrated Giant fans went on a rampage after their team played its final game at the Polo Grounds on September 20.

Milwaukee's Hank Aaron is greeted by the dugout after a three-run homer in game 4 of the '57 Series in County Stadium.

Pitcher Burdette is mobbed by teammates after his Series-clinching shutout in the final game of the '57 Fall Classic.

1958

The national game finally achieved coast-to-coast status in 1958 with San Francisco and Los Angeles joining the senior circuit. The first matchup between the two went to the Giants, 8-0, at tiny Seals Stadium in San Francisco. Tragedy had struck the Dodgers in the pre-season as All-Star catcher Roy Campanella was permanently disabled in an auto accident. The world champion Braves also were smitten late in the season when second baseman Red Schoendienst was sidelined with tuberculosis, which almost ended his career. Former baseball greats who passed away in 1958 included Chuck Klein (in March), Tiger radio co-announcer Mel Ott (in November) and Tris Speaker (in December). The baseball writers failed to nominate anyone into the Hall of Fame, a rare occurrence.

Briggs Stadium paid tribute to its Detroit heroes of the past with an old timer's day in May. Most of the living Tiger legends of yesterday (Cobb, Crawford, Davey Jones, Gehringer, Schoolboy Rowe, Greenberg, et al) participated in the festivities. The great Stan Musial signed for a record $100,000, then reached a personal milestone in 1958 by delivering his 3000th hit. The only new manager when the season opened was Bobby Bragan at Cleveland and he was replaced by Joe Gordon in mid year. Three other pilots failed to complete the schedule and were replaced by Bill Norman (in Detroit), Jimmy Dykes (in Cincinnati), and Eddie Sawyer (in Philadelphia). Trader Frank Lane had worn out his welcome in St. Louis and was succeeded there by Bing Devine. Lane moved on to try his luck as general manager in Cleveland. Several clubs made important front office changes after the 1958 season ended. Lee MacPhail relieved Manager Paul Richards from GM duties in Baltimore. Parke Carroll assumed the added role of GM at Kansas City. Cleveland's Frank Lane and Washington's Joe Haynes were named vice presidents of their respective clubs.

Baltimore's Hoyt Wilhelm (right) is congratulated by Mgr. Paul Richards on his Sept. 20 no-hit game. Catcher Gus Triandos is on the left.

A huge street parade welcomed the transplanted NY Giants to their new home in San Francisco for 1958.

39-year-old Ted Williams defended his AL bat title in '58 with a more modest .328.

White Sox lefty Billy Pierce came within one out of a perfect game—not done in season play since 1922.

Mel Ott, current Tigers' radio announcer and NY Giant legend, was killed in an auto accident late in 1958.

SF first sacker Orlando Cepeda was the NL's top rookie for 1958.

Record throngs poured into the LA Coliseum to witness the new West Coast version of Dodger baseball.

White Sox ace lefty Bill Pierce had a brush with immortality on June 27 when he retired the first 26 Washington batters, only to have pinch-hitter Ed Fitzgerald spoil it all with a two-base hit. Mickey Mantle added to his long-ball legend by hitting one completely out of Briggs Stadium, a feat accomplished only once before by Ted Williams in 1939. The lowly Cubs got a career year out of Ernie Banks in 1958, when he slammed 47 homers and batted in 129 runs—a performance that gave him the league's MVP honors. Jackie Jensen of the Red Sox was the AL's MVP with 122 RBIs. The Yanks' Bob Turley won the coveted Cy Young Award as baseball's premier pitcher of 1958. No-hitters were turned in by Detroit's Jim Bunning on July 20 and Baltimore's Hoyt Wilhelm on September 20. Aging Ted Williams won the last of his many batting titles with a .328 average, while the Phils' Richie Ashburn led the majors with a .350 mark. The All-Star game at Baltimore went to the American Leaguers 4-3 with Gil McDougald driving in the winning run. Hometown favorite Billy O'Dell retired the last nine NL hitters to close out the game. The top rookies of 1958 were little Albie Pearson of last place Washington and the Giants' new slugger, Orlando Cepeda.

The Milwaukee Braves, despite the loss of Schoendienst and injuries to center fielder Billy Bruton and pitcher Bob Buhl, repeated as NL flag winners by eight games over surprising Pittsburgh. The reliable aces Spahn and Burdette held the pitching staff together with 22 and 20 wins respectively. The Yankees also coasted to another pennant with Mantle's 42 homers leading the barrage. The speedy White Sox finished 10 games back but asserted themselves as genuine contenders for the second year in a row. The new Los Angeles edition of the Dodgers stumbled badly in their new surroundings, barely escaping the cellar, but as time would tell, it was simply an off-year and not the beginning of the end of the Dodger dynasty.

The 1958 World Series was to be an encore match-up between the Braves and Yankees. It looked like a repeat for Milwaukee as they quickly took a commanding three-games-to-one lead. But for the first time since 1925, the Yanks overcame those seemingly hopeless odds and rallied for three straight wins and yet another world championship. Warren Spahn was brilliant in the early going but the New Yorkers got revenge on 1957 nemesis Lew Burdette, routing him in game five, then sent him packing with a clutch three-run blast by Bill Skowron in the finale.

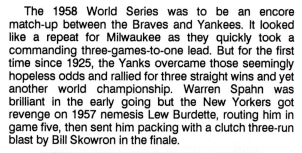

All the living Tiger heroes of the past gathered for Old Timers Day at Briggs Stadium in May. Former managers posed (left to right): Cochrane, Cobb, O'Neill, Moriarty, and Del Baker.

All-Star heroes for the AL's 4-3 win at Baltimore celebrate their triumph. (L to R): Gil McDougald, Billy O'Dell, and Nelson Fox.

Mickey Mantle became only the second player to propel a fair ball completely out of Detroit's Briggs Stadium. Ted Williams had performed the feat in 1939.

Stan Musial joined the exclusive 3000-hit club in 1958.

Over 46,000 fans jam Milwaukee's County Stadium for their second consecutive World Series appearance vs. the Yanks.

Bill Skowron was the Yanks' hitting hero in the final game win.

Bob Turley won 21, then pitched brilliantly in the Yankees' come-from-behind Series victory.

1959

The winter of 1958-59 witnessed a changing of the guard at the top of the American League as Will Harridge retired and was succeeded by Joe Cronin. Harridge, at age 72, had served as AL chief executive for 28 years. Bucky Harris was named to succeed Cronin as Bosox general manager. John Quinn left Milwaukee to assume GM duties with the Philadelphia Phillies. John McHale was lured from Detroit to replace Quinn at Milwaukee. Rick Ferrell took over as new Tiger GM. Branch Rickey, ever the visionary, proposed the formation of a third major league to be called the Continental League. The growing pressure of expansion in many new urban markets and the reluctance of the two existing leagues to respond were the catalysts in the formation of the proposed third league. New York, Houston, Toronto, Minneapolis, and Denver were the charter cities for the Continental League. In retrospect, historians have speculated that it was a calculated bluff on the part of Rickey and other principals to accelerate inevitable expansion.

A new wrinkle was added to the All-Star game format for 1959 as two games, both in one league's home parks, were scheduled for July and August. The Dodgers established a new single-game attendance record when 93,000 fans filled the Coliseum to pay tribute to Roy Campanella and watch an exhibition contest with the New York Yankees. Zack Wheat was the lone Hall of Fame inductee for 1959. Deaths of baseball notables included Nap Lajoie in February, Howard Ehmke in March, Ed Walsh in May, and Jim Bottomley in December. Flamboyant Bill Veeck finally purchased controlling interest of the White Sox from the Comiskey family and gave South Side fans a year to remember. Solly Hemus was the new Cardinals manager for 1959 and three more new pilots were introduced after the season was underway—veteran Jimmy Dykes replacing Norman in Detroit, Billy Jurges replacing Pinky Higgins in Boston, and Fred Hutchinson replacing Mayo Smith in Cincinnati.

The Boston Red Sox became the last major league club to break the color line in 1959 with new infielder Pumpsie Green—shown here with Manager Billy Jurges.

Branch Rickey (seated with cane) poses with the backers of a proposed third major league to be called the Continental League. O.B. bigwigs Ford Frick, Warren Giles, and Joe Cronin are included in the group.

Rocky Colavito of Cleveland tied a long-standing record with four homers in a 1959 game against the Orioles.

The Pirates' Harvey Haddix pitched 12 perfect innings in May, but lost the game in the 13th.

For the second successive year, the SF Giants showcased the league's top rookie—Willie McCovey, another slugging first sacker.

Elroy Face added to Pittsburgh's pitching laurels with a sparkling 18-1 WL record.

Retiring AL President Will Harridge (left) confers with his replacement, Joe Cronin.

The Cubs' Ernie Banks was a repeat choice for the NL's MVP award.

The White Sox' Nellie Fox made it an MVP sweep for Chicago, winning AL honors.

On May 26, Pittsburgh's Harvey Haddix hurled an incredulous 12 perfect innings against Milwaukee, only to lose in the 13th inning on a Joe Adcock extra-base hit. Pitching teammate Elroy Face posted a remarkable 18-1 win-loss record. On June 10, Cleveland's Rocky Colavito tied a major league record with four home runs in a game at Baltimore. The two All-Star games were a draw as the NL won game one at Pittsburgh 5-4, then yielded to the AL, 5-3, at the LA Coliseum. Ernie Banks had another productive season for the 5th place Cubbies, banging out 45 HRs (one less than ML leader Ed Mathews) and driving in 143 runs—totals which garnered him the league's MVP award for the second straight year. Across town little Nellie Fox sparked the White Sox to their first pennant since 1919 and was voted the AL's MVP. But it was ageless Early Wynn, 1959's Cy Young winner, who carried the pitching load in the Sox pennant drive, winning 22 games. Detroit's Harvey Kuenn restored a Tiger tradition by winning the club's 21st individual batting championship with a .353 mark. Washington's Harmon Killebrew tied Colavito for the AL HR honors with 42. Bob Allison of the Senators and Willie McCovey of the Giants were selected as top rookies of 1959.

The L.A. Dodgers rebounded from a forgettable maiden season in '58 by tying the Braves for the league lead at season's end, needing only 86 victories to do so. Some new heroes emerged to help in the Dodger resurgence—namely outfielder Wally Moon, whose numerous round-trippers over the infamous "Chinese Wall" at the Coliseum coined the descriptive phrase "Moon Shot." Reliever Larry Sherry and rookie Ron Fairly also made solid contributions to the cause. For the first time since 1951, a three-game playoff was required to determine the NL championship. LA dispatched the Braves in two straight to earn the right to face the speedy "Go-Go" White Sox in the Fall Classic.

The favored Pale Hose, behind Early Wynn, thumped the Dodgers soundly in game one, 11-0, at Comiskey Park. Newly acquired slugger Ted Kluszewski flexed his mighty muscles with a pair of home runs to lead the bombardment. But the Dodgers rebounded, winning the next three behind the stellar relief pitching of Larry Sherry. Bob Shaw out-dueled Sandy Koufax in a 1-0 victory in game six. Then Early Wynn had apparently run out of gas as he was driven out by a Dodger assault in the final game, 9-3. Once again, Larry Sherry was the man of the hour, pitching the last six innings brilliantly in relief of a shaky Johnny Podres. In only the second year of West Coast baseball, the world championship came to rest in Los Angeles.

In the NL's first post-season playoff since 1951, the LA Dodgers dethroned Milwaukee with a two-game sweep. Catcher John Roseboro (masked) is applauded by teammates Wally Moon (left) and Maury Wills after his winning HR in game 1.

Pale Hose pilot Al Lopez (center) rejoices with winning pitcher Bob Shaw (left) and Dick Donovan following the fifth game of the '59 World Series.

Ageless Early Wynn was the bulwark of the pennant-winning White Sox' 1959 pitching corps with 22 wins and the Cy Young Award.

Don Drysdale was the victor in game 3 for the Dodgers.

In '59 World Series action at Comiskey Park, Wally Moon sneaks past Nellie Fox at second base.

More '59 Series action at the LA Coliseum—Jim Landis is out at second on a fast double play executed by Charley Neal (left) and Maury Wills (far right).